ESSAYS ON
LOVE AND KNOWLEDGE

PIERRE ROUSSELOT

ESSAYS ON
LOVE AND KNOWLEDGE

EDITED BY

ANDREW TALLON & POL VANDEVELDE

TRANSLATED BY

ANDREW TALLON, POL VANDEVELDE, & ALAN VINCELETTE

VOLUME III OF THE COLLECTED PHILOSOPHICAL WORKS

MARQUETTE
UNIVERSITY
PRESS

MARQUETTE STUDIES IN PHILOSOPHY

No. 32

ANDREW TALLON, SERIES EDITOR

LIBRARY OF CONGRESS CATALOGING-IN-PUBLICATION DATA

Rousselot, Pierre, 1878-1915.
  Essays on love and knowledge / Pierre Rousselot ; edited by Andrew Tallon & Pol
Vandevelde ; translated by Andrew Tallon, Pol Vandevelde & Alan Vincelette.
      p. cm. — (Marquette studies in philosophy ; no. 32)
  Includes bibliographical references and index.
  ISBN-13: 978-0-87462-655-1 (pbk. : alk. paper)
  ISBN-10: 0-87462-655-2 (pbk. : alk. paper)
  1. Philosophy, Medieval. 2. Love—History—To 1500. 3. Love—Religious as-
pects—Christianity—History of doctrines—Middle Ages, 600-1500. 4. Knowledge,
Theory of—History—To 1500. I. Tallon, Andrew, 1934- II. Vandevelde, Pol. III.
Title.
  B738.L68R67 2008
  194—dc22
                                                                                              2007051766

MARQUETTE UNIVERSITY PRESS
MILWAUKEE

The Association of Jesuit University Presses

TABLE OF CONTENTS

ACKNOWLEDGMENTS

Archives de Philosophie 42 (1979) 91-126, for pages 103-126 of "Un inédit de P. Rousselot: 'Idéalisme et thomisme,'" par John Michael McDermott, S.J. McDermott wrote pages 91-102, as his introduction.

Archives de Philosophie 23 (1960) 573-607, for pages 574-607 of "Théorie de concepts par l'unité fonctionnelle suivant les principes de saint Thomas: Synthèse aperceptive et connaissance d'amour vécue."

Revue de Philosophie 17 (1910) 225-240, for "Amour spirituel et synthèse aperceptive."

Revue de Philosophie 17 (1910) 561-574, for "L'être et l'esprit."

Revue Néoscolastique de Louvain 17 (1910) 476-509, for "Métaphysique thomiste et critique de la connaissance."

Recherches de Science Religieuse 4 (1913) 1-36, for "Remarques sur l'histoire de la notion de foi naturelle."

Dictionnaire Apologétique de la Foi Catholique tome II (1914), columns 1066-1080, for "Intellectualisme."

SERIES EDITOR'S NOTE

The Thomist themes that Rousselot developed on cognition and love (love as affection more than as volition) in his two books of 1908 were continued and further developed in the articles written in the years immediately following 1908. Readers of this third volume in Marquette University Press's series The Collected Philosophical Works of Pierre Rousselot will be pleased to learn that Series Editor, Andrew Tallon, was fortunate in having an opportunity to visit the Archives and, with the kind permission of Father Robert Bonfils, SJ, was able to bring back photocopies of much of the unpublished Rousselot materials there in the Archives. I scanned the photocopies and exported PDFs which can be greatly enlarged on computers, making it easier for Pol Vandevelde to decipher Rousselot's extremely small handwriting (see the Appendix to this volume for a sample of Rousselot's handwriting). The editors of the present volume have begun reviewing these digital versions in order to choose which of the unpublished materials add significantly to our understanding of Rousselot's thought. Our intention is to transcribe, edit, and translate the best of those materials. Father Bonfils requested that we publish both the French (for the first time in any form) facing the English translation. Numbers in square brackets refer to pages in the original documents.

FOREWORD

CONNATURALITY: INTUITION OR COGNITION & AFFECTION IN PARALLEL?

ANDREW TALLON

INTRODUCTION

The aim of this brief foreword is to ask what Rousselot has to say to us today. For Rousselot the model or ideal of knowledge was intellectual intuition, enjoyed in perfection by God alone, by angels to a lesser degree, and by humans not at all.[1] Yet despite our total human lack of this ideal, for Rousselot it remained the model. Should it? Let us accept the standard definition of intuition as "knowing without reasoning," extended by some to include "union of knower and known," and sometimes "attainment and possession of the known by the knower." Let us accept with Kant that humans have only sense intuition, i.e., knowing by seeing, hearing, touching, etc., and that we have no intellectual intuition, the Thomist doctrine that Maréchal and Rahner professed with Rousselot.

Problems arise when we make intellectual intuition the model or ideal of knowledge and then find that humans come up short. We should question whether we vainly pursue (and why should we?) the ideal of cognition as intuition and incorrectly compare our best cognitive efforts unfavorably with this speculative paradigm. The comparison may be harmless or it may lead to mistakes in how we understand our own modes of knowing, especially our compensations for missing intellectual intuitions. We have two options open to us when turning to Rousselot as a resource. We can take a negative approach, reject the primacy of intuition, and fault him for espous-

---

1 The Scholastic notion of the hierarchy or continuum of spirits says that each level of spirit at its highest operation just touches the lowest operation of the next higher spirit.

ing it, or we can consider the positive possibility that he was too constrained by his time (including his shortened life) and training to work out a theory to explain (more fully than he did) his experience of a kind of knowing that *resembled* intellectual intuition; with the second approach we could also ask whether there is contemporary confirmation that he was on the right track. Let us take the negative approach first.

1. Intuitionism

Is it a mistake to make intuition the model of cognition (Sheehan 1997, 311)? It may be instructive to consider how Rahner took Rousselot's intuitionism to what might be its logical conclusion. Heidegger naturalized and historicized the infinite and eternal *theos* of onto-theology into finite and temporal being and beings, a move that Rahner followed to the extent of saying that theology must begin from below as anthropology. Assured by faith that we are, to use Rousselot's term, *capax Dei*, Rahner did not follow Heidegger all the way. The human soul-spirit as *Vorgriff* (anticipation) only *quasi*-intentionally[2] "attains" the horizon of being/God by anticipation, touching the horizon without grasping. Faith accepts as a gift and comes to rest in what intellect can only stretch out toward and touch, the ultimate horizon (of being) that Rahner called God. If we bracket faith, however, we are left with finitude, a continuing in space-time, for all we know a permanent anticipating with no assurance, only hope, that our minds and hearts will find eternal rest. As Sheehan (ibid.) says, "for better or worse, Rahner's *Geist in Welt* (GW) imports into the discussion of man and metaphysics the presupposition that cognition is first and above all a matter of intuition. Riding behind that presupposition is the Aristotelian understanding of the divine as a self-intuiting intuition, a perfect self-coincidence in a unity of being and self-knowledge. The transcendental turn in GW is thus scored on a hidden premise: that man is an intuition *manqué*, that he is movement only insofar as he approximates the ideal state of beingness, which is the perfect self-presence of the divine." If we forgo the hidden premise the movement is all there is,

---

2 "Quasi" because the term or target of the intending, being, is not an object [being as a verb, not a noun] but a horizon projected by the kinetic activity of cognition.

and no intuition, no coincidence of being and knowing, is in our future since there is no God or angel to instantiate it and hold it up to us as a credible ambition who dwell at the low end of the spiritual continuum. If we question Aquinas's intellectualism, which is really an intuitionism, and take the human situation as we experience it, then motion, *kinesis*, becoming are the defining notes, not stillness, rest, being. Perhaps Rousselot, like Rahner, "rested on a metaphysics of stable presentness (*ousia*) rather than on a vision of the movement that issues in *ousia*. The question about naming the term of man's movement becomes, in that case, a matter of how seriously one takes the issue of *kinesis*" (ibid.). Rousselot and others in the intellectualist/intuitionist tradition could (and did) turn to faith to remedy finitude: a deficient angel (*un ange manqué*) is still a spirit, *capax Dei*, and when the Word enters history and speaks the word we can hear it (*Hörer des Wortes*). The historical "break-in" by God is a revelation that invites us to redefine the horizon, to rename it from a verb (being) to a noun (God); Rahner continues onto-theology rather than undoes it. It is instructive to observe how Rousselot's Thomist intellectualism plays out in Rahner's *Erkenntnismetaphysik* and eventually in his theology. It is also instructive to observe how Levinas, another student of Heidegger, also followed the teacher only part of the way, naturalizing the divine (onto-theological) infinite by relocating it from eternal heaven to space-time earth, not in a Messiah/Word but in the ethical other: the divine infinite comes near in the neighbor and becomes present in the face of the other. That Levinas retains the infinite (albeit as the ethical) shows that his was only a partial naturalizing of the divine (Moyn, 2005; Tallon 2008).

Did the relatively easy availability of a teaching about God and angels that is less obvious today mislead Rousselot? If we bracket theology and angelology, we can still discover, in Rousselot's sympathetic knowing and its Thomist origin, knowing through affective connaturality, a solid contribution to philosophy and theology today.

2. Connaturality.

Rousselot used the tools and concepts at his disposal to expand from a dyadic to a triadic concept of the soul, at least that is what this reader finds between the lines in his works, especially the articles in this volume. He tried to make sense of our common human experience of something *like* intellectual intuition, viz., a higher knowledge than sense knowledge that is a knowing without reasoning, even a kind of union, based on connaturality, of knower and known. As everyone is aware, neuroscience has recently shown how essential affection is to making decisions that are not self-destructive and socially and ethically ruinous.[3] Rousselot's greatest insight, I submit, was to take Aquinas's connaturality and turn it into a theory of affection and cognition in a parallel processing, an operational synthesis that was sometimes presented as serial but at other times not, leading to an extraordinarily contemporary concept akin to the way neural nets process and evaluate (weigh) external and internal inputs. In Rousselot's language we can speak of a higher intuition (higher than sense intuition) not in the "strict" sense of angelic or divine near-perfect or perfect identity of knower and known, but something *like* a spiritual knowing through one's essence or nature. Knowing through one's nature would *approximate* angelic knowing (angels knowing through their essences is standard Thomist angelology, and God, of course, has to know everything in that fashion). Connaturality as knowing *per modum naturae* is this sort of knowing—but it is a knowing through one's *human* nature, a decidedly material and physical nature rather than a purely spiritual nature. That connatural *knowing* is the hallmark of Rousselot's epistemology. The rest of this brief foreword will first summarize the idea of Thomist connatural *knowing* as a step toward a more general understanding of connaturality as applicable to a triadic concept of consciousness, and thus to affectivity, not just to cognition. The following few words about connaturality can be brief (and probably unnecessary) for readers of this volume.

Aquinas's *Haupttext* on connaturality is *Summa theologiae* IIa IIae q. 45. a 2:

> Wisdom denotes a certain rectitude of judgment according to
> the Eternal Law. Now rectitude of judgment is twofold: first, on

---

3 The list is now long and familiar. Damasio, for example, shows that one can *know* with (to simplify) a damaged amygdala, but one cannot *decide* well, sometimes not decide at all; this supports reading Aquinas and Rousselot as not saying that affection (love) is essential to deciding. The bibliography offers some of the more accessible books and articles.

account of perfect use of reason, secondly, on account of a certain connaturality with the matter about which one has to judge. Thus, about matters of chastity, a man after inquiring with his reason forms a right judgment, if he has learnt the science of morals, while he who has the habit of chastity judges of such matters by a kind of connaturality. Accordingly it belongs to the wisdom that is an intellectual virtue to pronounce right judgment about Divine things after reason has made its inquiry, but it belongs to wisdom as a gift of the Holy Ghost to judge aright about them on account of connaturality with them: thus Dionysius says (*Div. Nom.* ii) that "Hierotheus is perfect in Divine things, for he not only learns, but is patient of, Divine things." Now this sympathy or connaturality for Divine things is the result of charity, which unites us to God, according to 1 Corinthians 6:17: "He who is joined to the Lord, is one spirit." Consequently wisdom which is a gift, has its cause in the will, which cause is charity, but it has its essence in the intellect, whose act is to judge aright.[4]

I interpret this text to be about two ways to *decide* (rather than only *judge*) what to do in the two realms Aquinas chooses for his examples, the ethical and the mystical ("Divine things" [*res divinae*]). With Lonergan I take the first three levels of consciousness to be the cognitive levels of experience, understanding, and judgment; the fourth level is the volitional level of decision. In this article Aquinas is taking us

---

4 Respondeo dicendum quod, sicut supra dictum est, sapientia importat quandam rectitudinem iudicii secundum rationes divinas. Rectitudo autem iudicii potest contingere dupliciter, uno modo, secundum perfectum usum rationis; alio modo, propter connaturalitatem quandam ad ea de quibus iam est iudicandum. Sicut de his quae ad castitatem pertinent per rationis inquisitionem recte iudicat ille qui didicit scientiam moralem, sed per quandam connaturalitatem ad ipsa recte iudicat de eis ille qui habet habitum castitatis. Sic igitur circa res divinas ex rationis inquisitione rectum iudicium habere pertinet ad sapientiam quae est virtus intellectualis, sed rectum iudicium habere de eis secundum quandam connaturalitatem ad ipsa pertinet ad sapientiam secundum quod donum est spiritus sancti, sicut Dionysius dicit, in II cap. de Div. Nom., quod Hierotheus est perfectus in divinis non solum discens, sed et patiens divina. Huiusmodi autem compassio sive connaturalitas ad res divinas fit per caritatem, quae quidem unit nos Deo, secundum illud I ad Cor. VI, qui adhaeret Deo unus spiritus est. Sic igitur sapientia quae est donum causam quidem habet in voluntate, scilicet caritatem, sed essentiam habet in intellectu, cuius actus est recte iudicare, ut supra habitum est.

through to the *end* of the cognitive levels, *to* the judgment, showing us two ways to put everything in place for deciding and acting. *Reason's* way to decision is to move from experience through understanding (questions, insights, concepts) to judgments. The *second* way, which Aquinas seems here to present as actually the first and best way (and in the real world it is probably the more common way people decide in practice), is by virtue, by good habit (or by whatever habit), by second nature. Second nature is a positive attunement or improvement (or at least an attunement; it could be for the worse, vicious rather than virtuous) of their first nature. First nature may become second in two ways for Aquinas the theologian: habits may be acquired by our own efforts (the ethical) or may be given by grace (the mystical) as Gifts of the Spirit [the gifts of the Spirit are virtues]). In the first, ethical example, virtuous persons feel a resonance (Aquinas's word is *compassio*), harmony, "vibes" in and between their (second) nature and the acts they can perform (chaste or not). In the second example, one's human nature is "divinized" (connaturalized) by grace that makes us adopted children of God, so that we share a common nature with God, the divine parent, at least by participating through the gifts of the Spirit (the first of the seven gifts is wisdom). Now Rousselot's book on love (2001) describes love as a phenomenon of union: either persons are apart and ecstatically move toward union (the love of friends) or they are already one in nature (members of the same family or just of the same species) and therefore love one another (*physis*, physical or natural love: con–natural, as shared nature). Friends and lovers love by going out from separateness toward union. Parents and children, already united in their shared nature, find love arising from the pre-existing union. Personal, ecstatic, love-toward-union is antecedent; connatural love-from-union is consequent. In practice love can, of course, be both. This affective connaturality, this attunement—sometimes foreground as feelings and emotions, sometimes background as moods and dispositions (*Stimmungen, tonalités affectives*)—operates in parallel with cognition; there is a functional synthesis of the two distinct intentionalities.[5]

---

5 It would be interesting to trace whether Heidegger's duality of (cognition) *Verstehen* and (affection) *Befindlichkeit, Stimmung,* and *Grundstimmung,* the fundamental mood or attunement, have roots in the idea of connaturality, which of course goes back to Platonic "like knowing like."

The important point in all this is, of course, the addition of affectivity, emotion, compassion, empathy, feeling—affection in general—to cognition, and not in a serial subordination but in a synthesis here expressed in terms of intentionality rather than in terms of a faculty psychology that is too constraining. Rousselot's connaturality thesis is a major contribution to (Thomist) epistemology, a direction Rousselot himself was taking (and which Rahner did not follow except on mysticism [Tallon 1995]). Rousselot did not live long enough to work out his own position and it is not clear, given the baggage he was dealing with, sometimes rather ambiguously or just incipiently or developmentally, that he would have liberated himself fully from his influences, including Bergson's intuitionism. But there are signs that we should try to get past his Scholastic language to a positive reading based on what he wrote about connaturality, sympathetic knowing, and apperceptive synthesis; I offer a brief argument next to try to show why this is a plausible reading.

SYMPATHETIC "KNOWING" = AFFECTION + COGNITION. The synthesis of affection and cognition as sympathetic knowing is, in practice, I submit, what Rousselot proposes as his own ideal, indeed as the actual substitute for a missing (intellectual) intuition enjoyed by higher spirits (angels and God). Scholastic Aristotelians usually spoke of a dyadic spiritual soul, i.e., a soul endowed with only two faculties, intellect and will. (Augustine at least had a version of a tripartite soul adapted from the Platonic triadic soul.) This creates a problem of how to locate the affections and how to explain the interaction of affection and cognition. The medieval Scholastics, with only intellect and will to work with, either made the affections cognitive or appetitive, attaching affectivity to intellect or to will, on the one hand, or kept *affectus* solely in the body, as sense appetite, on the other; rejecting substance dualism allows the spirit-matter barrier to be crossed so that "spiritual affections" are not automatically ruled out; since experience makes it impossible to deny spiritual affections, they end up attached to intellect or will, but nothing forbids affection being an equal intentional partner with cognition and volition once we replace faculty psychology with intentionality analysis. In the text above, Aquinas attaches affect to intellect; at other times he goes with will. Neither solution is correct: affectivity has its own irreducible intentionality and should not be reduced to the so-called spiritual faculties just because they happen to be the only available options under his current faculty psychology. Lonergan has suggested that we leave behind faculty psychology for intentionality analysis,[6] and offers what he calls "Newman's Theorem" to help explain what occurred in a similar context (*The Idea of a University*). Newman was asked what would happen if theology were removed from the university curriculum. As Lonergan put it:

> Positively, Newman advanced that human knowing was a whole with its parts organically related, and this accords with the contemporary phenomenological notion of horizon, that one's perceptions are functions of one's outlook, that one's meaning is a function of a context and that context of still broader contexts. On the negative side, Newman asked what would happen if a significant part of knowledge were omitted, overlooked, ignored, not just by some individual but by the cultural community, and he contended that there would be three consequences. First, people in general would be *ignorant* of that area. Second, the rounded whole of human knowing would be *mutilated*. Third, *the remaining parts would endeavor to round off the whole once more despite the omission of a part* and, as a result, they would suffer *distortion* from their effort to perform *a function for which they were not designed*. Such was Newman's theorem (Lonergan 1974, 141-42; my italics).

"Ignorance, mutilation, and distortion" happened under the dominance of a dyadic paradigm of human consciousness: first, expulsion of affection from the spiritual soul led to its being practically ignored

---

6 "A faculty psychology divides man up: it distinguishes intellect and will, sense perception and imagination, emotion and conation, only to leave us with unresolved problems of priority and rank. Is sense to be preferred to intellect, or intellect to sense? Is intellect to be preferred to will, or will to intellect? Is one to be a sensist, an intellectualist, or a voluntarist? The questions vanish, once one has ceased to think in terms of faculties or powers. *What is given to consciousness, is a set of interrelated intentional operations.* Together they conspire to achieve both cognitional and real self-transcendence. Such is the basic unity and continuity" (from Bernard Lonergan's unpublished "Faith and Beliefs" 8-9 [in the Lonergan Archives of the Lonergan Research Institute at Regis College, University of Toronto]; my italics).

as an available explanatory principle along with intellect and will; second, the received way of conceiving the soul became mutilated, dyadic instead of triadic; and third, the functions properly belonging to affection were forced either under cognition (e.g., emotions as judgments) or under volition (e.g., love as a will act). Only when the triadic structure of human consciousness is restored will these mistakes be corrected. In his own time and in his own way, Rousselot took steps to restore the affections to a place in consciousness, but he continued to work within a faculty psychology. This he calls the synthesis of sympathy and knowing a "sympathetic knowing" rather than, say, "intelligent sympathy," or some other term.[7] Despite these failures to replace *formally* a two-faculty soul with a three-intentionality soul, Rousselot did *materially* almost as much, and probably all he could. We can read him as trying to integrate affect into life and action by adding it to cognition. I conclude that the dominant place of Aquinas's connaturality in the ethical and mystical examples in ST IIa IIae 45, 2, suggests that we propose a parallel rather than serial alignment. In other words, instead of saying affection follows cognition sometimes and affection leads cognition at other times, which would be a serial alignment, we should think of three intentionalities in "parallel processing."[8] The dyadic tradition lacked a spiritual faculty ("heart" was always metaphoric unlike mind and will, which were taken as literal faculties).[9]

If we analyze the ethical and mystical examples Aquinas offers, we note that while the reasoning mode passes from experience through understanding to judgment, the connatural mode goes right to judgment without passing through understanding: as Lonergan and

---

7 Indeed, what *shall* we call the synthesis? Even contemporary approaches continue to speak of basic "affect programs" and "higher cognitive emotions" in the context of neuroscience's questioning whether emotions are "natural kinds" at all and whether the names for emotions refer to anything but social constructs (Griffiths 1997; Brothers 1997; 2001).

8 For Lonerganians the affections parallel the four levels of consciousness and could be diagrammed as extending along the right side of the levels and operations (Tallon 1997, 210, 216).

9 J.B. Lotz (1978) states unequivocally that there is no third intentionality: *keine dritte Intentionalität*. This is a consistent position to hold from within dyadic concept of the soul, mind and will but no heart.

Doran have clarified, insight is to truth what feeling is to value. We experience feelings or emotions that are connatural resonances or dissonances, attunements or discords between oneself and a contemplated act; the emotion itself is not a judgment but feelings and emotions make value judgments possible without using concepts: a feeling or sense of rightness replaces or substitutes for a concept. Indeed, we should probably reverse the priority and say that our usual way of deciding in familiar and repeated occasions is "intuitive" in this sense of a synthesis of affective and cognitive intentions (connaturality), and we should consider this way the default way. Only in unusual, novel, unfamiliar cases are we forced to use reason to supplement our connatural resonances.

In connaturality, the feeling takes the place of understanding; without an act of understanding, no concept is formed; as Maritain has noted (1953; 1953), this kind of "knowing" is non-conceptual (whence his application of connaturality theory to his analysis of art, poetry, and mysticism). It would *have* to be non-conceptual if there were no acts of understanding: no insights hence no concepts, since concepts, ideas, hypotheses, theories, etc., are the products of insights, and this "half" of the apperceptive synthesis is the affective half. An emotional response takes the place of a cognition (Meinong 1972). Since we normally experience no neutral feelings (flat affect, autism, and psychopathic or sociopathic responses are abnormal), the affective intentions bring along the evaluative component in combining with the cognitive. They are *parallel* inputs, with the affections as evaluations of our world as in tune with us or not (hedonic tone, pleasant or not, good or bad, etc.).[10]

---

10   If we try to think our way out of faculty psychology and its talk of *ratio, intellectus*, etc., and into intentionality analysis, we can ask why it is that no intentionality has any direct control over any of the others. We find both affection and volition opaque, outside of our ability to understand them, to reduce them to our ideas of them. Affection cannot feel thoughts or will acts. And volition is incapable of commanding understanding (try telling yourself that you are going to master Einstein's two relativity theories in the next few minutes) or feeling (like cognition, one can negotiate time and effort to bring understanding about and one can diplomatically prepare and dispose oneself to respond affectively, but no emotion is available "at will"). Refer to Lotz and *keine dritte Intentionalität*.

The confirmation by neuroscience today must broaden beyond the internal workings of the single brain and include an externalist's awareness of the social matrix in which human consciousness originates and operates. Only a field theory can do justice to the social and ethical (Tallon 2008), to show that consciousness, including self-consciousness is emergent or supervenient not in an isolated brain but on a field co-constituted by and together with other human brains (Brothers 1997; 2001; Rockwell 2005; 2007; Tallon 2008).

Aquinas's connaturality and Rousselot's elaboration of it illustrate the same thing: persons otherwise limited to acting solely on the basis of conceptual knowledge experience a great improvement in their ability to act, and to will (virtuously) because they acquire a habit, chastity, or receive it as a gift (wisdom as a gift of the Spirit). Habits as second natures allow us to operate the way nature does, with a kind of "natural appetite" instead of an "elicited appetite" (elicited by a [sense] image or an [intellectual] idea), hence Aquinas's speaking of *per modum naturae*, which we could translate loosely as "a nature's way" of acting, a natural rather than conceptual way, or by consulting one's whole nature rather than only one's mental inventory.

Knowing by attending to one's body's resonance adds another intentionality in order to secure a better way to decide and act. The human soul was a kind of "associate member" in the Thomist intellect club (whose "full members" are angels and God). Given the lack of empirical evidence for the existence of the full members, evolution may be thought to enter the scene offering a natural hierarchy and continuum, and what prevents our speculating, in the fashion of Ray Kurzweil, Bill Joy, and others, that we are not the end point of evolution, that we are perhaps approaching a time of "spiritual machines" who will succeed us, outdoing our highest level of operation perhaps so effortlessly that we could be said to represent the low end of what our robotic "children" can achieve (and some include affective computing in this scenario; Minsky 2007).

Conclusion

I take Rousselot's major thesis not to be the primacy of intuition but the thesis that affection and cognition are inseparable in a synthetic act that he calls an apperceptive synthesis (which ends in a synoptic concept [*synopse conçue*, literally a "conceived synopsis," more freely translated as "conscious synopsis"].[11] Reference to context is a good answer, given that Rousselot aims to inject love into knowledge as a necessary condition for all knowledge, with the corollary that the knowledge is better to the degree that the love ingredient in it is conscious (he mentions art and religion as examples of when we are more aware).

"Apperceptive synthesis" is less a cognition with an affective tone added than a concrete functional union of two intentionalities that can be distinguished abstractly; but we should not conceive the synthesis as something we consciously put together from separate faculties operating independently. Rather the union pre-exists the distinct intentions and the intentions are only given together. We would have to do something like a freeze frame to stop the kinetic flow. The synthesis of the two intentionalities may vary in degrees of affection and cognition dependent on the subjects or objects intended. We should stop *separating* the two intentions, even though we may *distinguish* them phenomenologically; whether they remain distinct "all the way down" to the neural nets is debated; at the level of neural nets both cognition and affection are weighted and neurochemically washed synapses. Rousselot's sympathetic knowing calls attention to the affective within consciousness, whether peripherally, in the margins of consciousness, as moods, or more dominantly. We should, then, accept Rousselot's apperceptive synthesis and sympathetic knowing as descriptions of human experience, without needing to accept immaterial spirits as models. In other words, we replace the elegant notion of a (top down) hierarchy of spirits, with God at the top, angels at next level down, and human souls as the lowest ranking, with a (bottom up) messy evolutionary perspective where consciousness is emergent on human brains in social fields.

---

11   Lonergan solved a similar problem in much the same way, choosing the term "apprehension" to refer to an affective experience (in *Method in Theology*) when he elsewhere uses the term "feeling." He says feelings are apprehensions of value; clearly he intends to use apprehension as a neutral term, one applying to both cognition and affection. Cognitions apprehend truth (meaning, information); feelings apprehend worth (value, importance). In a history of philosophy dominated by cognitive theory, we need patiently to seek the right word.

The apperceptive synthesis is a synthesis of affection and cognition that aims at decision (volition) and action. It is a looser way to speaking that allows one to say that we cannot know without love; we can try not, but we cannot act well without love.[12]

BIBLIOGRAPHY

Brothers, Leslie. 1989. "A Biological Perspective on Empathy." *American Journal of Psychiatry* (January 1989) 146 (1): 10-19.

————. 1997. *Friday's Footprint: How Society Shapes the Human Mind*. Oxford: Oxford University Press.

————. 2001. *Mistaken Identity: The Mind-Brain Problem Reconsidered*. Albany: State University of New York Press.

Damasio, Antonio R. 1994. *Descartes' Error: Emotion, Reason, and the Human Brain*. New York: G. P. Putnam.

————. 1999. *The Feeling of What Happens: Body and Emotion in the Making of Consciousness*. New York: Harcourt Brace.

————. 2003. *Looking for Spinoza: Joy, Sorrow, and the Feeling Brain*. Orlando, FL: Harcourt.

Darwin, Charles. 1955. *The Expression of the Emotions in Man and Animals*. New York: Philosophical Library.

Davidson, Richard J., Klaus R. Scherer, & H. Hill Goldsmith, editors. 2003a. *Handbook of Affective Sciences*. Oxford; New York: Oxford University Press.

————. 2003b. "The Neuroscience of Emotion" in Goleman 2003: 179-204.

DeLancey, Craig. 2003. *Passionate Engines: What Emotions Reveal about Mind and Artificial Intelligence*. New York: Oxford University Press.

Goleman, Daniel. 1995. *Emotional Intelligence*. New York: Bantam Books.

————. 2003. *Destructive Emotions: How Can We Overcome Them?: A Scientific Dialogue with the Dalai Lama*. New York: Bantam Books.

Griffiths, Paul E. 1997. *What Emotions Really Are: The Problem of Psychological Categories*. Chicago: University of Chicago Press.

Guillaumont, Antoine. 1950. "Les sens des noms du cœur dans l'antiquité." In *Le cœur*, 41–81. Bruges, Belgium: Desclée de Brouwer,

---

12 "Il découvre non seulement qu'on ne peut connaître sans aimer, mais encore que connaître vraiment, c'est se laisser éclairer par l'amour, accepter d'être illuminé en consentant à aimer" (Holstein 1965, 124 [460]. Needless to say throughout this Foreword the presumption has been that for Rousselot love is much more than an act of the will, despite his "dyadic lapses," if I may call them, where affection is ascribed to the will. If one thing is clear to this reader at least, for Rousselot love is misunderstood if affection is reduced to volition.

Heidegger, Martin. 1995.*The Fundamental Concepts of Metaphysics: World, Finitude, Solitude.* Trans. William McNeill & Nicholas Walker. Bloomington: Indiana University Press.

————— 1999. *Contributions to Philosophy (From Enowning).* Trans. Parvis Emad & Kenneth Maly. Bloomington: Indiana University Press.

Held, Klaus. 1992. "The Finitude of the World: Phenomenology in Transition from Husserl to Heidegger." Trans. Anthony J. Steinbock. In Dallery 1992: 187-198.

—————. 2002. "The Origin of Europe with the Greek Discovery of the World." Trans. Sean Kirkland. *Epoché* 7, 1: 81-105.

—————. 2007. "Phenomenology of 'Authentic Time' in Husserl and Heidegger." *International Journal of Philosophical Studies* 15, 3: 327-347.

Holstein, Henri. 1965. "Le théologien de la foi," In *Mémorial Pierre Rousselot, 1878-1915.* Paris : Centre National de la Recherche Scientifique: 86 [422]-125 [461].

Humphrey, Nicholas. 1992. *A History of Mind: Evolution and the Birth of Consciousness.* New York: Simon & Schuster.

Johnston, Victor S. 1999. *Why We Feel: The Science of Human Emotions.* Cambridge, MA: Perseus Books.

Kurzweil, Ray. 1999. *The Age of Spiritual Machines: When Computers Exceed Human Intelligence.* New York: Viking.

—————. 2005. *The Singularity Is Near: When Humans Transcend Biology.* New York: Viking.

LeDoux, Joseph. 1998. *The Emotional Brain: The Mysterious Underpinnings of Emotional Life.* NY: Touchstone.

—————. 2002. *Synaptic Self: How Our Brains Become Who We Are.* NY: Viking.

Lonergan, Bernard. 1972. *Method in Theology.* New York: Herder.

—————. 1974. *A Second Collection. Papers by Bernard J. F. Lonergan, SJ.* Ed. by William F. J. Ryan & Bernard J. Tyrrell. Toronto: University of Toronto Press.

Lotz, Johannes Baptist. 1978. *Transzendentale Erfahrung.* Freiburg im Breisgau: Herder.

Maritain, Jacques. 1952. "On Knowledge through Connaturality." In *The Range of Reason*, 22–29. New York: Scribner's.

—————. 1953. *Creative Intuition in Art and Poetry.* New York: Pantheon Books.

Meinong, Alexius. 1972. *On Emotional Presentation.* Trans. with an Introduction by Marie-Luise Schubert Kalsi. Evanston: Northwestern University Press.

Minsky, Marvin. 2007. *The Emotion Machine. Commonsense Thinking, Artificial Intelligence, and the Future of the Human Mind.* New York: Simon & Schuster.

Moyn, Samuel. 2005. *Origins of the Other: Emmanuel Levinas between Revelation and Ethics.* Ithaca: Cornell University Press.

Rockwell, W. Teed. 2005. *Neither Brain nor Ghost: A Nondualist Alternative to the Mind-Brain Identity Theory.* Cambridge: MIT Press.

———. 2007. "Reply to Review of *Neither Brain nor Ghost*" in *Education and Culture* 23.1: 87-89.

Rowlands, Mark. 2003. *Externalism: Putting Mind and World Back Together Again.* Montreal: McGill-Queen's University Press.

———. 2006. *Body Language: Representation in Action.* Cambridge: MIT Press.

Rousselot, Pierre. 2001. *The Problem of Love in the Middle Ages. A Historical Contribution.* Trans. with an Introduction by Alan Vincelette. Reviewed and corrected by Pol Vandevelde. Milwaukee: Marquette University Press.

Rummel, Rudolph J. 1975. *Understanding Conflict and War.* Volume 1: *The Dynamic Psychological Field.* 1976. Volume 2: *The Conflict Helix.* Beverly Hills: Sage Publications.

Sheehan, Thomas. 1987. *Karl Rahner: The Philosophical Foundations.* Athens: Ohio University Press.

Tallon, Andrew. 1992. "The Heart in Rahner's Philosophy of Mysticism." *Theological Studies* 53: 700–28.

———. 1997. *Head and Heart: Affection, Cognition, Volition as Triune Consciousness.* New York: Fordham University Press.

———. 2008. "Levinas's Ethical Horizon, Affective Neuroscience, and Social Field Theory." Jeffrey Bloechl, editor. *Levinas Studies.* Volume 4. Pittsburgh: Duquesne University Press, forthcoming.

INTRODUCTION

BETWEEN EPISTEMIC VIRTUE AND METAPHYSICS OF KNOWLEDGE: THE PLACE OF LOVE IN PIERRE ROUSSELOT'S EPISTEMOLOGY

POL VANDEVELDE

This volume is the third of Pierre Rousselot's Philosophical Works. It includes seven essays written between 1908 and 1914, one year before his death (Two were published posthumously: "A Theory of Concepts by Functional Unity" and "Idealism and Thomism."). These essays offer a complement to Rousselot's views on epistemology, which he presented in *Intelligence* and constitute the core of his Neo-thomistic philosophy. However, besides making his views more clear and specific, these essays also go further than what we had in *Intelligence*. It is an effort to offer a systematic view on knowledge as the fusion of the knower and the known. These views go significantly beyond St Thomas' doctrine and some of them are rather daring, like Rousselot's notion of an Angel-humanity.

The common thread of these essays is the role of love in knowledge and this is what I would like to examine in this introduction. Rousselot's expands St. Thomas' view on knowledge "on the mode of nature" (*per modum naturae*) or connaturality and understands love both as an attitude of the knower, who must be in a certain disposition toward the object, and a characterization of the relationship between knower and known. As an attitude love is a virtue—an epistemic virtue as it were—as a quality of the knower who has to be benevolent toward what can be known. As a characterization of the epistemic relationship, love is this state or atmosphere in which both knower and known are caught and which allows for the correlation of the subject and the object to function successfully. These two aspects—the emphasis on the attitude of the knower and the focus on the type of relationship required—make his epistemology significantly different from what we are accustomed to in the sense that his is also a metaphysics of knowledge. He does not only explain how the mechanics of knowing works, but also on what this mechanics relies.

Regarding the first aspect of love as an attitude of the knower, we can appeal to a new brand of epistemology, called virtue epistemology, in order to show the relevance of Rousselot's position. Virtue epistemology is modeled after virtue ethics and stresses the importance, besides moral virtues, of intellectual virtues. This model is motivated by what it sees as the shortcomings of a view on knowledge that only takes into account some necessary and sufficient conditions like the traditional view of knowledge as justified true belief. Its goal is to show that an account of knowledge can only be complete if it integrates the qualities or "excellences" of the knower. (See, among others, Zagzebski 1996).

The introduction of virtues into epistemology may be traced back to the need to take into consideration the reliability of the means we use to have knowledge. Edmund Gettier showed negatively that we cannot just limit the set of necessary and sufficient conditions for knowledge to following: that, first, what is claimed to be known is the case; secondly, the knower believes that what is known is the case, and, thirdly, the knower is justified in believing it. As Gettier showed, we may be justified in believing something and that may be true, but without it being knowledge, because, as in his examples, one of the propositions we entertain as part of our justification is false. And other scenarios have been provided in which no false proposition is involved, like those farmers in Wisconsin who set up three fake barns for any real one in order to increase the appearance of wealth. A driver on the highway may form the belief, "This barn is quite nice," would be justified in believing it, and it may be a real barn, but it would not be knowledge, since three out of four of those barns are fake.

One attempt was made by Keith Lehrer to distinguish what is justified according to one's own acceptance system and what is justified according to the verific system in place in the community (Lehrer 2000). This solution indeed communalizes the problem, so that I may be personally justified given what I know, but if I knew what others know, I would not be. However, this only pushes the problem further, for we would have to define what the verific system is, who establishes it, and on what ground or authority. All these attempts point to the importance of the reliability of the means we use to gain knowledge. Plato's example in the *Theaetetus* of a jury convicting a criminal on the basis of an eyewitness was already an effort to show that knowledge has to come from what is a reliable source.

Reliability has been linked to the proper function of our faculties. This led Alvin Plantinga to reformulate the problem of justification through what he calls "warrant": "I therefore suggest initially that a necessary condition of a belief's having warrant for me is that my cognitive equipment, my belief-forming and belief-maintaining apparatus or powers, be free of... malfunction. A belief has warrant for you only if your cognitive apparatus is functioning properly, working the way it ought to work, in producing and sustaining it" (Plantinga, 2000, 446). In addition, Plantinga insists on the link between the environment and the belief-forming apparatus. "Your faculties must be in good working order, and the environment must be appropriate for your particular repertoire of epistemic powers. It must be the sort of environment for which your faculties are designed—by God or evolution (or both)" (Plantinga 2000, 448). This is a version of naturalized epistemology with a design component.

Such a model relies on a strict causalist view of knowledge: our knowledge is caused by faculties and these faculties were themselves caused by evolution or God. The usual problem of causality is that it is supposed to explain how we move from the physics of things impinging upon our senses in the form of sense data to the semantics of representations in our mind. But the nagging question has always been what the law or the rule or the principle of explanation is that allows us to make the connection between the order of things acting upon our senses and the order of representations, which consists of beliefs. In "Two Dogmas of Empiricism" Quine has questioned what he sees as dogmatic empiricism in its claim that our concepts and the objects we see around us can be directly derived from sense data. And phenomenology on the continental side has made an analogous case against reductionism by introducing the notion of intentionality and the necessary link between consciousness and object.

What virtue epistemology introduces in the framework for defining knowledge is some qualities or excellences of the knower, and not just faculties and powers. But what do we mean by virtue? According to John Greco "a virtue is... an ability. An ability, in turn, is a stable disposition to achieve certain results under certain conditions" (Greco 2000, 468). Traditionally, intellectual virtues include wisdom and understanding (See Zagzebski 1996, 49-50). Alvin Goldman lists some specific epistemic virtues and vices: "I shall assume that the virtues include belief formation based on sight, hearing, memory, reasoning in certain 'approved' ways, and so forth. The vices include intellectual processes like forming beliefs by guesswork, wishful thinking, and ignoring contrary evidence" (Goldman 2000, 440). Another list was proposed by Montmarquet, summarized by Zagzebski as follows: "They are the virtues of impartiality, or openness to the ideas of others, the virtues of intellectual sobriety, or the virtues of the careful inquirer who accepts only what is warranted by the evidence, and the virtues of intellectual courage, which include perseverance and determination" (Zagzebski 2000, 462). Thus virtue epistemology widens the scope of epistemology by introducing certain requirements on the side of the knower. But it still remains within the causal framework of cognition. It still considers the knowing subject and the known object as two separate entities and related by some causal links.

Rousselot's understanding of love as an attitude can be understood as deepening the scope of epistemology by uncovering certain elements that force us to renew or reformulate the very process of cognition making it very difficult to confine the process of knowing to a strictly causal model. While building upon St. Thomas' understanding of love as a love for God, Rousselot also suggests that love is an attitude of the knower in the sense of a benevolence toward things. The main effect love as an attitude has epistemically is to do positively what Heidegger presented negatively as the "step back" (*ein Schritt zurück*) or the "letting be" (*Gelassenheit*) of things, by which the knower accepts to put herself in the attitude of being addressed by things instead of forcefully categorizing them. This attitude was itself a reformulation of Husserl's *epoche* by which the knower no longer participates in the world as it goes, with this difference that Heidegger recognized, what Husserl did not, that we are always approaching things from within a web of beliefs, so that the neutral attitude Husserl advocated is merely methodological and not a real attitude to adopt.

The attitude of love in epistemology would thus be the positive side of Heidegger's willful disengagement from things in their social, cultural, and scientific entanglements. It would mean that the knower has to have an attitude of benevolence toward things and a willingness to look for more than what is strictly given. For, givenness is always framed in some fashion and it requires a particular attitude of benevolence for envisaging the possibility of other modes of givenness. Any object is always given or approached in a certain attitude. For example, a financier can buy a Stradivarius as investment and put it in a safe in a bank as investment, just as I can use with respect and emotion an otherwise old and worthless aluminum kitchen knife that belonged to my grandmother. This affective status, always specific, makes salient some aspects of the object but at the expense of others. Different from this state of being affected love is the attitude that allows us to transcend these specific affective states and give things credit: things may be richer and more meaningful than they presently appear and there may be other modes through which they may be given, of which I am not yet aware. Such an attitude of love is what guides the knower in trying to apprehend things without grasping them in available categories. In addition to the negative Heideggerean stepping back—which is the moment of disengaging from the world and no longer participating in its business—we have with love a positive acknowledgment of the integrity of things, of their resistance to any particular approach.

This attitude of love is of course by definition vague, because it is an attitude that cannot be defined by necessary and sufficient conditions. But this attitude is also rigorously a twofold recognition: First, against methodological solipsism, it is the acceptance that I do not perceive, believe, or otherwise think in isolation and cannot thus generalize to others what I would find true for me; I perceive, believe, or otherwise think from within a community, a culture, and a tradition.

I may perceive the Zeus temple at Paestum, in Heidegger's example, but I do not perceive what the ancient Greeks who believed in Zeus and other gods perceived. The fact that causally I have the same sense data as ancient Greeks does not explain the specific perception of this as a temple to worship Zeus at the sacred place of Paestum. As Heidegger famously said, this world of the temple is no longer. And, secondly, things themselves are part of a world in which they are interconnected through our beliefs, thoughts, and habits. When these webs of beliefs change, it is not so much that things change, but that they gain a different outlook. And given the first point, the outlook (their *eidos*) is also part of what they are (their essence). These two points in fact slightly reformulate the creed of phenomenology that consciousness is always "of" something and that things are always "for" consciousness.

Rousselot's understanding of love in knowledge can be discerned by following two threads. The first one is a continuation of the traditional account given by Aquinas, which we can find, through the influence of Rousselot, in Maréchal's transcendental version of Thomism (Maréchal 1949).[1] When Rousselot says that the "desire for God is the dynamic and active element of knowledge: we understand things only insofar as we desire God" (123 in this volume), he reformulates Aquinas's view that God is ultimately the cause of knowledge. Both subject and thing have been created and wanted into existence by God. Only with an affinity with God's plan can the subject fully recover God's intention in the object. This is what Maréchal reformulates when he sees the love of God motivating us as a "latent love in us and operating no less mysteriously outside us: we discover it in us only through the mediation of finite objects where this love is refracted to the infinite without being absorbed; we discover it in things only through their correspondence to the attempt we make on them of our own tendency toward God, i.e., by knowing them and wanting them" (Maréchal 1949, 463).

This model appeals to the model of potentiality-actuality, which puts forth the view that we come to actuate by our mind what is potentially intelligible in the thing. Rousselot assents to Aquinas' understanding of connaturality. "Indeed intellection, as Thomas often says, requires, as does all knowledge, a certain identity, connaturality or resemblance of knower and known. There could in no way be knowledge if the soul did not express itself by expressing the object, and this or that object" (136 in this volume. On Aquinas, see *Summa theologiae* IIa IIae q. 45 a.2). This model of potentiality-actuality in a causal framework assumes a kind of pre-established adequacy between mind and world, so that what our mind actuates was already a possibility and this possibility was previously actuated, usually by God, who is the first absolute performer of the act leaving us the second-order task of retrieving these possibilities and re-actuating them. From a strict epistemological perspective this first performance is precisely what we want to be explained and to make of it a posit or a postulate will not satisfy contemporary epistemologists.

There is, however, a second thread in Rousselot's views, which is quite original. Love is not only an attitude of the knower causally explainable, but also a character of the relationship between knower and known. It is the epistemic relationship that is permeated by love and this is not exclusively an attitude or a virtue of the knower. Beyond Aquinas Rousselot reconnects with the tradition started by Plato in *Phaedrus* and the *Symposium* which link love and knowledge. These Platonic views were in turn taken over by romantics, especially early German romanticism, which brought out the view, expressed by Schlegel, that an object has an inner sense (*Sinn*) and through perception "the sense immediately shines, the thou speaks in the moment *the essence in its totality is understood by the ego*, addresses the ego and *manifests to him the essence of its existence*" (Schlegel 1964, 350).

In the case of Rousselot, we can hear this second thread in the quote given above: beside the desire for God, Rousselot mentions a "dynamic and active element of knowledge" (Rousselot 1910, 229). This second thread is what I will pursue.

LOVE AS A CHARACTERIZATION OF THE RELATION
BETWEEN KNOWER AND KNOWN

In this thread the love of God becomes a love for the object. This view of love is more inchoate in Rousselot's essays, but clearly present and it suggests that love does not work exclusively in a causal way nor in the framework of potentiality—actuality, but instead teleologically. This aspect makes of Rousselot's epistemology a metaphysics of knowledge and represents a genuine contribution to any theory of knowledge. This contribution sustains itself independently of the assumptions of Neo-thomism, so that Rousselot's religious vocabulary can thus be translated in non-religious epistemic terms.

What the love for the object does is to motivate us to look further and transcend the different modes of givenness toward the fullness of the object. By inviting us to go further love also explains and justifies the trust we have in our senses and the conviction that things are as we know them to be. Love in a sense grounds our trust that, although there is more to what I see, what I see is also what is the case. Through love the indefiniteness of the object is reconnected with its fullness.

With love as one of its components cognition becomes an existential event in which we may be one with things. In Rousselot's explanation "love" is what allows us to reconnect the "what" of things with the fact "that" they are, their essence with their *esse* (i.e., being or existence). This existential component reconnects knowledge with life. "I above all wanted to bring to light the inanity, from a Thomist perspective, of the opposition between *intellection* and *life*; I wanted to show that intellection is only fully itself if it is action in the full sense... I defined in these terms ideal cognition: To know is chiefly and primarily to grasp and embrace in oneself another who is capable of grasping and embracing you; it is to live of the life of another living" (quoted in Lavalette 1965, 129).

This existential character of cognition manifests itself in the reliability of our beliefs and knowledge. While the general framework of justified true belief appeals to some mechanisms to insure the reliability or warranty of our knowledge (See Alston 1995, Plantinga 1993), they have to stop at a level of belief that is qualified as highly probable. What this model does not explain is that what we experience in our perceptions in not a high probability that what we see is as we see it. In our experience perceptions are neither hypothetical nor probable when we have them: we just trust them, even if we constantly amend and modify them and even if we know they are sometimes wrong. This indicates that the fluctuation of our perceptions from vague to clear and their susceptibility to being false does not appear at the level of experience, but rather only at the level of reflection, and usually when we are forced to reflect because the experience we are having does not make sense anymore. In these instances the pattern our perceptual experience was following dissipates and we are forced into a search for a new pattern; however, this attempted correction does not follow the model of a hypothesis having been tested and refuted. In other words, the way we live our perceptual experiences relies on a trust we have, a trust which Descartes, for example, placed in God, who he thought would not have given us deceiving faculties. Rousselot's existential account of knowledge, which blurs the boundaries between intellection and life, allows him to move beyond the causal model of cognition (of St. Thomas and Descartes, for example) and show that cognition is not merely an effect of things on the intellect but an activity of human existence directed towards a certain end.

The starting point for Rousselot is the correlation between things and the soul. "Being, thing, object, all this means: object for the soul, being for the soul. It would be the formula of subjectivism if one meant by this that the being of things is reduced to what is actually perceived of them" (105 in this volume). with these formulations Rousselot seems very close to phenomenology: the thing is for the soul, but this is not traditional subjectivism or idealism. Husserl's phenomenology made a significant contribution to epistemology by showing how it is in the appearing itself, in its consistency and harmony (or lack thereof) that the stability and identity of things gives itself to us. But Rousselot also offers an explanation for the reliability of our faculty of knowledge, what phenomenology does not do. What such an explanation has to account for is that, in addition to the harmony of experience and the constant focus of multiple conscious acts, there needs to be something that guarantees the identity and stability of objects.

Rousselot reminds us that human cognition is mostly representation. By representation he means that "intelligence fabricates in itself an image of the object to be contemplated and considers its object *in* this image" (112 in this volume). Representation is different from two other forms of apprehension: grasping and intuition. "There is grasping if the intelligible Reality is identical with the very idea one has of it: if God exists, this is how He knows Himself. Physically there is intuition if there is no objective intermediary between the idea and the object, even though the idea is not the same physical reality as the object itself" (112 in this volume).

More specifically, Rousselot differentiates four components in human intellection: 1) the representation in our mind of what the thing is, for example, a thing perceived; 2) the act of synthesis in our mind producing this representation; 3) a desire and 4) an act of anticipation.[2] The last two, desire and anticipation, are of particular importance because they explain how an act of knowledge is an existential event. Let us start with the first two components, which are presented by Rousselot in the expression "for the soul": "Thus, if we say that a thing is, we also say that it is for the soul" (114 in this volume).

In the expression "for the soul" we have two relations that are intermingled: on the one hand, what a thing is is "related" to the soul as well as to the "that it is." There is a relativity of things to the soul to the extent that "corporeal essences do not exist by themselves; they are *things for a self*" (62 in this volume). It thus means that the thing in its substantiality needs the soul in order to be said, i.e., to be thought. Without the soul the thing would not be a substance. Conversely, on the other hand, the soul is such a soul only if it is related to things. As Thomas Sheehan puts it, "the point is to find the soul within the world and at the heart of material beings." It is, he continues, Rousselot's "interiorized Scholasticism" (Sheehan 1987, 60) according to which one finds oneself "thrown outside into active affinity with things" (60). We thus have a twofold interaction: there is in the thing an eye tagged to it as its principle of intelligibility and in the soul there is this intrinsic link to things. Thus, whether we start from the soul or the thing, both are intermingled: "if we say that a thing is, we also say that it is for the soul; if we say that it is for the soul, we say that it is" (114 in this volume).

The mutual dependency between things and soul relies on the saying (*dicere*) that is proper to the soul. It is this "saying" that both testifies that the thing is and makes this existence intelligible. Rousselot calls it, after Kant, the synthesis of apperception and establishes the following equivalences: "In the Word=to be=to be said=to be considered=to be generated (*In Verbo = esse = dici = considerari = gen-*

erari, (111 in this volume). Thus, a representation is such "because it is in its word, being, that the soul contemplates the thing it wants to consider" (112 in this volume). The expression "for the soul" thus means: "said by the soul."

In the sentence, "*To say that a thing is, is to say that it is for the soul,*" Rousselot emphasizes that the sentence "must be taken as a whole and without canceling the phrase *to say.* It does not mean that things are only as far as they are the actual object of the perceptions of the soul (which is false), but rather that to affirm the reality, the *entity* of a thing, is to affirm, whether one wants it or not, the possibility that this thing enters in combination with the synthesis of intellectual apperception" (110 in this volume) In a footnote Rousselot writes: "I do not claim that a thing *is* existing only through its actual relation to the soul, but that this relation (represented as possible) is found at the ground of the affirmation of the being or the possibility of a 'thing.' (Thing = object for me, unifying my consciousness, potentiality... of unifying me, potentiality... of entering in the synthesis of my apperception)" (106 in this volume).

This *dicere* that is part and parcel of things is the manifestation of the soul in the things. "To say a thing (to say in the Thomist sense: *dicere* [to say] = to think) is not to have said, but to have apperceived the soul under the thing, the soul supporting the thing, the soul informed by the thing" (111 in this volume). He qualifies this correlation between soul and thing as transcendental. "Being entails the soul as certainly (if not as expressly) as the notion of son entails the notion of father, as right entails left and selling entails buying. This transcendental relation (unequally reciprocal) does not cancel the identity of the two terms any more than the previously mentioned examples do" (106 in this volume).

Because this correlation between thing and soul is irrefragable, there is no strict unthinkable and unknowable; it can only be a manner of speaking to qualify some things as unknowable or unthinkable since they are "said" unthinkable and unknowable within a relation of thinking and knowing. "Thus, if the soul imagines the possibility of possessing an absolutely *unthinkable being,* it innocently falls into the same mistake one makes when asking: 'Were the flowers of the desert island blue and the leaves green before Robinson came ashore?'

The one who asks this question, through the very fact that he asks it, that is to say, that he speaks of *color,* substitutes, hides in the question itself an eye, a potentiality of vision. In the same way someone who imagines an unthinkable being thinks something thinkable which would be unthinkable, something representable which could not be represented" (111 in this volume). In short, "when it says being, the soul thus hides itself under it without knowing it through a kind of innocent and unconscious ruse" (111 in this volume).[3]

This character of things to be "for the soul" in the form of "being said" introduces in the act of knowing the act of affirmation and this means that, as we saw above, knowing is an existential event. To know something then is to affirm that it is and at the same time to affirm that I am among things. "All this is in intellection, because the soul, which says being, is perceived at the same time as generating, as constituting its word, which is being, and as generating it in a way from its proper substance, generating it without expressing it outside, finding itself in it and *being* it in a certain manner" (111 in this volume). The soul before knowing affirms being. In Maréchal's formulation, "in affirmation we commit ourselves to a certain manner of being of the object" (Maréchal 1949, 325).

We should not understand this affirmation of being as a voluntary act. Rather, it derives from the proper use of my faculties. I perceive a tree and, despite the specificity of the givenness (from my perspective, now, under this light) I affirm the existence of the whole tree and act upon my perception. This affirmation of being is the correlate of the trust I have in my faculties: that the object, although given incompletely, is completable in a manner I clearly anticipate. As Rousselot insists, we do not have a relativizing of the soul to things or of things to the soul; to the contrary, the mutual interaction between them makes them relational. Regarding things, "to say that corporeal essences, animals, plants, minerals, are *things for a self,* is to say that they are at the same time substances and relationships to human beings (non-"predicamental," but "transcendental" relationships) (63 in this volume). Instead of a derealization of things Rousselot suggests that the thingness of things or their substantiality as persistence is of the nature of a relationship. "These corporeal beings, *being relationships, are substances*" so that there is a "formal coincidence of their substantiality and relativity" (63 in this volume). An interesting consequence is that God himself, in order to understand substances, has to go through the human soul. The human soul is thus not merely an inferior mode of knowledge compared to God, but a component in God's intellection.

"The first word of the soul is neither *Cogito* [I think] nor *Sum* [I am] but *Est* [it is]. But this *Est* has no meaning if *Sum* cannot come out of it and there is no truth in this *Est* if there is no truth in *Sum*" (109 in this volume). The *Sum* is the synthesis of apperception manifested by anything and the *Est* is the affirmation of existence at the ontological core of a thing. By synthesis of apperception Rousselot means that any positing of being is performed by someone, and hence: "To say: 'This is,' is to say: '*Someone who would see all of being would see this there.*' Forming this synthesis is equivalent then to presupposing, to presuming, to imagining [*rêver*] the absolute creative Truth—Every act of intellection presupposes not only that reality is intelligible, that reality can be brought to light, but also that reality is somewhere understood, somewhere completely brought to light: therefore it presupposes God" (171 in this volume).

As suggested above, we do not need to understand God in religious terms here, since we are dealing with a structural issue about cognition as a metaphysical fact. If it is correct to say as Rousselot does, and as I think it is, that any talk about a thing involves a talker, the talker or speaker or positer of things, or more simply, the observer, is immediately split: there is the observer who now perceives a thing, but this observer is then connected with another, let us call him the "ideal" observer who would know all perspectives about the thing now observed from a specific perspective. This is what was meant by desire and anticipation, the last two of the four components of human intellection mentioned above. Although structural, the anticipation of the whole is also the anticipation of another act of knowledge performed by another ideal subject. "This is not" means "Someone who would see the whole of being would not see this there"" (170 in this volume). In any act of perception we thus have this collaboration between an imperfect observer seeing things from a particular perspective and the ideal observer able to see the whole, so that at the moment I perceive there is a transcendence of the perspective. Trusting my faculties I can also affirm the being of the thing observed. I may be a split subject when I reflect upon my faculties, but I am existentially a full subject during the exercise of my faculties. But who or what is this ideal subject who sees the whole so that I, seeing from a perspective, do not see piecemeal, but anticipate the whole?

The anticipation of the whole of being that an ideal subject would see means that the whole must also be accessible to imperfect subjects. That is the reason why the desire for God as the means to reconnect with the fullness of the object in a causal model is not fully satisfactory for Rousselot, because this model does not account for the fullness I can experience of the object in an otherwise partial perception. Given that he rejects any unthinkable, the ideal subject cannot be a mere postulate; it is itself "said" by me and thus accessible to me. This means that an intuition of such an entity must be possible. I can anticipate the whole of the object by intuiting the one who would see the whole. This already significantly reformulates Aquinas' view that God is such a perfect subject, since God cannot be intuited. Rousselot then makes an interesting threefold claim: first, this ideal subject is not necessarily God; second, in some sense I am this ideal subject; but, thirdly, although it is a transcendence within me, this remains an existential fact, and not a transcendental device of cognition. Rousselot sometimes calls it the "angel-humanity." I will return to this.

This threefold claim shows that every act of cognition involves a transcendence of the knower from the particular perspective he has of the object. It is this transcendence that explains the fact that I never merely see a perspective but always the whole objects. This anticipation of the whole of the object is structurally included in the representation I have of the object precisely to represent "an" object (and not a fragment of a shapeless something). In this sense this anticipation is transcendental. But it is not just a transcendental device of cognition, because this structural anticipation is also linked to an ideal subject who would see the whole. Thus, the anticipation of the whole of the object is ultimately made possible by an intuition of the ideal subject who would see the whole. Now, as an actual subject not seeing just a part of things, but seeing them fully in flesh and blood, I have at the core of my perceptions another eye completing my vision. This ideal subject, which is, to repeat, neither merely a structural component of cognition (a transcendental device) nor a mere Kantian regulative idea guaranteeing the totality of the object, is collaborating with me in a living process. Thus, I have to be this ideal subject, although only through anticipation. The mode I can be this ideal subject is precisely love. How does it work?

This question of how a perspective on an object gives the whole object has been addressed by phenomenology and Gestalt theory. And now neurosciences struggle with the same problem. But all tend to treat the issue as a structural puzzle: the whole is already in the parts. The difficulty with such an exclusively structural approach is that the parts or perspectives cannot be exhaustively mapped, because they are also in part intermingled with other aspects of the life of the knowing subject, her culture, customs, and tradition. So the whole of the thing would have to be made of fluctuating and innumerable parts.

Husserl offered a solution, followed by Searle, by introducing the notion of horizons of perception (what Searle calls background). But this again seems rather to name the problem than to offer a solution. How does the horizon "complete" my partial perspective?

Rousselot offers two different kinds of solutions. The first one is the traditional causal model of potentiality-actuality, according to which the other unseen possibilities of the object are in potentiality in the object. As I mentioned above, this entails that they have been or are in act for an ideal subject. This ideal subject knowing in act as ideal can only be a real subject and this is God. He knows the totality of the thing *in actu* before I can see it from my perspective and my partial seeing is both subsequent and consequent to His. This belongs to the first thread we discussed above of love as love of God.

However, Rousselot also suggests another solution, rather daring, which he does not make fully explicit, but which derives from his views that the subject who would see the whole object is not God, but what I call the ideal subject and what Rousselot calls the Angel-humanity. In this model the other perspectives on an object are not merely structural components pre-inscribed in my horizon and already included implicitly as a hologram in the particular perspective I have now. These other aspects are what another ideal subject would see and this ideal subject, which is not God and thus not inaccessible to me, is in fact made of other human subjects, the totality of them. The whole is what humanity would see as the sum of all possible human perspectives. Because it is human this ideal subject is something I could be virtually at the very moment I perceive from my perspective.

Rousselot does not explicitly state this, but suggests it: love is precisely what allows me to be virtually the ideal subject. This love is both a desire for completion and a love for things. It is a desire for completion because I feel that the subject who now sees is also striving toward being an ideal subject who would see the whole object. And it is also a love for things, because I have to let things be more than what I can see of them and to let them unfold before my eyes before categorizing and classifying them. These two directions of love explain why love for Rousselot is not simply an attitude, but also a character of the epistemic relation between knower and known. Let us examine the love for things first.

Love for things

The mode of knowing *per modum naturae* gives the soul access not just to the essence of things (what representation allows), but to the *esse*—that is why to perceive a thing from one perspective is to affirm the being of the thing as a whole—although the *esse* is not generated by the soul. Love allows the knower to have access to what something or somebody is and to the fact that the thing or the person is. This is how the soul is not just a recipient for things but an ontological appendage to things. Love is supposed to explain the homogeneity between the knowing subject and the known object at the ontological level: that the soul is for things and things for the soul or that the soul is "saying" (affirming of existence) and things are "sayable." But love is more than an affinity, which would only mean negatively that the soul and the thing known are not of a different order or are not unrelatable. Love in the strong sense "makes" the subject such as he can know the thing as it appears to him or her. "Love blinds.—Affection gives eyes in order to know. Love makes us see. These two truisms, while apparent opposites, in reality only express two sides of a single truth, one of considerable philosophical importance, and one we could formulate in these terms: *every knowing* [connaissance] *is defined by a love*]" (119 in this volume).[4] Because it is in part a disposition of the knower "love, which renders the subject *such*, makes the object appear *such*" (119 in this volume). However, it is not exclusively a quality or virtue of the knower, but a state of the relationship between knower and known (it is the metaphysical fact mentioned above).

All cognition, Rousselot claims, has two components: "the *attitude* moment and the *knowledge* element" (136 in this volume), the attitude moment being the sympathetic or loving moment and the knowledge moment being the strictly representational element (136 in this volume). Love makes the object appear as the knower sees it. By "sympathetic" or "loving moment" Rousselot does not mean the affective state of being taken by an object, like my grandma's kitchen knife. To the contrary, love means to let go of the object, so that the object, as it grabs me, can also be the full object, object "for other souls."

Rousselot compares such knowledge through love with Kant's aesthetic knowledge. "As Kant so rightly observed, the pleasure that characterizes aesthetic knowledge does not depend on some new note perceived in the object: for aesthetic perception as such adds no new note. It consists in at least implicit consciousness of the harmonious play of our faculties, which make us vibrate, as it were, in unison with the object and installs us, so to speak, in its essence" (128 in this volume). Love does not actually make me see other properties that I would not see otherwise, but makes me aware of the existence of other possibilities. It brings me to a state antecedent to the categories I can use or it brings me back to an existential state in which I can be in unison with the fullness of the object not yet spelled out in terms of categories or perspectives. When I begin to love but do not know it yet, "I feel vaguely and as through a fog that I am seeing things otherwise than before. A certain strange quality is spread all over the objects like a light mist.... But what is new is myself; it is as though I have acquired a new category and it is because of it that I imperfectly penetrate my objects. When I become conscious of my attitude, i.e., of my love, the *meaning* of things will appear to me. I will see myself loving and take pleasure in it; everything will be clear to me, the object and the act, the object through the act. To the attitude, to the unconscious inclination there corresponds the imperfectly penetrated object; to the conscious inclination there corresponds the *possessed, understood,* concretely known object" (142 in this volume).

Knowledge through love is at the opposite of a passive knowledge in which I would be caught. I am not so much grabbed by love as invited by love to follow the hidden threads in the paste of things, allowing them to be more than I can grasp. In this sense love is an effort to do justice to things, to attend to the indefinite pool of their givenness, to care for them epistemically. This existential attitude will become in Maréchal's understanding a categorizing capacity: "when saying 'this is,' I experience and recognize 'this' as something *due* (exigible), something on which I have control and which I raise in terms of possible action, of objective means for my final end; in short, I experience and recognize 'this' globally as *value*" (Maréchal 1949, 525-26). For Rousselot, the thing is not due and not valued. I am the one who is transformed at the contact with things and as things they matter to me, the value I may attach to them being a subsequent fact.

This anticipation of the complete object, permeated by benevolence and good disposition, gives rise to a sort of ontological principle of charity, analogous to the principle of charity in interpretation. Just as we are asked in interpretation to assume that speakers or authors have at least as much intelligence as we have, the ontological version Rousselot suggests here asks us to presume that things may be denser, richer, and more complex than they appear to be. The completion of the object is also a completion of a desiring and loving subject.

This indicates the extent to which Rousselot wants knowledge to be a living knowledge and why knowledge is first of all an existential event before being a state of the soul or a state of mind. "Fundamentally, this state consists in living" (85 in this volume). When Rousselot says that love provides a new category (142 in this volume) we should understand him as speaking of a new categoriality in the etymological sense: a new set of ways to address things and to let them appear such as they are. This means that the synthesis at the level of conception or representation is supported and nurtured by the synthesis of apperception, instead of being merely made possible transcendentally as in Maréchal: "The synthesis of apperception is inseparable from the perceived synopsis... and the intuition of my modification, of my act, is physically identical to the conception of the thing. But if only the moment of *perception* is considered, the essence and the *esse* [existence], the reality and the *suchness* [talité] are indissolubly welded together, perceived together; the affirmation is not added to perception, the distinction of the real and the possible has not yet arisen" (85 in this volume). Rousselot calls the apperception of the knower in the knowing "a knowledge that is not expressed": "it is a knowledge engaged in action, indissoluble from action, all vitality, all living, without conceptual residue, lastly: one of those Aquinas calls *cognitio per modum naturae* [knowledge by way of nature]" (101-102 in this volume).

Rousselot gives several examples showing how love gives access to the *esse* by allowing for a fusion of the knowing subject and the object, but his examples are somewhat heteroclite. In one example Rousselot compares what a normal French person feels when perceiving, and what an "aesthete" who is passionate for anything French perceives. The aesthete, who has learned anything he could find about French culture, has an affinity with details of French culture of which the man-in-the-street, who lives in it, is not directly aware. For, as an aesthete "you penetrate to the core of a song, a conversation, an anecdote, where the national genius comes to expression. You can taste it because you vibrate in unison with anything the least bit French, *recognizing yourself therein*: a mere hint, a gesture, an intonation, the banter of a child passing by, will suffice to move you profoundly with an emotion full of intelligence, to make you almost faint with joy in the keen perception of the French quality" (143 in this volume).

In another example Rousselot describes a man going to the window and looking at an acacia. "Some might find him dumb and others intelligent: he stares. He does not appear particularly absorbed and if his little daughter rushes into the room in order to announce a visit, he will not wake up as if from absentmindedness. And now, see, it is already over. He leaves the window and resumes his work" (84 in this volume).[5] With this example Rousselot in addressing his readers hopes that "this has all of a sudden, in the strike of a quick intuition, brought you back to an afternoon of your childhood with the full materiality of the state in which you were. I hardly dare call it *psychological* and still, it lies at the heart of life: the confused presence or rather, more simply, the *known* presence of the white overall that protects you, the familiar heap of sand, cups and shovels, the hands full of this fine sand which is sticky and wet, life on the go" (84-85 in this volume). In this experience we are brought into a state where our common ways of classifying and categorizing things have no hold. It may be called an antecedent stage, as Rousselot suggests by mentioning children, but it is in fact a component of the metaphysical fact of knowledge: before the act of cognition there is this moment of positive indifference when knower and known are still fused, where the knower is immersed and overwhelmed by the *esse*, by the brute and wild existence of things. What makes this indifference positive is the fact that the knower is conscious of himself as fused, that he is conscious of himself as a lover. It is thus a positive and active attitude of fusion, analogous to what the full intuition of the thing would be (what God has). As a component of knowledge, but not reducible to cognition, this positive indifference nurtures the good use of cognition, as it were. By contrast, the indifference of the French man-in-the-street is a negative attitude—blurring differences—and derivatively—ignoring what is accessible.

The difference in the two attitudes of positive and negative indifference lies in the status of apperception. In the negative indifference there is no apperception, in the sense that the man-in-the-street is also oblivious of himself. By contrast, in the positive indifference, the knower is brought back, so to speak, to the arising of what becomes for him an object of knowledge. Through love the knower can attend to the birth of the object of knowledge as if at the dawn of the world.

I said above that Rousselot's use of love was the positive side of Heidegger's notion of stepping back. Heidegger's stepping back is negative because it is a disentanglement from the world and from the objects in this world. It leads to the awareness that our world is only, as it were, a possible world, which has been disclosed as a particular configuration of being, without necessity and without telos. But it is difficult to live in such an attitude of suspension or disentanglement from the world and even more difficult to re-enter a world we know to be a mere guise of the unfolding of being, let alone to love it. By contrast in Rousselot the indifference is fusion, not withdrawal. Foremost it is a loving embrace of the object so that the knowing subject assents to its own cognitive unraveling and to its being engulfed in the paste of things.

But then Rousselot gives two other examples suggesting that this positive indifference, which is action and affirmation, is a skill. He takes one of these examples from Aquinas: a chaste person compared to someone who has taken lessons on morality. Faced with a situation asking for a decision regarding the best way to behave the person who has learned chastity intellectually will seek to classify the case under consideration according to some principles. By contrast the person who just knows how to be chaste, who has the habit of chastity, "will feel a reaction of an affective order" telling him "instinctively" what is appropriate and what is not (102 in this volume). The second example Rousselot gives is of a player unable to explain a rule of a game in the abstract, but able to apply the rule and then within the concrete situation of the game able to explain it. He concludes from these two examples, the chaste person and the player, that "a true knowledge preexisted… immanent in the action itself (or in habit or in nature), which should not be confused with the theoretical extraction one can give of this knowledge when posed a question. This knowledge is independent of the extraction, since it precedes its extraction; and this knowledge could subsist without its expression" (102 in this volume).

If we now return to the first example discussed, one could wonder why the indifferent French in the street cannot have that kind of habit, since he lives the French culture and also, like the player, he may not immediately explain a particular French custom, but if asked about it *in concreto*, he most likely will be able to say something like: "We do not hug very much around here, but we shake hands quite a lot."

The ambivalence Rousselot manifests in choosing his examples is another illustration of the two threads I mentioned above in his understanding of the role of love. In the last two examples he seems to entertain the traditional causal model of knowledge through poten-

tiality and actuality: the chaste person like the player has the knowledge in potentiality and this potentiality can be acquired, as Rousselot grants: "One can find at the origin a theoretical teaching, but
then that the content has become naturalized through habit" (103
in this volume).[6]

We saw before that the love for the thing is itself derived from a
desire for completion in an ideal subject. How does this completion
take place?

LOVE AS DESIRE FOR COMPLETION

If the anticipation of the ideal subject is already immanent in any
perception, is that not another version of Kant's synthesis of apperception, the fact that an "I think" must accompany all my representations? Not quite. Rousselot laments: "We remain stuck at an
insufficient notion of apperceptive synthesis, we identify it only by
a derived property, when we explain it by saying that all intellectual
representation can be accompanied and informed by the conception
of the judgment: I think." (133 in this volume).[7] In the "I think"
there is also a non-subjective synthesis of apperception. The subject
is split and longing for its ideal part. However, this does not mean
that the subject is a truncated one, deprived of some vital ideal part
and thus impotent until it reconnects with the missing part. There
is no relativization of the knowing subject to the ideal subject compared to which it would appear as imperfect and no relativization of
the object to the completed object compared to which it would appear as incomplete. The completion of the subject and object works
by attraction. Neither do I try to re-build a parceled out object nor
am I a deconstructed subject trying to fix myself. Both subject and
object are complete, but perfectible; both are full, but completable.

We saw that this completion of the subject would take place as
and through the intuition of the ideal subject and would give me the
object fully. I can virtually be this ideal subject, which is not God. It
is thus an idealization of myself. This is what Rousselot describes as
being *in via*, being a wayfarer or *viator*. This does not mean that my
human knowledge is only a stage toward a completion that another
ideal subject would enjoy. It means that knowledge is the way itself
and knowing is a process of transformation of the subject itself: I

have to anticipate all human subjects when dealing with things. This is how I strive toward the ideal subject, this striving being an existential event, a fact of life.

We recall the difference between types of cognition. God knows things exhaustively in their *esse* while we know them inexhaustively in their essence. "God knows things by their *esse* [existence], by what they *are*. This means that God knows them exhaustively; but it also means that God knows them by what is 'deiform' in them. *God knows them by loving himself in them.* God's knowledge is love" (129 in this volume)." Maréchal turned this relationship between *esse* and essence as a transcendental one. "To affirm essence is to affirm indirectly *esse*, the act of the essence; to affirm the finite *esse*, as a limited act, is to affirm implicitly pure Being, the necessary perfection of the act; to affirm the pure Act as supreme rational condition, as ideal *par excellence*, is to affirm logically the pure Act as absolute reality... Any affirmation that would stop at any of the inferior levels of actuality would thus enter into conflict with the affirmed content and would ruin itself" (Maréchal 1949, 346).

Here Maréchal goes beyond Rousselot in his effort to show the anticipation of the whole by God as a transcendental component of any cognition. By contrast, the transcendental element in Rousselot is life itself and in life the incompleteness of knowledge and of things is also of the essence of knowledge and things. Since things are relationships to us and since the soul is part of the being of things, things are substances precisely because they can be known only inexhaustively. The anticipation of the whole for Rousselot cannot be God's perspective as it is in Aquinas or Maréchal, because God knows things exhaustively. The *esse* he knows obviously includes the whole, but is not identical with the whole. And God can only know substances through our mode of knowing. Aquinas' distinction between two types of truth, one for perfect intelligence and one for our imperfect intelligence, or what Maréchal calls "ontological truth" and "logical truth" (Maréchal 1949, 107) gives way in Rousselot to a third way: besides what I can actually know (logical truth) and what God knows (ontological truth) there is what an idealization of myself would know, which I can virtually be.

We saw that on the side of things love was an attitude of letting them be more than what is actually given. On the side of the knower we already surmise that love is not a link between an actual imperfect subject knowing partially and an ideal subject who would know the whole, since it is the same subject. Love is rather what guides the actual imperfect subject in the process of knowing so that the actual subject knows how inexhaustive his knowledge is and strives toward completion. For, knowledge will never have at its disposal the whole of what is to be known about the object. This would amount to being like God and knowing what is deiform in them, but not knowing them as they are "for the soul." Thus, love guiding the subject does not offer the anticipation of a totality of the object, which totality the subject can only see piecemeal. This is how it is for Maréchal, for whom the anticipation of the whole is a structural component of the whole. If this were merely the case, then love in this sense would only function like a Kantian transcendental idea, regulating the process of knowing. Rather for Rousselot love also gives the actual imperfect subject confidence in his knowing abilities. The "new eyes" love gives him do not so much open to something different than what is seen, as they provide confidence in the subject's knowing faculties that what is seen is indeed as it is seen. "Love does not make us judge falsely objects first seen in clear light; it colors the very light or the very atmosphere, in which we see objects. It makes us draw forth, as by nature, a new term of knowledge. I would say, in Scholastic terms, that *it elicits a new faculty of abstracting and prescribes for the knowing subject a new formal object*" (120 in this volume).

When Rousselot qualifies a thing as being "for the soul," it now means that "a thing is for the soul insofar as it is infinite, i.e., inexhaustible and incomplete. To affirm the thing insofar as it is *being* is thus to affirm it insofar as it is inexhaustible and incomplete. The being that is conceived thus has these two characters. Everything that being is, it is such for something else; and it is inexhaustible, that is to say, exhaustible, but indefinitely." (114 in this volume). This last phrase is crucial for what Rousselot tries to do. He wants to avoid traditional idealism—"for the soul" would mean "for me and you and them," but God sees the thing exhaustively and we don't; and

Rousselot wants to escape dogmatism that simply states that God is already the principle of unity within our finite knowledge.

The difference between God and the ideal subject, among others, is that God knows the thing exhaustively and at once, while the ideal subject sees the thing also exhaustively, but indefinitely and this means: not at once. Or we can say that the ideal subject sees the thing exhaustively, but through an indefinite sequence of acts analogous to mine. The ideal subject is, thus, more like me than like God: it is ideal in the sense that it does ideally what I do, as an upper limit of my capacities. And since I anticipate the whole of the object once I have a perspective, I already make use of this idealization of my capacities, although I do not know how and have no guarantee that it is the whole that is actually there. "We humans tend toward [the totalizing unity] by multiplying laborious acts: their natural end is to actualize through them the power of the spirit, to arrive at the maximum of consciousness" (Rousselot 1999, 45).

Left to my own devices without this natural tendency I would have to burden my perceptions with qualifiers which would be as many disclaimers: "there is a duck there, but although it looks like a duck and walks like a duck and quacks like a duck, it could be something else." And I would have to fall back on some form of community consensus (as in Rorty) or coherence (as in Lehrer). For Rousselot the trust I have in my perceptions indicates that the performance of the ideal subject already works as a prosthesis in my knowledge. The ideal subject completes my knowledge not in the sense of making up for my conceptual infirmity by providing what I could not see myself. It completes me by making me confident that both my limited perspectives on things and their incompleteness belong to our respective essence and thus, becoming aware of this, I also have access to the *esse* of things as well as to mine. I am a wayfarer in matters of knowledge neither as a link in a larger chain, in which those after me would see more, nor as a stage to be overcome by better knowers, but by accepting the inexhaustibility of things and my necessary consecutive perspectives. I thus accept that the sequences of perspectives may be continued without changing the essence of things and invalidating my actual knowledge.

But I can only trust this fact that, on the one hand, my particular perspectives do not threaten the integrity of knowledge and that the incompleteness of things does not compete with their identity if I have some link to that other ideal subject. "*Affirmation* of a being which is infinite by inexhaustibility is absolutely incoherent and *nonsensical* (deprived of meaning), if such an affirmation does not implicitly rely on a deeper affirmation of a being that is infinite by spirituality. Since *being* means *knowable...*, I claim that the affirmation of a represented knowable has in fact only one meaning, namely: a means for reaching an intelligible possession, which can only be the intuition of oneself." (114-115 in this volume). This intuition of myself relies on another totalizing synthesis performed by what Rousselot calls the "Head of Humanity" or "the Angel-Humanity as an unrealizable Ideal" (71, 78 in this volume) or the first Adam.

It is an angel or the first Adam because this exhaustivity is indefinite and consecutive and thus human in its mode of operation, although super-human in its status, like an angel between humans and God or Adam as the first one fallen from the hands of God. As Sheehan notes, "angelic knowledge functions in Rousselot's works less for its own sake (i.e., as an angelology) than for the purpose of defining the telos of human knowledge" (Sheehan 1987, 66). Although for Rousselot this head of humanity is Jesus, this identity is not necessary. "There needs to be a head of Humanity... The necessity of an intuition that is superhuman in a sense and preternatural [*préternaturel*] in order to ground the natural life of humanity, is in full harmony with Aquinas's whole doctrine about the human being. But *supernatural* and *preternatural* should not be confused and one should not believe that the doctrine I just sketched postulates the Incarnation for the solidity of the human world. If one puts the totalization of the world in Jesus Christ, furthering the beautiful thought of Blondel (See also Aquinas. III q. 10, a. 2, q. 11 a. 1 ad 3), the Savior did not fulfill this role precisely as Emmanuel, but as the second Adam" (71 in this volume).

This ideal of the angel-humanity is unrealizable, but it is manifested as a living ideal and its life is love. It is our own attitude towards things that brings with it its own anticipation of completion and the more disposed we are, the more sympathetic and loving even, the more sophisticated the completion will be. Since, however, the completion is made by other human perspectives my love for things is predicated on my love for those bearers of as yet unknown perspectives. The Angel-Humanity is thus less a super-ego outdoing me in the game of knowledge than an upper limit of hyper-benevolence that already informs me and attracts me, so that things tell me more of their story, as I tread along as a wayfarer.

Works Cited

Alston, William. 1995. "How to Think About Reliability" *Philosophical Topics* 23 (1995), 1-29.

Goldman, Alvin. 2000. "Epistemic Folkways and Scientific Epistemology," in Ernest Sosa and Jaegwon Kim, *Epistemology: An Anthology.* Oxford: Blackwell, 438-444.

Husserl, Edmund. 1998. *Ideas Pertaining to a Pure Phenomenology and to a Phenomenological Philosophy.* Dordrecht: Kluwer.

Lavalette, Henri de. 1965. "Le théorecien de l'amour," in Mémorial Pierre Rousselot, *Recherches de Science Religieuse LIII, no. 3, 126-158.*

Lehrer, Keith. 2000. "The Coherence Theory of Knowledge," in Sven Bernecker and Fred Dretske (eds.), *Knowledge: Readings in Contemporary Epistemology.* Oxford: Oxford University Press.

Maréchal, Joseph. 1949. *Le point de départ de la métaphysique. Leçons sur le développement historique et théorique du problème de la connaissance.* Cahier V *Le Thomisme devant la Philosophie critique.* Bruxelles: Desclée De Brouwer.

Plantinga, Alvin. 1993. *Warrant and Proper Function.* Oxford: Oxford University Press.

Rousselot, Pierre. 1910. "Amour spirituel et synthèse aperceptive" *Revue de Philosophie* 16 (1910), 225-240.

———. 1910b. "Métaphysique thomiste et critique de la connaissance" *Revue Néo-scolastique de Philosophie* 17 (1910), 476-509.

———. 1910c. "L'Etre et l'esprit" *Revue de Philosophie* 16 (1910), 561-574.

———. 1960. "Théorie des concepts par l'unité fonctionnelle suivant les principes de saint Thomas" *Archives de Philosophie* 23 (1960), 573-608.

———. 1979. "Idéalisme et Thomisme" *Archives de Philosophie* 42 (1979), 103-126.

———. 1999. *Intelligence: Sense of Being, Faculty of God*, trans. Andrew Tallon. Milwaukee: Marquette University Press.

Schlegel, Friedrich. 1964. *Philosophische Vorlesungen (1800-1807).* Erster Teil. Kritische Friedrich-Schlegel-Ausgabe, vol. 12, ed. Jean-Jacques Anstett. München-Paderborn-Wien: Ferdinand Schöningh/Zurich: Thomas-Verlag.

Zagzebski, Linda, *Virtues of the Mind.* Cambridge: Cambridge University Press.

Notes

1 On the link between Rousselot and Maréchal, see Thomas Sheehan, "Rousselot and Maréchal: Transcendental Thomism" in Id., *Karl Rahner, The Philosophical Foundations.* Athens, GA: Ohio University Press, 1987. Here us how Sheehan sees the general distinction between the two: "Rousselot is more the pioneer who opens up a new land, while Maréchal is more the colonist who settles the territory" (57).

2 This is how he explains the four components: "Dans toute intellection naturelle je trouve en plus de 1. l'élément représentatif, perçu, synthétisé, *verbum operatum inte* l'idée même) 2; l'élément actif et synthétisant, qui n'est autre que l'acte d'intellection et 3. un désir qui non seulement rend raison de l'exercice, mais de l'essence même de l'acte et 4. une sorte de prolepsis, de préjugé d'anticipation, qui fait que l'intelligence, tout en se suspendant à son désir comme futur, s'y appuie cependant comme possible" (Rousselot's unpublished Manuscript "Note sur l'analyse de la foi," HRO 50, 8).

3 He suggests that the soul is "as it were the material cause with regard to the essence of the thing" (111 in this volume) or that "In intellection the soul is both efficient and material [111 in this volume] cause."

4 In a footnote Rousselot writes: "love is taken in the metaphysical sense of *appetite* in general." (119 in this volume).

5 In another example (84-85 in this volume) he quotes Victor Hugo's "La Rose de l'Infante"

> She is so very small. A duenna looks after her.
> She holds in her hand a rose and stares,
> At what? What is she looking at? She does not know. The water,
> A basin shadowed by the willow and the birch tree,
> What she has before her, a swan with white wings.
> The murmur of the waves under the song of the branches.

6 In addition, Rousselot also claims that "in all knowledge *per modum naturae* [by way of nature]... a judgment is made about the object through the act" (103 in this volume), something he seems to deny at other places, for example, as mentioned above, when he writes: "One cannot stop at conceptual clarity: 'light of being,' 'evidence of principles'" (134 in this volume), adding in a note: "the question of knowledge is not exhausted" with the question of judgment. To qualify perception, which is affirmation, as a skill seems to deny or at least to downplay the teleological function of love that the other examples illustrated.

7 See also this excerpt, expressed in theological terms: "If every look at an object is also by definition a look at the soul, the soul and the object are seen quite differently... Love would therefore play a double role in intellectual knowledge. It would actuate intellectual knowledge, as the appetite for God actuates every passage from potency to act. It would specify intellectual knowledge by indicating its formal object for it. The love of God who is Truth [*Dieu vérité*], naturally imprinted on our essence, is what makes us see in every truth our good and actively operates the synthesis in us" (133 in this volume).

[103] **IDEALISM AND THOMISM**[1]

If it is true that Idealists despise Scholastics as unrefined and enslaved to a wholly corporeal and sensible conception of reality, if they think that the School has an idea of the spirit less pure and less exquisite than theirs, does the fault lie with them alone? No doubt, one cannot seriously read Aquinas without acknowledging that his system is a powerful synthesis of traditional spiritualism. If we have penetrated his principle: *Scientia Dei est causa rerum* [The knowledge of God is the cause of things], we acknowledge that for a Thomist Divine Intelligence is what gives the real all its reality. Still, one has to admit that we have not reached a deep enough understanding of the relationships between spirit and material realities considered as realities. How many people attempt to do that every day! The very multitude of the attempts emphasizes the depth of the need.

Some believe nowadays that Scholastics are so little known that the systematic differences have to be put aside and only the theories common to the diverse schools should be presented. Such is not my method. I believe that by extending the most particular, the most systematic and apparently the most paradoxical doctrines of Aquinas one will manage to discover some principles of truly logical and original solutions to our urgent problems. But I also believe that by taking this route, the alleged oppositions between the necessary dogmatism of the School and some affirmations in which modern philosophical thought stubbornly persists, as if these were its most precious and definitive acquisitions, will disappear like ghosts.

For, those who only have a superficial knowledge of Scholastics will probably deem such a manner of proceeding strange, if they do not even reject it *a priori* as absurd. Nevertheless I venture in these

---

1 Rousselot's text is preceded by an introduction (pp. 91-102) by John McDermott, who edited it from the handwritten manuscript preserved in the Rousselot section of the Jesuit Archives in Paris. The translators have accepted McDermott's readings. So that readers might have an idea of what McDermott had to decipher, we include a sample page from the Archives as Appendix 1.

pages to give a sample of this method by studying the relationships between corporeal reality and human intellect.

I

By "world of bodies" or "external world" I always mean what the Scholastics understand when [104] speaking of "material substances." The external world so defined does not include God nor spirits, but is not reduced to accidental sensible qualities either, like sounds, colors, warmth, resistance, etc.

To say that the external world "does not exist" is a formula not only repugnant to common sense, but contradictory in terms, if it is true that our idea of existence is suggested to us precisely through what we call bodies (Plato). If we draw the notion of "being" first of all from bodies, we have to grant in some way that they "are." We can thus turn away from this formula, usually abandoned in any case, without granting it further examination. But the problem remains intact, for the whole question is to know *how* the external world is, or *what* it is.

The response of standard realism consists in saying not only that this world exists, not only that it is not identical with the human spirit and not convertible with it, but also that it exists *outside* human beings: a proposition which is readily transformed into this one: the world could exist *without* human beings. Or it is claimed—and again in order to exclude this identity of world and the soul, this fusion of things in the soul, which is the idealist paradox—that the external world is real *like* the soul. Material essences are thus countable like the minds and as it were juxtaposable to them. Thus, the relationship of human beings to the world is conceived as similar to the relationship of two substances *quantae* [quantified], impenetrable to each other. The same holds, moreover, when one wants to determine the relationships between the world and God. "God is not the world." This is the principal truth to be salvaged. But this negative expression easily suggests the other formula: "The world is outside God and God is outside the world"; and this other formula as well: "God and the world make two beings." It may seem that one has to say this in order to maintain the substantial distinction and avoid pantheism.

This last remark already suggests the correct way[2] to represent the relationships of human beings and the world according to the Thomist doctrine. From a Scholastic point of view, we know the reservations the following statements call for: "God and the world are two, the world is outside God." The first formula can be criticized because the counting-together [*connumération*] supposes a certain [105] univocity[3]: and the second, because divine immensity encompasses the world, that is to say: divine action posits the world and maintains it as spatial, just as it posits the world as real, sonorous, colored. Creation is completely relative to God. The being of created things is only an analogical *participation* in divine Being, *scientia Dei est prior rebus in quantum sunt res* [The knowledge of God is prior to things insofar as they are things]. As Aquinas says, the world is only "a real expression of divine ideas" (CG IV, 42). It is a rather bad representation of the relationships between God and the world if we see these relationships as between two impenetrable substances, since what is most intimate to the world—its very being—is constituted as such only through the penetrating action of divine Spirit. Although criticizing the above formulae as inadequate, in doing so I still want to affirm as strongly as possible the substantial distinction between the world and God. The perfect reality of the two terms is thus salvaged, a reality which is *analogical* and such that if one of the two terms—God—can dispense with the other, the other on the contrary only has meaning, consistency, reality, through its relation to God.

Following Aquinas's familiar method, let us now move from the consideration of divine science to that of angelic knowledge,[4] and

---

2 It is clear that by using this formula or others similar to it, the author of the present essay does not claim to deny the understanding of what Aquinas thought to those who would not adopt his conclusions. Precisely because Aquinas did not articulate what, according to me, follows from his principles, I can offer a new interpretation of these principles related to partially new problems.

3 See Aquinas's doctrine on number, *In Quartum Metaph.,* lect. 1; Cp. I q. 30 a. 3.

4 Aquinas's theory of intelligence cannot be understood without studying his doctrine on angels. Needless to say, a modern reader is free to consider all this doctrine as a hypothetical construction, as a scaffold that will have to be removed once it has served its purpose. The solidity of the principles

then to human knowledge. This process will not yield for us right away the demonstrated and definitive formula of the relationships between the material world and man, but it will shed light for us on the way to proceed and will allow us to discern the right direction.

As is well known, the doctrine of "separated substances" in Aquinas could be defined as a kind of Platonism with inverted formulae. He does not say that ideas are beings, that is to say: he does not admit the existence of a Lion in itself or a Rose in itself in order to explain lions and roses. When saying that beings are ideas, he means that, in the society of purely intuitive minds, which constitutes the most noble and considerable part of the universe, each being coinciding with its nature is, according to him, both intelligent activity and "subsisting intelligible." This property is what defines the substances superior to space, which are thus at the same time object and subject of pure intellection, pure Ideas and pure spirits. We have to be accustomed [106] to see in this notion the keystone of the intelligible world, if we want to measure the metaphysical and noetic import of the Thomist theory of the principle of individuation, however bizarre, however gratuitous at first glance it may be, but which bears in itself the principle of all critique of knowledge as well as of all ontology.

According to Aquinas, each angel thus constitutes an original intelligible world. Now, this world is complete in itself, not in the sense that the angel would be ignorant of other beings, but in the sense that the angel learns nothing through *external* reception, is not in potency with regard to objects which would impress on the angel their resemblance. The proper and specific act of the angel consists in knowing itself. The angel is always present to itself. If it were infinite Being, it would know everything by knowing its own essence. But it is finite, and there needs to be representations added to this fundamental personal intuition, which are accidental to it and which, poured in it by God, allow the angel to know the nature of substances realized outside itself. Besides, "the more sublime a separated substance is, the more similar its nature is to the nature of God,

---

laid out in this doctrine is independent of the real existence of angels. They are introduced here just as Kant introduces in his *Critique* the idea of an intuitive intelligence, in order to make us understand what perfection he refuses to the human mind.

the less then the separated substance is constrained and restrained, being closer to universal, perfect, and good being. For this reason, the ideas of the more sublime angels are less multiplied and more universal," more universal, naturally, not by generalization, but by condensation (C.G. II, 98). In the last angel, the notions of things are at the maximum of multiplicity. They are more removed, more distinct, more *detached* from its substance. Its intelligible world is less concentrated in it than in superior angels. However, nobody will say that these ideas, these accidents which perfect its intellectual potency, are *external* to it. These ideas are not its substance. However, they are not *outside* its substance. And even less are they realities *like* its substance.

Now the human soul, in the same doctrine, is an intellectual substance of "minimal efficacy" and it has been put in a body precisely because it could not reach an actual intellection that would be perfect enough without a body. If God, Thomas says, had granted the human soul infused ideas, these ideas would have remained in it confused and vague and would have represented real beings only commonly, confusedly (I q.89 a.1 *De Anima* A.15 and 20; see CG III, 81). The body is thus for the intelligent soul, and the external world is for the soul through the body. Body and world, submitted to space and time, allow for a receptive and progressive knowledge: this is their whole role, their whole function. *If finality measured the degree of being*, what would these things be that give their ideas to human beings? What would a *material substance* be? The two taken together, "thing" and its "idea," one actualizing the other, would have a value [107] analogous to the value of infused notions in angelic intellect—an analogous value, but inferior. Being superior to progress, the angel rests from its creation in the contemplation which is natural to it, and the way [*voie*] for it is not distinguished from the end; by contrast, material essences are not given to us as having a final value, so that our mind could settle on them, but as *means for progress* toward an intellectual perfection, which through them we will never reach absolutely; this intellectual perfection would be self-intuition, the intelligible synthesis of our nature. If again the finality of material essences measured their essence, it would be to misinterpret their notion entirely to consider them as realities that are juxtaposable to the reality of souls. Analogous to the angelic *species,* they would have, so to speak, a value of *quo ens* [that by which a being (is)]; if they existed more in themselves, more apart from their subject, it would be precisely because, the human order being inferior to the angelic order, the intelligible *perfectiva* [perfections] are in the human order more removed, more detached from intelligence, less concentrated in it.

Now as we conceive things in this manner, we have to say that, if human beings came to understand the external world perfectly, this world would at the same time cease to exist apart from human beings. For, human beings would then completely possess their nature, they would perfectly coincide with themselves, as Angel Gabriel coincides with "Gabriic̄ity" and fulfils his nature by perceiving it through an intuition which exhausts it. Then, matter would vanish or, more exactly, it would strengthen, realize itself in the intelligible. Spatial distension would cease with imagination, which is correlative to it. All the lions would enter into each other; and all would enter into human beings. All human beings, space having disappeared, would also enter into each other. There would only be one human being left; it would be the Angel-Humanity. All these strange conclusions would only be the consequence of the doctrine of the principle of individuation.[5]

What has been said so far is grounded on the consideration of the order of finality which, in the theistic intellectualism of Aquinas[6] cannot be *adequately* separated from the order of being. When we consider the situation in the spirit of medieval metaphysicians, this would be the point at which we reach the most profound reason of the total relativity of the corporeal world. However, it is a systematic insight based on the analogy of the world, not a rigorous demonstration.

---

5 In order to be rigorous: Finality measures essence, i.e., *the being of things is the meaning they have for God.* God does what he wants at some time—the being of a thing is defined by what God wants (his intention, *intendit* [what he intends]) it to be. Here intrinsic finality cannot be distinguished from extrinsic finality. With regard to the absolute order, from the divine point of view, this distinction does not hold.

6 See also Bonaventure II d. 1 a. 1 q. 2.

❄

[108] The same result can be reached in a contrary way through an apodictic manner, if we no longer start from the metaphysical Platonism of Aquinas, but from the Peripatetic elements of his doctrine; if we ascend from the senses to the mind, instead of judging the essence of knowledge at first glance through its finality.

According to Aristotle's doctrine, the sensible and the sensing are essentially correlates. If they are in act, one cannot be without the other. *Sensus in actu est sensibile in actu* [The sense in act is the sensible in act]. Aquinas repeats this after his master. To know the sensible is thus to feel. Now, a question, which did not trouble Aristotle, arises necessarily for the Christian Philosopher: the question about the relationships between God and the sensible. On the one hand, it is affirmed that God knows the sensible in its own and total knowability. On the other hand it is claimed that God does not sense. For example, strictly speaking, God does not *see* the white, and still nothing escapes him of what is original, specific, inexpressible in the sensation of seeing white. In the same way, he exhausts everything that is immanent, concrete, lived in the sensation of feeling cool in the sea, as a small fish experiences it at one point of space and duration. And still, God is neither plunged into the wave nor submitted to continuous time nor restricted to the nature of the fish.

The explanation is quite easy: God knows the sensible by knowing the sensing, which is for its part supposed to be intelligible. God knows whiteness through the consciousness of human beings, deer or bird. He knows the coolness through the fish. But let us note that by salvaging God's omniscience, this answer also establishes the relativity of sensible qualities. For, the priority of divine science compared to things compels us to say that if God does not know the sensible as such apart from the sensing, the sensible as such *is* not apart from the sensing. Besides, this conclusion does not bring anything new, even for Scholastics. I am here only interested in the reasoning.

For one has to extend it further. The sensible quality, I said, is known to God only through finite consciousness. Thus the sensible quality is not outside finite consciousness and the transparency of a sensible actual ego is the necessary means for a color to be. However, since I am interested not in sensible qualities, but in material substances, does one have to affirm of corporeal essences, or of extended matter, which is their necessary condition of existence, that they express an intrinsic relationship to a conscious subject in which their reality is impossible? Are material substances relative to the human mind?

[109] Maybe one could say first that the quite common affirmation of the relativity of sensible qualities already inclines a follower of Aristotle to answer in the affirmative, since it is proper to a Peripatetic on the question about universals not to separate the sensible element from the substantial element of bodies.[7]

But I refrain from developing this first general view, because a thesis of Aquinas provides a demonstration of this vaguely suggested truth that seems sharp and radical. Why could the soul of an animal, he asks, not exist without its body? He answers: because it would be at once intelligible by itself, *intelligible in act*, which is repugnant to the concept of such an essence.[8] But to say this is to say that the

7 See the fragment of Theophrastus' *Metaphysics*.

8 Aquinas writes, C.G. II, 82: "Omnia forma separata a materia est intellecta in actu... Sed si anima bruti manet, corrupto corpore, erit forma a materia separata. Ergo erit forma intellecta in actu. Sed in separatis a materia idem est intelligens et intellectum, ut Aristoteles dixit. Ergo anima bruti, si post corpus manet, erit intellectualis, quod est impossibile" [Every form separated from matter is understood in actuality ... But if the soul of the animal remains when the body is corrupted it will be a form separated from matter. Therefore it will be a form understood in actuality. But in things separated from matter the understanding is identical to what is understood as Aristotle said. Therefore the soul of the animal, if it remains after the body, will be intellectual, which is impossible]. The second part of the reasoning which brings into sharp light the equation of *intelligible* and *intelligent*, to which Aquinas many times refers, helps us understand that the Thomist theory of being lies in this triple correlation: *actuality, intelligibility, intelligence*. Nothing exists if it does not live by a mind, if it does not bathe in this transparent and palpitating duality that intellectual life is. But the "identity" of which Thomas speaks (*idem est* [it is identical]) is not a convertibility. An angel knowing another angel is not substantially transformed into the other angel. This "identity" is comparable to the union of matter and form (I q. 55 a. 1 ad 2um). The human mind supports the world in this manner, as I said, without being substantially identical with it. All spatial representation has to be banished and the idea of *distinction* preserved. See III q. 75 a. 6. "Si autem (forma panis in Sacramento) remaneret a materia separata, iam esset forma intelligibilis actu, et etiam intelligens:

animal, as it is in itself, cannot be an object of pure intellection. Thus, it is to presuppose that the beast cannot be known intellectually without intrinsic and necessary reference to a being which is not *uniquely* intelligent. It is thus to deny implicitly that the beast could be the object of divine intellection without connotating a relative and spatial knowledge. Lion, tiger, olive tree, "mountains, forests and waters," Aquinas says equivalently, cannot exist in a pure, intelligible, spiritual state, but only, so to speak, in a *cashed in* [*monnayé*] state. There are only individuated, quantified lions, and the *quantum* [*quantified*] is not intelligible in itself, but only imaginable. As *intelligi actu* [being understood in act] is an *a priori* condition of existence, it remains then that material being can only acquire consistency and reality through a consciousness that would be both imaginative and intellectual. This is the definition of human consciousness.

One could also examine the problem from another angle and say the following. When Aquinas so rigorously applies the principle of the essential convertibility of *intelligent* and *intelligible* in order to reject [110] the hypothesis of a beast existing without matter, he at the same time presupposes, clarifies, and justifies another of his doctrines, often enunciated but too little noticed: the one that attributes to intelligence as its object not all "quiddity," but *substantial* quiddity, and to sensible potencies the material accidents which are "proper or common." He expressly denies that the quiddity of accidents is directly an object of the mind.[9] This negation entails that, if material extension, if quantity is intrinsically necessary to the *fieri* [being made] or to the *esse* [existence] of any substance, this substance can only be known by God, and thus can *be*, to the extent that it is enveloped in the intuition of a consciousness that brings together in its unique immanence both the senses and the mind. Just as an animal is necessary for mediating the reality of sensible qualities like color or perfume, in the same way the human mind is necessary in order

---

nam omnes formae a materia separatae sunt tales" [But if (the form of bread in the Sacrament) would have remained separated from matter, it would then have been a form intelligible in act, and also intelligent: for all forms separated from matter are such].

9 *Opusc.* 25 *De princ. indiv.* 1. *C.G.* III, 56, 4. III q. 75 a. 5 ad 2 um. In 12 *Metaph. lect.* 5.

to mediate the reality of the *quantum* [quantified], both relative and substantial, of the resisting and colored thing.

Let us conclude this first part.

Note: So as not to be accused of having "*veiled* my thought under flowers" or even hidden contradictions under metaphors, let me summarize all my reasoning in syllogistic propositions linked together according to the School. The Scholastic form is disastrous, if it is considered as the only means in all orders of reaching the truth. It is useless if it is applied to the critique of a doctrine, before attempting through means other than the syllogism to understand the terms, to assimilate the concepts of other people. But once these conditions have been fulfilled, the syllogistic form is incomparable in order to make one's own thought vigorously precise. Once one has abandoned oneself to the love of this barbarian woman[10] one will never leave her grip. My proposal is thus to condense syllogistically the ideas I developed above, although I still maintain that the previous pages are necessary for the intelligence of the words.

The reasoning on sensible qualities can be formulated in this way: "Aliquid esse formaliter a parte rei, nihil aliud est, nisi illud esse obiectum intellectionis Dei" [Any thing existing formally as an object is nothing other than that thing existing as an object of the intellection of God].

"Atque sensibile, qua tale, et sine sentiente, non est obiectum intellectionis Dei."[11] [And the sensible as such and without the sensing is not an object of the intellection of God]. "Ergo sensibile, qua tale, et sine sentiente, non est formaliter a parte rei" [Therefore the sensible as such and without the sensing does not exist formally as an object].

---

10   "De cette barbare." Rousselot plays with the word *BARBARA*, which is the name of a syllogism, and *barbare*, which means "barbarian," here in the feminine.—Translators' note.

11   It is needless to distinguish here science of vision and science of simple intelligence. For, one has to speak of the latter as of the former and say, for example, that the possible white is known by God only through the possible human being. From the second reasoning it follows that the Ideas of material essences "in the Word" (the Idea of rose, for example, or horse) should not be envisaged as juxtaposed to the Idea of human being, but as subsumed under it, depending on it, and striving in some way to integrate it.

[111] "Ad minorem: Sensibile, qua tale, sentitur. Sed Deus non sentit. Ergo" [For the minor: The sensible as such is sensed. But God does not sense. Therefore].

For material essences here is how one could express it:

"Ut intelligitur a Deo, ita res est" [As it is understood by God, so a thing is].

"Atqui, substantia quanta non intelligitur a Deo sine homine" [Yet a quantified substance is not understood by God without a human].

"Ergo substantia quanta non est sine homine" [Therefore a quantified substance does not exist without a human].

"Probatur minor. Omnia cognita a Deo sunt obiecta intellectionis purae" [The minor is proven thusly: All things known by God are objects of pure intellection].

"Atqui substantia quanta sine homine non est obiectum intellectionis purae. E" [Yet a quantified substance without a human is not an object of pure intellection. Therefore].

"Probatur minor. Eatenus substantia quanta sine homine esset obiectum intellectionis purae, quatenus esset per se intelligibilis. Atqui, non est per se intelligibilis. E" [The minor is proven thusly. To the degree that a quantified substance without a human would have been an object of pure intellection, to such an extent it would have been intelligible through itself. Yet it is not intelligible through itself. Therefore].

"Probatur minor" [The minor is proven]. See Aquinas's reasoning above, CG II, 82.

Besides, I observe that what is said here of space could also be said of time. Those of our judgments that express a relationship to time are true judgments; positions in time are real, but their reality is absolutely identical to their reciprocal relativity. This is unimaginable and this is certain. As Aquinas says, "Quidquid in quacumque parte temporis est, coexistit aeterno, quasi praesens eidem *etsi respectu alterius partis temporis* sit praeteritum vel futurum" [Whatever is in any part of time coexists with the eternal as present to it, *though with respect to another part of time*, it would be past or future], (C.G. I, 66). Now, if one made known to God material things otherwise than through human beings, one would lower God to the rank of imaginative beings.

So to make God perceive temporal positions without human beings would amount to turning him into a successive being.

While staying on the field of the most intransigent Scholastic, we have arrived at an assertion that could be formulated in this way: "Ponere mundum materialem existere sine homine, est ponere contradictoria esse simul" [To place the material world in existence without the human is to place together being and its contradictory]. Intellectualization through human consciousness is a necessary condition of the existence of the material world. Corporeal essences do not exist by themselves; they are *things for a self*.[12] It remains to show *how* this relativity, which is an established fact, does not take anything away from the reality of these essences; how, on the contrary, there is formal coincidence in this case between relativity and reality. Once more, the most systematic conceptions of Scholastic metaphysics will put us on the right track to find an explanation.

[112] II

To say of substantial essences that they are wholly relative does not represent anything shocking to a Scholastic. As is well known, Scholastics possess a deep and original theory of relation (Aristotle's πρός τι, *ad aliquid* [to something]).[13] Aquinas teaches us about the mystery of the Trinity that relation is the only one of the last nine predicaments that does not entail accidental imperfection, the only category that could coincide with that of substance.[14] The Scholastic transcription of the assertion mentioned at the end of the previous paragraph is thus quite simple. To say that corporeal essences, animals, plants, minerals, are *things for a self*,[15] is to say that they are at

---

12   In English in the text.—Translators' note.

13   This is not the place to emphasize the theory of "predicamental relations." Let me only point out that the attribution of a proper reality to these entities, which is one of the great scandals of Scholastic metaphysics, is all the more shocking as one conceives metaphysics in the quantitative manner of the Nominalists and Cartesians. On the contrary, the more spiritually and the less spatially we conceive reality, the less we feel aversion to admitting that "order," for example, could be a "reality" in its own right, as well as "ordered things."

14   I q. 28 a. 2; Quodl. VII a. 1.

15   In English in the text.—Translators' note.

the same time substances and relationships to human beings (non-"predicamental," but "transcendental" relationships). My whole task now is to show how these corporeal beings, *being relationships, are substances*, to show the formal coincidence of their substantiality and relativity. This is how we will assign to them their definite place in the hierarchy of beings and establish their solidity against phenomenism.

What is the particular substance in Aquinas's philosophy? It is what is properly susceptible to "esse, id quod habet esse in se" [existence, that which has existence in itself]. It is what is properly composed of essence and being. I maintain this notion not only against those who would say that bodies "do not exist," but also against those who would attribute being to them only through a participation in the act of human existence, through a kind of hypostatic union to a human being, in which they would become our accidents. I preserve for bodies their quality of hypostases besides their *esse* [existence].

But allow me to observe that all substantial essences are not susceptible to *esse* [existence] in the same way. No doubt, any finite essence is radically incapable of giving itself existence: powerlessness is equal in all degrees. But stronger and higher essences require fewer *alien* conditions in order to exist than lower essences. They are more capable of being actualized *alone*. Essence is all the more immediately [113] ready to receive *esse* [existence] when being is less feeble, less potential, more in itself, closer to God. The less the external being or *the other* created enters intimately into the constitution of an essence, the more this essence is freed from the rest, the more it is in itself, gathered, immanent, concentrated in itself, the more unity it has, as well as intelligence and freedom.

Material accidents only exist through conjunctions of things. For example, whiteness is absolutely not immanent, absolutely not for itself and in itself, although it is necessarily in a subject, it is that "cuius esse est inesse" [whose existence is to be in]. This subject, which is not the color itself, still enters into the definition of color, just like the nose in the traditional example enters into the definition of the pug-nosed. Since white is only white that is seen, its formal being is only obtained in a consciousness which, because it is not "body," is not properly "white." Thus, the essence of whiteness, that is to say:

the material cause, the subjective potency of its *esse* [existence] is con-stituted by something *other* (by the conjunction of some corporeal determinations with a sensible potency). This is the reason why the accident is not properly composed of essence and *esse* [existence]; it is absolutely not in itself, but, so to speak, extrinsic to itself.

At the other extremity of the chain of beings, the angel is on the contrary a potency of intellectual immanence of a certain tone. It does not necessarily belong to a system; it can be independent of any other creature; it is in itself.[16]

As far as we, human beings, are concerned, for *esse* [existence] to be infused into our essence, for us to be, it is necessary that God cre-ates with us a world of material essences, the "external world," which allows us to actualize ourselves. It is necessary that God determines us through what is other than ourselves. Our essence is thus less im-mediately ready to receive *esse* [existence] than the angelic essence. Our essence is more engaged in *the other*, which amounts to saying that we are less fully immanent, that we have a body. However, one has to note that this extra substantial substitute [*suppléance*], which allows us to exist, remains *contingent* with regard to its existence. What I mean is this: if a whole material world necessarily connotes human species, humanity for its part does not necessarily connote *that world,* but only a world. Intelligence could extend to natural species other than those which are realized. We can only become [114] conscious of ourselves through a material world, but no ma-terial world fully expresses humanity. The world thus depends on us more than we depend on the world. The "relationship" between these two terms is reciprocal as far as it is "real," but not as far as it is "transcendental."[17]

---

16 In its permanent and personal perception the angel does not apper-ceive as *existing* the beings which have been co-created with it. These beings are represented by it as *existing* through the notions God superadds to its nature. Thus, its existing essence, which suffices to constitute it in itself, does not suffice to put it in relationship with the real "external." God adds something "intentional" to the angel. By contrast, for us to enter into re-lationship with our peers, and even for us to exist, it is necessary that God puts besides us something substantial (i.e., the world of bodies).

17 Thus, the human mind does not constitute the world through a neces-sary dialectic evolution. By *mediating* the world humanity is neither deduced

This being granted, what degree of relativity and essence is suited for material substances, for the oak, for example, or for a lion? Such a being is at the same time such that matter is extrinsic and co-substantial to it, and such that one can extract from it an intelligible idol, a simulacrum of spiritual Reality. On the one hand, it connotes a material whole, which encompasses it and, on the other hand, a mind to which it relates. The lion is more independent, more immanent, more in itself than sound or whiteness, but it is less than a human being. Being neither intelligent nor purely intelligible, the lion is not totally in itself; it is correlative to *the other*, and not only to a determinative of inferior and subordinate species, but even to a created determinative, which supports it from the inside and without which it is unexplainable, because without this determinative it could participate neither in intelligibility nor, therefore, in being. As material, the lion (like whiteness and like a human being) connotes a system of necessitating determinations in which it is caught. As intelligible, it connotes a mind that understands it. As intelligible and material (that is to say: intelligible in potency and not purely—"conceivable"), it connotes a consciousness both sensible and intellectual, which alone can mediate its unity. The relativity of the lion as a *quanta* [quantified] substance thus consists in its *conceivability*. It is truly what it is for the one who perceives it as a corporeally realized intelligible, as *conceivable*.

I say: as *conceivable*; I do not say as *conceived*, and this distinction is capital. It is imposed on us by facts of intellectual experience. The coincidence between reality and relativity is quite different in the case of the oak or the lion from what it is in the case of whiteness. Of whiteness it can be said without taking anything from its reality, "esse eius est percipi" [its existence is to be perceived]. Of the lion it cannot be said, "esse eius est concipi" [its existence is to be conceived], but rather: "esse eius est posse concipi et percipi" [its existence is to be able to be conceived and perceived]. For, white is only white that is seen; the lion is something else than the conceived lion, since it is at the same time the lion that is seen, touched, etc. and even the visi-

---

nor exhausted. However, while actualizing the human intellectual potency through the perception of species—species God chooses to be such—God by the same token limits the actual expression of our essence.

ble and tangible lion. And in order to form any idea of the individual lion, we are compelled [115] to envelop in a reflex act [*acte réflexe*] the general conception and the determinate perception, according to the well-known doctrine of Aquinas on the intellection of particular things. Perception is exhausting, while conception is essentially inexhausting; it is an effort to synthesize multiple possibilities of perception, which it can never manage to conquer, to subsume, to absorb completely in itself (*aufheben*). Whiteness as such is everything to the seeing being; it is its good, its thing, its captive, it fully penetrates it. The same does not hold in the case of the lion or the oak with regard to the conceiving being. The conceiving being is aware of the imperfection of its act and feels in its object a mysterious remnant [*fond*], which escapes it. The synthesis of white in each perception is perfect, but we are powerless to make the synthesis of the lion. That is why its essence is not its *concipi* [being conceived], but its very conceivability. That is why *it is relative,* not to multiple conceptions of which it is the object in time, but *to the totalizing intuition which would determine it in perceiving it and which precisely would determine it as conceivable.*[18]

My view will become clearer if I present it in a slightly different form.

The middle term between relativity and substantiality of material essences is their intelligibility, but in the sense of their special intelligibility, which is intelligibility in potency or conceivability.

Relativity = Conceivability = (some) intelligibility = (some) substantiality.

---

18 It can be said that, for the white thing to be known and justified *as white*, it only needs to refer to the consciousness of a subject who sees what we see every day. On the contrary, the natural substance does not find its explanation and justification, *even as such*, in the consciousness of a subject who only *conceives*. I say *as white* and *as natural substance*, and the assertion is true only with this restriction. For, conceiving the white thing only as white is to form an abstraction. White escapes us to the extent that it is in an object if this object escapes us. To the extent that it connotes a perceiving subject, white escapes us insofar as our perception escapes us too, because our perceiving ego is not wholly clear and we do not perceive ourselves as the total reason of being. Any being whatsoever, when considered with regard to being, i.e., in its entirely true reality, can only find its explanation, its "justification" in God.

The first and last link of this threefold equation does not present any difficulty. For, what prevents the substances *quantae* [quantified] from being directly and in isolation susceptible to *esse* [existence], like angels, what prevents them from being realizable without human beings, as was shown in the first part of this essay, is the fact that they imply a necessary relation to imaginative knowledge, that they are not intelligible *actu* [in act]. But they can be [116] realized, they can have being; this is how they participate in intelligibility. And we can indeed see that, as substances *quantae* [quantified], they are objects of a certain sort of intellection, which connotes an imaginative perception: they are conceivable. Thus, when considered under the aspect of reality, under the aspect of the spirit, of God, relativity in them = conceivability.

On the other hand, the notion of substance in the world of bodies is reduced to what? The most vulgar, primitive, irreducible form is the following: substance is "what is underneath the accidents." In other words, substance is a reality that is not convertible with the sensible phenomena that manifest it, and is impenetrable to the limited and subjective knowledge of the senses. We find here again the Thomist notion on which we drew attention above. *Substance is object of the mind.* It is an intelligible remnant, the source of accidental manifestations. What is an object of the mind necessarily participates in the in-itself, in *perseitas* [perseity, i.e., through-itselfness]. Substance and mind: these two terms are correlative. *Substantiality = intelligibility.*[19]

Thus, we have secured the first and last link of our chain. What remains is to unite them, to complete the chain by the middle, to show how the conceivability of material substances is some intelligibility. If one can see farther than the words, this is the most delicate part of my task. "Intelligible in potency": this is easily said, but how does this explain that the relative and the imaginable, albeit not intelligent, participate in the in-itself? Or, to formulate the problem in the same terms as above, how can imagined, spatial beings be objects

---

19 It does not follow from this account that "whiteness" itself, because it can be an idea, becomes a substance. Indeed, whiteness can only be conceived separately through a contrivance of reflecting reason, which attributes to the accident the mode of being of substance in order to reason comfortably. See Aquinas, *In 5 Metaph.* lect. 7 and *In 7 Metaph.* lect.1.

of divine intellection, which is *a priori* necessary for them in order to exist?

It is not sufficient to answer that they are made intelligible in act through *a posteriori* conceptions of human beings. Vision can "justify" color because it grasps it in its unity, because it perfectly makes the synthesis of it. But conception does not make the synthesis of its object, it does not perceive it in its unity. The individual lion, i.e., the real lion, does not directly unify intellectual consciousness. Thus, the lion is not totally relative to human beings who know it *a posteriori*. Thus, with regard to our conceptions and reflex [*réflexes*] intellections, the relativity and the reality of the lion do not coincide.

[117] On the contrary, if there existed a consciousness which would totalize in its unity all conceivable being and condensate the intelligible and the perceived through the superior force of a unifying intuition, then the oak and the lion would be totally relative to it. With regard to this consciousness, their reality and relativity would coincide. It would make for them, with a force of grasping of which they themselves are incapable, the synthesis of their idea and their manifold. This consciousness would thus perceive the lion and the oak as relationships to itself. It would perceive them at the same time as substances, i.e., as centers of natural and specific activity, as permanent sources of phenomenal manifestations, as giving themselves to human beings under a double aspect: presenting an inexhaustible remnant to the perceptions of human beings and allowing the intelligence of human beings to extract from these relationships an idol, a blueprint of a pure idea, a simulacrum of spiritual Reality.

Thus, the essence of the lion is not its *concipi* [being conceived], but its conceivability (which implies its perceivability). It is not purely what it is for a conceiving subject, that is to say for a subject which unifies conception and perception without succeeding in fusing them. *The lion is what it is for the postulated and unknown perception that grounds the possibility of human experience.* The lion needs to be somewhere understood in act, if it has to be for us intelligible *potentia* [in potency].

Let us now examine as briefly as possible the conditions of this primordial intuition, since it is only according to it that we can form a correct idea of what the realities of the corporeal world are.

III

Any explanation of the world in the idealistic or relativistic sense runs afoul of, as we know, a difficulty which seems insurmountable. How to reconcile the unity of the world with the plurality of conscious subjects?

The most naïve form of idealism would consist in having the world constituted by the forms of consciousness we know, by *a posteriori* conceptual and temporal knowledge. The unity of the world, its continuity in space and duration are thus unexplained. For, everything here below connotes an "elsewhere" and a "past" to which it is related through necessary laws and of which the mind has no awareness of being the source. All the usual refutations would hold against an idealism thus conceived.

Are we going to say that the mind unconsciously produces the world? Besides the fact that the notion of an action which would be both wholly spiritual and unconscious is unthinkable, the difficulty we encounter is not removed. For that to be the case, the mind would have to be *one* in its [118] productive operation and then multiply itself in the subjects who know *a posteriori*. To speak of an unconscious work of the universal mind means to deny this definite solitude, this eternal independence of all that is created, which is the most certain character of the spiritual substance. There cannot be "one single agent intellect for all human beings."

It is clear after all that the world cannot be unified, totalized through the very fact that it is subjected *at the same time* to several collaborating consciousnesses. Of itself, the manifold is not the principle of unity and the *specific* similarity of these consciousnesses is not sufficient in order to account for the *substantial* unity of their residue. The harmony among them would have to be pre-established and reside in a conscious state of a superior intelligence.

Thus, it remains that we can reconcile the unity of the corporeal world with the plurality of conscious subjects (to explain bodies both as relations and as substances) only in putting into a singular consciousness the global intuition that makes possible all the particular experiences and mediates the consistency of the whole. Because corporeal things are *a* system of relations, they must be relative to *a* subject. In order for them to be things, for them to have an objective value relative to several subjects, the perception of this singular consciousness must connote, encompass and, so to speak, assume all particular perceptions and conceptions, which will inform conscious subjects *a posteriori* about the beings of the universe. It is necessary that everything that is *cognoscibile potentia* [knowable in potency] be somewhere and previously (this is of course a *logical anteriority*) *cognitum actu* [known in act].

Can this totalization be sufficiently explained through divine consciousness? As shown above, to affirm the existence of a corporeal world known by God apart from human consciousness is to unite two contradictories. But if we subsume under divine intellection only a collection of consciousnesses, which know the world *a posteriori*, one cannot explain the substantial unity of any being of nature or the unity of the world as spatial and temporal. Once again, for the material substance to be one and substantial as material, it has to be *unified* in a consciousness both sensible and intellectual. In order to salvage the consistency of the material world, the consciousness which unifies it and allows it to be must be caught in the network of the world. In other words, for what is cashed in [*monnayé*], quantified, for what is a successive continuum to be *real* in its own way and in its order, the plurifying principle, space, must be *prius in aliquo signo* [prior under any sign] to the totalizing principle, the mind. These two causes are in a relationship of reciprocal priority. One is as it were the matter and the other as it were the form. A mind that is in all respects prior to the manifold [119] is not capable of totalizing it. The manifold in presence of the mind would no longer be totalizable, i.e., substantial and material; it would *only* be relative to the mind. One would have something like an "intentional" angelic world; one would no longer have a human "real world." On the contrary, in order to have reciprocal priority, the unifying being, not as unifying but as being, must itself be constituted through pluralization. In other words, the totalizing mind must have a body; it must be human.[20]

---

20 There needs to be a head of Humanity. The necessary metaphysical role I grant such a head is not without analogy with the role Scholastics ascribes to the First Human Being as educator of humanity by giving him the perfection of all conceptual sciences in order to fulfill his role well (See Aquinas I q. 24 a. 3). But a deeper critique of knowledge, just as it re-

It could be replied that even in this way I do not avoid the difficulty, because the dissemination, the exteriority, the spatial multiplicity cannot be regarded as *first* in any respect, because it is inconsistent that one of the two terms be posited from the start as totalizable and detailed. I grant that we need a cause of pluralization in the order of intelligibility and that this cause could not be the totalizing mind. But this cause is not absent: it can be found in the other human minds connoted by the intuition of the First Human Being. These human minds are there, since the reason for demanding this primordial intuition was precisely the necessity to justify the ideas human minds have of the world, to make them objective by making them supported by the totalizing consciousness. Several minds *as minds* can be known and posited by God without mediation nor any connotation. As several of the [120] same species, they necessarily express a relationship to space, according to the doctrine of the principle of individuation. By the very fact that they are in space,

---

stores the speculative value of concrete perceptions, compels us to put in the first Human Being the particular intuitions the ancients refused him: "puta quod lapilli jaceant in flumine, et alia huius modi" [suppose that gem stones would lie in the river, and other things of this kind] (Aquinas, l.c.). The necessity of an intuition that is superhuman in a sense and preternatural [*préternaturel*] in order to ground the natural life of humanity, is in full harmony with Aquinas's whole doctrine about the human being. But *supernatural* and *preternatural* should not be confused and one should not believe that the doctrine I just sketched postulates the Incarnation for the solidity of the human world. If one puts the totalization of the world in Jesus Christ, furthering the beautiful thought of Blondel (See also Aquinas. III q. 10, a. 2, q. 11 a. 1 ad 3), the Savior did not fulfill this role precisely as Emmanuel, but as the second Adam.

[In the first version of "Scholasticism and Idealism" (p. 11) a similar note included the following interesting paragraph: (French editor's note.)]

"It does not seem necessary to say, as Blondel did in *Action*, that the totalizing human Consciousness must be the consciousness of a divine person and thus that the Incarnation is necessary for the solidity of the human world. Adam could suffice. However, one could say that, according to the analogy of divine plan, Adam has been replaced by Jesus Christ, or better, subordinated to Jesus Christ. The Savior would thus have played this role precisely not as Emmanuel, but as the Second Adam. Why as Emmanuel, since the union is not made in nature, since there are two consciousnesses, *consciousness* not constituting personality?"

that they have bodies, they connote the totalizing act.[21] Thus, both minds, to the extent that they are several human beings, can only exist through their implication in the consciousness of our metaphysi-

---

21   To the extent that the First Human Being seeing the totality of the world sees in it conceptions and perceptions which are part and parcel of this world, he sees the acts of other conscious subjects. To the extent that these acts are representative, the First Human Being exhausts them and even confers upon them their objectivity, since the spiritual force of his intellection is what allows those natural determinations, which actualize conscious subjects in those acts of consciousness, *to be*. But to the extent that these acts are subjective, the First Human Being does not exhaust them and does not ground them. He encounters, so to speak, his equal, a being as substantially spiritual as he, and capable as such of being supported directly by God. This limitation is precisely what makes the world *spatial*, that is to say, substantially common to several beings, what prevents it from being all intentional and relative to a single being. This limitation, a necessary element of the totalizing intuition of the material world, is also what necessitates a totalizer other than God. The world is not relative to "Adam" alone, because it includes elements for which "Adam" does not account by himself alone: these elements are the conceptions through which other minds enter the world, and which necessarily connote the *esse in se* [existence in itself] of those minds; these conceptions are parts of the total reality. In order to mediate the indivisible unity of each of them, there needs to be another mind working with "Adam," the effect being "totus ab utroque secundum alium et alium modum" [wholly from both according to one way or another]. The same reasoning holds for the perceptions of animals. Being endowed with a sensible *consciousness*, animals help to mediate each other; they collaborate in the constitution of the world to which they belong. And if only sensible perceptions *as such* needed an explanation, animals would sufficiently account for them. But they cannot account for the *intelligibility* of anything whatsoever and of themselves. They have to be taken in totality, related to the human being, understood *actu* [in act] by "Adam," in order to become conceivable separately and *a posteriori* (*intelligibilia potentia* [intelligible in potency]). This last point is also true of insensible corporeal substances, plants and minerals, which, besides, are more powerless to mediate themselves than animals, since they do not feel, do not enter consciously in the whole, and do not account for colors and sounds, even *praescisive* [presciently]. Let us recall that no finite being, not even the totality of the global intuition, can suffice in order to account for the lesser term of the series as existing, as being (or, in other words, since *being* equals *intelligibile actu* [intelligible in act], in order to account for the *actuation* of the Adamic consciousness); one has to go back to God.

cal Adam, and this Adam cannot be human, if there are no other human minds.[22]

[121] In concluding, these explanations allows us to determine more precisely the degree of essence and reality that pertains to material substances.

The first principle for judging this matter is the following: *they are in themselves what they are for totalizing consciousness.* Now, the totalizing consciousness does not perceive them in isolation, but as a whole. Moreover, it does not see them diluted in a kind of homogeneous fluency, but as taking their place in the total network of natural determinations, as relative centers of totalization, intrinsically connoting the whole, also acting upon the whole and contributing to make the whole what it is. It follows that the material individual does not have consistency apart from the whole. Any time the metaphysician persists in seeking a resisting, solid, intelligible foundation for it by considering it in its singularity, the metaphysician wastes his time. The *individual* lion is not intelligible *actu* [in act]. To make the metaphysical point of view and the point of view of the concept coincide is to establish a contradiction in natural being.

And still, since the whole task of totalizing intuition is to constitute conceivable essences, since the metaphysical Adam is for humanity, one has to go through the concept in order to have a correct idea of what a body is. For the concept after all has its place in nature, an

---

22 It is clear that the explanation I offer here does not lead as its consequence to the view that all the human souls have to be created *at the same time*. One cannot speak here of time, since we try to ground the possibility of space, which is logically prior to time. For the same reason there is no impossibility that a world totalized by intuition in intensive ("aeviternal" ["*éviternelle*"], not temporal) duration is identical to the world which successively unfolds in time. According to Thomist principles, these two durations are not reciprocally independent, since time entirely "flows" from the *aevum* [eternity] and is possible only through the *aevum* [eternity]; but neither are these two durations in a relation of *before* and *after*, which subordinates the former to the latter and compels the First Human Being to live in his body from one end of time to the other. The same doctrine also allows us to suppose that the Human Being, when his temporal consciousness wakes up, finds himself within a temporal matter far *older* than he.

important place to boot.[23] What are we really doing when we indulge in conceptual parceling out? How do we treat material substances? Instead of seeing them implicated in the whole, we hypostatize them into subsisting Ideas; we treat each of them as if it were capable of actuating the intellect by itself alone, as if we could make a perfect intelligible synthesis of them.[24] And still, we do not make that synthesis. Thus, while an intellectual substance is a synthesis that is made or makeable, the lion is a synthesis that is ideal and impossible. Both intelligible and cashed in [*monnayé*], the lion would be in its pure state a conceptual reason, which would perfectly coincide with itself. This cannot be the case. The lion is a tendency toward synthesis, the dream of actuation of a spiritual potency which seeks itself, the mirror that is fabricated by an intelligence that does not see itself [122]. The lion *in its conceptual state* is the human being seeking itself.

In the state of the intelligible *actu* [in act], in totalizing intuition, its relationship to humanity does not disappear. It still is for the Human Being a means of knowing itself. It is true that in this intuition the human being "finds itself." However, it does not coincide *immediately* with itself. (Otherwise, "Adam" would no longer be individual, but would be the Angel–Humanity). It understands itself by mirroring itself in the world God reveals to it, and which is the condition of its existence as well as its intellection. This world is thus relative to human beings. Nevertheless, it is "external" to them. The world has this property because, as already mentioned, it can be opposed to them, it is spatial—a property it has because of the multiplication of the souls within the species, because of the limitation of human beings by one another, since the conscious acts by which human beings enter the whole are an element which is necessarily encompassed in the totalizing intuition. However unintelligent it may be, the world is thus substantial, since it directly unifies the ego of "Adam" and

---

23   If it is wrong to make the conceptual point of view the definitive point of view, as ancient philosophy too often did, it is also wrong to treat the conceptual point of view as a mere perversion or falsification of nature, as the new philosophy sometimes seems to do. The concept is in nature. To act as if the concept had been expelled from nature is to give oneself up to the vice of "parceling out" and to commit the sin of "abstraction."

24   This is the very reason for the *rigidity* of our ideas of essences in conceptual knowledge.

because it is irreducible to this ego. Besides, each of the material substances plays its role as image in the totalizing intuition as well as in the concept. However, by virtue of space, a substance has the *quantum* [quantified] in itself. It is thus not purely intentional and relative to a singular being; but it is maintained in equilibrium, in a solid state, in the state of being through the opposition among different minds. The lion is thus intrinsically correlative to these knowing potentialities, which naturally will hypostatize it into a subsisting intelligible. Because the lion is only possible through the totalizing intuition, the lion is relative. Because it is capable of founding conceptions, that is to say, after all, intellections, although small, the lion is substantial.

This manner of viewing things will not seem strange, if one admits the Thomist theory of the finality of the world expounded in the first part. What is the purpose of the world? To make human beings conscious of themselves in it. The world is thus like the mirror of the human being, but it is a natural mirror, the nature of which is only to mirror, a mirror which does not go beyond its object, which has no other figure, no other dimension, no other essence than those of the image it reflects of itself, without being thereby identical to the object it mirrors.

This metaphor of the adequate mirror, of the *speculum adaequans*, is not unknown in the Scholastics. It is used in the theory of the *word*, created and uncreated—word meaning naturally not the act of intelligence, but the residue of the intellectual operation, according to Aquinas's doctrine. I could not express better in a Scholastic fashion the finality of the world than by saying: the world is like the word of the human being. What holds for the divine Word also holds [123] for the world; its quality of word is identical to its relativity. On the other hand, the quality of the word expresses in it both substantiality and exteriority, because, by contradistinction with angelic ideas, it is too detached from the mind to be a mere determination of it (*quo ens* [that by which a being is]) and by contradistinction with divine Word, it is not equal to productive Intelligence, but is *apart* from it. Let me repeat in conclusion and in order to prevent once again possible misunderstandings: I do not claim here that the mind is sufficient for producing its word. On the contrary, I maintain that

God himself is the one who gives the word to the mind, who actuates human beings through the world and the world through them, just as, by creating the material composite he actuates matter by form, although he could not produce one or the other without its correlative (See Aquinas, Quodl. 3 a.1). For the nature of corporeal substances demands that they not be "intelligible in themselves," but that they be made intelligible through their unification in the consciousness of a being both sensible and intelligent. Thus, before conceiving their subjective potency (essence) as susceptible to the divine effect (*esse* [*existence*]), one has to conceive their subjective potency as already engaged in the network of the reciprocal determinations, which form the unit where the Human Being becomes aware of itself.

Only in this manner can the corporeal essence be realized. *Human beings thus mediate the essence*, that is to say: make it possible; *God gives being*. To say that God gives being means that he gives all of reality, and it is not necessary to insist on this point in order to show to the disciples of Aquinas that the theory I expounded here takes nothing away from creative action or the entire domain of the creator.

(Completed in this form in February 1908)

❋

[Here follows a note by Rousselot from 1911 appended to the article with continuous pagination.—Editors' note]

... After considering things in this manner for some time, although it did not fully appease my mind, I wondered whether the source of all my difficulties did not lie in this: through a remainder of "the ecstatic" prejudice I was always attempting to ascribe to the sensible world an *esse* [existence] totalized *extra mentem* [outside of the mind], completed, finished, wrapped up, in itself—whereas incompleteness was intrinsic to it, precisely because humanity was intrinsic to it. It then appeared to me that the sensible world must be conceived as essentially referring not to a singular humanity, which would totalize it in actuality, but to the idea of Humanity, which wants it as an end κινεῖ ὡς ἐρώμενον, but as a purely [124] regulative and really unrealizable end, since the Angel-Humanity cannot be.

(Besides, after clarifying this concept philosophically, it would be necessary to find out whether there remains any truth in the idea of an ontological role played by the First or Second Adam, and whether the resurrection of bodies, apparently postulated by the beatific vision, does not become possible for us through a special consolidation of the material world effectuated by Incarnation).

Does the fact that the sensible world can be explained by the attraction of a purely regulative and really unrealizable ideal not account for both the infinity of powerlessness, which is intrinsic to things of this world, and, consequently the antinomic character of human reason?

This can be suggested by comparing the sensible world with the play of a game, a tennis game for example. Tennis rules essentially presuppose the idea of an ideal, perfect game, which would be played faultlessly and indefinitely. This perfect Game is the supreme Goal toward which the activity of players strives; it is the essential measure of the objects used to play tennis; and as Ideal and first Measure it also makes us decide the value of the different moves composing the real games. But if tennis rules necessarily presuppose that this perfect game can be played, they also as necessarily presuppose that this game cannot be played: for no tennis game would move forward, *would take place*, would last, if the perfect Game was being played; the game would always be at a standstill and there would never be victory or defeat.

Does the implicit and simultaneous acceptance of these two contradictory presuppositions make the tennis game a repugnant and impossible thing? Not at all, since we play tennis. On the contrary, it must be claimed that accepting these two contradictory presuppositions alone makes the tennis game possible. If the first presupposition was alone true, there would be no tennis game anymore, but only some sort of impeccable and heroic exercise, which, as was said above, *would not move forward, would not take place*, and would suit angels rather than human beings. The possibility or rather the necessity of mistakes, by causing interruptions, makes it the case that the duration of the game is no longer simple and as it were "aeviternal" [*éviternelle*] ("operatio interscissione multiplicatur" [an operation is multiplied by a discontinuation], Aquinas says, Ia IIae q. 3 a.2 ad 4), but composed of different moves that are *generated*, determined by each other; in other words, it makes it the case that this duration is spatialized, is continuous. But the continuity of this duration is necessary for a tennis game to take place; this continuous duration is the very existence of the tennis game. For, *to exist* in the case of the tennis game, as in the case of beings composed of matter and form, means *to take place*, or, as Hegel says, *to hurry outside oneself*.

[125] Thus the necessity for mistakes to occur, or in other words, the irreality of the Ideal which moves as an end, is a necessary and intrinsic condition for the realization of the sensible world. That is why the sensible world only has *meaning* (intelligibility and existence) through the attraction of this unrealizable Ideal: The Angel-Humanity. The realization of this Ideal, by perfecting it, completing it, satisfying it, would cause it to vanish. It cannot be only the attraction of a completed and totalized mind which makes it live: for then it would not subsist, but would be at once robbed, consumed, and devoured (*aufgehoben*) with regard to its existence. Why? Because the intrinsic deficiency that matter is is the necessary condition of its existence, and the possibility of the existence of matter is mediated only through the irreality of the Ideal that moves by the mode of attraction. Under what condition is a particular material essence, lion, ox, or olive tree, susceptible to existence? Under the condition that it not be *totalized*, perfect, completed. The separated lion cannot be, because it would be intellectual (C.G. II, 82) and thus would no longer be a lion. Its essence is such that, being for itself, it would cease to be in itself. The same holds true for the sensible world. If it is sensible and conceivable, if it justifies the category of being of which it is the proper object, that is to say, if it is offered to totalization and still never totalizable, the Ideal to which it is suspended must be unrealizable. If the indefinite fraction 0.285714... managed to equal 2/7, at once the particular determinations founded by its very deficiency would vanish.

The gap between the ideal and the real is the field in which corporeal essences can be realized. This gap is matter itself: and yet matter is real, substantial, and not pure privation, precisely because, for the essences in discussion, it is the intrinsic condition of possible realization, the intrinsic condition of *esse* [*existence*]. Similarly, the gap with divine infinity is what allows pure Spirits to exist (See Aquinas *de Spiritualibus Creaturis,* Art. 8: "Omnes angeli ab invicem specie differunt secundum maiorem et minorem perfectionem formarum simplicium ex maiori vel minori propinquitate ad Deum qui est Actus Purus et infinitae perfectionis" [All angels differ from each other in species according to a greater or lesser perfection of simple forms due to a greater or lesser nearness to God who is Pure Act and of infinite perfection] (See *In Boet. de Trinitate* q. 4 a. 1).

Thus the common remnant of creatures considered as common is a nothingness, something negative: but not considered as informed, i.e., as actualized, divided, particularized.

I explained above how in the order of being the attraction of an unreal Ideal makes materiality possible, whereas the attraction of the infinitely real Ideal makes possible essentiality (ness-ness) and, consequently, the creature in general. The principle explaining material essence also explains conceptual knowledge, why [126] conceptual knowledge is bottomless, so to speak, why it can never yield for us the last word about its object. Because the effort of humanity seeking itself, the *intentio humanitatis* [the intention of humanity], is intrinsic to the ox and the lion, we cannot form a pure intelligible image of the essence of the ox and the lion. If we cannot purely understand it [*intelliger*], it is because we cannot completely disengage ourselves from it.

I assume as being granted that one cause of the essential imperfection of the concept, of its "infinity of powerlessness" is the incompleteness of our spirituality: if we do not clarify our object, it is because we have not clarified ourselves (See *Being and Spirit*). Those who grant this can understand it in two ways: either they can mean that the object is complete, totalized, in itself, but that the subject has a blurred vision because he still seeks himself. Or they can mean that the incompleteness, the *non-totalization* of the object is closely linked to the potentiality of the subject. The second manner of seeing things, which moves one farther away from current dogmatism and naive realism, better safeguards the truth of conceptual knowledge than the first. If our knowledge of the material being is bottomless, it is really true only if material being is itself bottomless.

The explanation of the synthesis of apperception through the role of attraction in knowledge shows us that this second way of seeing things is the true one. However, it should not be understood in such a way that by refusing to bodies a noumenal being in the mode of angels, one grants them a noumenal being in the mode of human beings; in other words, one should not believe that bodies are totalizable in another world. *Their actual non-totalization is all they can have as totalization.* They have here below the solidity that suits them. Their noumenal corresponds to the phenomenal of the soul, according to Leibniz' word: "The body is an instantaneous spirit." Thus, where there is for us infinity of powerlessness, there is for bodies all the finite that suits them (just as for the white, the sound, the scent, each in its order).

A THEORY OF CONCEPTS
THROUGH FUNCTIONAL UNITY
BASED ON THE PRINCIPLES OF AQUINAS:

APPERCEPTIVE SYNTHESIS AND LIVED KNOWLEDGE THROUGH LOVE

[The indented text below is a note added by the French Editor, i.e., John McDermott.—Translators' note]

[573] It has now been half a century since Father Rousselot with his thesis on *The Intellectualism of Aquinas* and his articles of 1910 immediately became part of the avant-garde of neo-Thomism. One could probably sort out "che è vivo e che è morte" [what is alive and what is dead] in his work, which was prematurely interrupted, or better discern the role he played in the progress of ideas. Some of those ideas which he pioneered are now a common good, other ideas did not outlive him. Before all else the philosophical world has much changed and we can only with difficulty go back fifty years in the past. The idealism he fought, the problematic of which he probably saw as a hindrance, has become quite dated. We are now confronted with very different problems. He himself who expounded his ideas with force and intrepidity and sometimes to excess, was also capable of self-critique. It is well known how he tempered quite quickly his affirmations on the irrealism of conceptual knowledge. No one can predict how he would have evolved later on. Certainly he would have continued to expand his theories. His work remains rich of promises. Let me only mention some of those chapters of his thesis on the knowledge of the particular, art, history and symbol.

[574] We re-read him somehow like the classics: in order to educate ourselves under an intellectual leader, even if we can go beyond his conclusions. Surely, unpublished pages will be of interest. These are incomplete at least in form. It would thus be somewhat unfair to judge them as works for which the author had assumed full responsibility by making them available to the public. One can at least find in these pages ideas, intuitions which were familiar to

him, but of which he felt the provisional character and which he attempted to clarify.

The excerpt from a letter to Maurice Blondel which is quoted in the appendix brings new information on the evolution of his thought and on his sources. A notebook in which he wrote down his readings tells us that he read Hegel's *Logic*, probably in Vera's translation (1874), *Logique de l'Encyclopédie,* in 1905 and some pages of 1908 deal with *The Secret of Hegel* by J.-H. Stirling, in which Rousselot extensively quotes the passage where Hegel speaks of the infinity of the fraction 3/7[1] (p. 562ff). We shall see how Rousselot takes advantage of this passage.

What the author added in the margin or between the lines is inserted <>. The words I could not decipher are replaced by ??. The words whose reading is in doubt are followed by [?].

[Here begins Rousselot's text.—Translators' note]

The broadening and the flexibility of psychology of the last years allows us to discover and clearly identify the initial mistake that totally or in part vitiated the research on this capital and unique problem of philosophy: "What do we know about the soul and God?" Scholastics suffered much from this mistake and Kant was not immune from it either. This mistake consists in considering that the work of the concept, the action of representing *one thing* to oneself is the typical fact or the characteristic action of the mental life. While this phenomenon is extremely important, it is nevertheless secondary and derived. For everybody a thing that is conceived is opposed to a thing that is real. The task at hand was then to find a process capable of bringing about the coincidence of the "conceived thing" and the "real thing." Concept and reality had to be *joined up end to end*. This is what the proponents of traditional [575] philosophy applied themselves to do and they took diverse ways to accomplish it. Some denied the critical

---

1 In this text and in a text appended to "Idealism and Thomism," published by McDermott, Rousselot speaks of the fraction 2/7, not 3/7.—Editors' note.

problem by attributing to human beings (in each case) an intellectual perception of reality that carries with itself its definite certainty. Others, more open and wiser, tried to reduce the opponent to absurdity by showing that this first link of intelligent life—the concept—is in solidarity with the whole dynamics of the mind; if we do not grant that it is solid then we must acknowledge the entire incoherence of mental life. Many have tried to "refute" Kant, but we only destroy what we replace and I do not yet see that a sufficient account has been given of the immense difference separating the two kinds of concepts for which (and often as one whole) "objectivity" is claimed: the concept of bodies and the concept of immaterial beings. The sensible origin of all ideas, following the Peripatetic and Scholastic traditions, is forcefully defended. However, the firmer one stands on this solid experimental ground, the more difficult it is to provide a theory of "analogical knowledge," whose coherence would not be purely verbal. How do we escape agnosticism?

In the present essay my first goal is to bring clarity. I try to present the explanations I believe to be correct in their clear-cut contour and in their uncompromising light. I thought the best way I could serve readers was to withhold from them as much as I could all possibility of misunderstanding my views. I prefer being accused of excess, apriorism, and presumption on a first reading than being praised for the insinuating charm of my discourse, but taxed with obscurity on a third or fourth reading. I did not find any better way to please serious readers; for, it is with their reason that readers read books. Is it permissible in exchange of this proof of good will to ask my readers a favor? Even if they are at first shocked by my method, that they accept to make the effort of forming a sympathetic representation of the doctrine I expound here as *an* intelligible *whole*. After that let them exercise, if they wish, their reasoning and refuting reason. But before doing this, let them not think that they have read me. I renew about this work the wish Jerome made: "legant prius, et postea despiciant" [Let them read first and despise afterward]. <See the end where I treat the problem of the will..??.. (which I accept)....??..>.[2]

---

2 J. M. McDermott in note 18 of his edition of Rousselot's "Idéalisme et Thomisme" lists a series of "corrections and additions" of the present article "A Theory of Concepts ...". He reads this text and, after examining the handwritten original, we concur: "Renvoyer à la fin où je traite de la valeur

[576] I

If there were in intellectual life a first fact and if it were to be taken, assuredly not as the unique basis for all of philosophy (what would ever justify such an exclusivism?), but as a starting point, as the measuring unit in order to start and as a provisional ideal type, it should not be "the fact" of "intellectual conception" and even not the fact of "sensation." There is a fact, or rather a state, which is prior to them and of which the intellectual conception and sensation can only be excerpts and abstracts, particular intensifications or differentiated transformations. This state does not really have a name in any language. The name that would be the least ill-suited—"life"—is too broad, since I elect at the beginning of my reflection to choose and isolate artificially one elementary fact in the total experience. This unnamed state can be described. Go to the window and look at the yard of your house. Your neighbor is at his window and looks too. It is an hour when the sun is shining fully and the beautiful acacia in the yard with its leaves of a tender green and white flowers stands out against the sky of a charming Parisian blue. The man at the window looks at the acacia, or rather, no, he just stares. Some might find him dumb and others intelligent: he watches. He does not appear particularly absorbed and if his little daughter rushes into the room in order to announce a visit, he will not wake up as if from absent-mindedness. And now, see, it is already over. He leaves the window and resumes his work. The particular state about which I want to talk seems to me (again) perfectly suggested by Victor Hugo's verses in "La Rose de l'Infante":

> Elle est toute petite. Une duègne la garde.
> Elle tient à la main une rose et regarde,
> Quoi? Que regarde-t-elle? Elle ne sait pas. L'eau,
> Un bassin qu'obscurcit le saule et le bouleau,
> Ce qu'elle a devant elle, un cygne aux ailes blanches.
> Le bruissement des flots sous la chanson des branches..."

> [She is so very small. A duenna looks after her.
> She holds in her hand a rose and stares,

---

des vieilles preuves (que j'admets)": See the end where I treat of the value of the old proofs (which I accept)."—Editors' note.

> At what? What is she looking at? She does not know. The water,
> A basin shadowed by the willow and the birch tree,
> What she has before her, a swan with white wings.
> The murmur of the waves under the song of the branches].

I hope this has all of a sudden, in the strike of a quick intuition, brought you back to an afternoon of your childhood with the full materiality of the state in which you were. I hardly dare call it *psychological* and still, it lies at the heart of life: the confused presence or rather [577], more simply, the *known* presence of the white overall that protects you, the familiar heap of sand, cups and shovels, the hands full of this fine sand which is sticky and wet, life on the go... Refrain from thinking that only children and savages know these states. This is the daily bread of mental life. However refined, complex, and subtle one is or deems oneself to be, it is rather easy to catch oneself or even to put oneself in such states almost at will. The quality and quantity of the previous experience do not change anything in this state. It can be found in the scholar as well as in the uneducated, in the impressionist and even in the naturalistic artist, who naively believes he can see things "as they are," but also in the one who exaggerates in order to retrieve the truer nature, the human and humanized nature, and in all others. For here it is: fundamentally, this state consists in living. Above I opposed to it "the intellectual conception" and I chose in order to give some sample of it, moments of apparent idleness; but one has to understand that this state is unceasing and that it persists under the "intellectual conception" and that one experiences it fully in action as in leisure. This state, which I represent here for the sake of simplicity as delimited in time and occupying the whole of consciousness, corresponds in all human intellection to the moment (intemporal: *momentum*) of *perception* as distinct from the moment of *conception*. In reality, the synthesis of apperception is inseparable from the perceived synopsis [?] and the intuition of my modification, of my act, is physically identical to the conception of the thing. But if only the moment of *perception* is considered, the essence and the *esse* [existence], the reality and the *suchness* [*talité*] are indissolubly welded together, perceived together; the affirmation is not added to perception, the distinction of the real and the possible has not yet arisen.

One can thus start the article with "La Rose de l'Infante" by saying that these examples are excellent in order to make Maréchal's theory intelligible; but for my part I will rely on such a perception-affirmation (pure knowledge) which is immanent to every intellectual operation.

To start by "La Rose de l'Infante" and then say: one seeks a "primitive fact." Then one realizes that this primitive state subsists under the conceptions supporting them [?]—as *cognitio per modum naturae* —conception can only [578] be manipulated in its relationship with this primitive fact. Introduction of the element of *duration*—of the vital flux instead of juxtaposed states, of the S. of the Hp^3 instead of the representation [?] of concepts.

Forgive me for this description. It might have been useless, for there is hardly any task to which psychologists nowadays have devoted themselves more felicitously than paying heed to the vital flux. I only wanted my readers to relive the apparent *stupor,* the indifference, the indistinctness with things that this experience involves and involved.

Stupor with regard to doubt: this stupor is an intense life. Not only in this state has the "problem of certainty" neither sense nor place, but even the dissociations made by the most ordinary reflection cannot be found in it—and this is the more interesting point. One cannot find in this state, it seems, any reflection or negation. Sensation and intelligence are so well blended that they cannot be distinguished. Nature and supposit [*suppôt*], body and soul, *real and possible*, object and subject: all these *oppositions* (I do not say all these *realities*) have vanished. Let us pay particular attention to the disappearance of the opposition between the real and the possible in the basic case of the man looking at the acacia. One will then understand the extent to which the above mentioned stupor is, through vital identity, a vigorous affirmation. And one will understand how right a psychologist recently was when he established quite astutely the following (about the feeling of presence in J. Maréchal, *Revue des Questions Scientifiques*): there is no need to seek a new and special psychological element which, *being added* to the representations of

---

3 McDermott (*loc. cit.*) reads, and we concur, "S. de l'Ap." [de la synthèse de l'aperception": "of the synthesis of apperception."—Editors' note.

consciousness, would be the cause of the "feeling of presence"; the first natural irresistible tendency before deceptions is to *affirm* everything and what needs an explanation is the representation of what is absent and possible rather than the knowledge of the real as such. The knowledge of the real is not made through addition; it is the idea of the possible which is formed through a subtraction.

These considerations are suitable for providing intelligibility to the notion of the *infinite* as Aquinas understands it in his metaphysical psychology. However, before explaining it, or rather before attempting to suggest it as concretely as possible, let us return briefly to philosophers who took conception as an elementary fact and as a starting point.

[579] II

These philosophers can be classified into two groups, those who only focus on concepts and those who manage to distinguish the *conceiving action* from the concept or the conceptual residue.

Unfortunately, most of those who endeavored to defend the Scholastic *analogy* in recent controversies fall in the first category.[4] The tactic of their opponents consisted in driving them to agnosticism and sometimes the task was all too easy. Indeed those who only consider the representative elements, if they also acknowledge that all the notes of representations are borrowed from sensible experience, can no longer hope to attain any conception of suprasensible realities through the way of "eminence and negation." Negation, they were rightly told, bears either on the whole representative content or only on a part. If it bears on the whole, what is left? Only a pseudo concept is left, which destroys itself like the idea of a square circle or an absolute evil.[5] If negation only bears on a part of the representation,

---

4 Analogy in Aristotle means proportion, but it is a commonplace in the School that the Scholastic meaning of this term was broadened and extended to the terms Aristotle calls ἐξ ἑνὸς καὶ πρὸς ἕν καὶ (See Cajetan, *De nominum analogia* and the Scholastic manuals, for example De San, *Tract. De Deos Uno*, I. Louvain 1894, p. 252. This author has a dissertation on analogy, p. 231-262).

5 The mere *existence* of the idea of God and the idea of the soul, proven by the language and beliefs of human beings, is not sufficient to guarantee their legitimacy. Manicheans could believe in the existence of absolute evil,

the other parts, although extracted from sensible experience, are then transported as such to the soul and to God. What has become of the notion of spirit? What especially has become of Divine transcendence? As long as one remained in the *representative* notes, there was nothing one could do against such a logic. One in vain [580] appealed to the idea of being, to the idea of reality, which could, it was said, subsist with the negation of the note of *sensible* and *material* being. For this idea of being itself, which is the most fundamental and common, was also in the doctrine drawn from experience and included in its representation the mode of corporeal being as internally implicated (the idea of being that forms the foundation of human intellectual knowledge, "primo in omnibus cognitum" [what is known from the first in all acts] is "ens concretum quidditati sensibili" [a concrete being of sensible nature]). As a consequence, this answer did not bring us any further and the idea of God still seemed to include a contradiction.[6] <One needs to introduce here for clarity's sake the term of *thing*. The question is: the legitimacy of the critical reference [?] introduced into the intimacy of the idea of *thing*. The legitimacy of the idea of a spiritual being, that is to say of a thing that would not be a thing.>

---

and yet today, when we expound their system, we understand what all this represented, what the word means. In philosophy itself there are indeed pseudo-concepts of this kind which habit, laziness, etc., conceal for the intellectual critique in the mist of a *Vorstellung* [*representation*]. The question is knowing whether the concepts of God and the soul are among them. It is said that for the minds imbued with modern culture, neither dogmatic statements nor fundamental notions of religion in their traditional form offer a meaning that can be thought. I do not deny that in the idea many an uneducated person forms of God and maybe many a philosopher (And here say "implicit critique")... [Incomplete sentence.—Translators' note].

6 The idea of a thinking subject was no more helpful than the general idea of being, either for the formation of the notion of God or even for the formation of the idea of a spiritual soul. For these philosophers kept the character of a finite and determined being for the human subject. Theodicy thus only escaped somatomorphism to fall into anthropomorphism. And in particular these philosophers only granted the soul an analogical knowledge of itself, which was itself also completely drawn from sensible experience. As far as nothing further was put forward, the objections mentioned above have not retreated by one line.

It was then necessary to give up this quantitative illusion which consisted in seeing only a content of the consciousness composed of juxtaposed *parts*. One started to grant its role in subjective activity and the claim was that thought transfers to God the notion of perfection it conceived (Wisdom, Goodness, Justice...), but by disowning, repudiating the lowness of its mode of conception.

Vain defeat! The opponent immediately responded: since the sensible image is according to you an *intrinsic* condition of all conception, "limits are essential in our concepts" (Le Roy, *Dogme et Critique*, p. 143, see p. 98), and you thus have no right to separate conceived *note* and *mode of conceiving*.

Here is the heart of the discussion. In order to proceed in full clarity one has to start by dispelling an inaccurate impression. When it is said that the human affirms of God the *res significata* [thing signified] and condemns the *modus significandi* [mode of signifying], we do not mean this *res* [thing] and this *modus* [mode] as they can be found in the very conception of the corporeal object. The *res significata* [thing signified] is not, for instance, life such as we have observed and conceived it in a plant or an [581] animal, so that when we knew the plant and the animal, what was known would have been infinite and the human mode of knowledge would have been limiting and restrictive. (What is correct is the contrary, as we shall see below). The *res significata* [thing signified] that is affirmed is the concept of life already submitted to reflection, to elaboration, to a preparatory purification. And the *modus significandi* [mode of signifying] which is disavowed is the imperfection which, after this first work, remains in the idea elaborated by the human subject. So the central point of the debate is *the possibility for human beings to criticize their own concepts.* Once the possibility of the first critique is admitted, the possibility of the second will easily follow. The first provides what the Scholastics would call the objective concept of life, which they claim to be one, although it is realized differently in the animal, the angel, and God. The second objection excludes the limitations proper to every creature so that the concept can only be verified about God. The mechanism of both critiques is rather similar. I shall start by devoting myself to the first objection.

Once we talk about the possibility of criticizing concepts or reflecting on concepts, we immediately see, if we understand ourselves, the radical insufficiency of all psychology that reduces consciousness to the juxtaposed presence of *representative elements*. As a matter of fact such a conception leads not only to making the idea of God and the idea of the ego impossible; it also leads to eliminate all intellectual life *and even all consciousness*. If this is so, the soul only has the form of a thing, *it is the thing*, no longer spiritually through transparence and palpitating duality, πωϛ, but is the thing, is truly and properly the thing *materialiter, in esse naturae* [materially, in natural existence]. The soul is thus stupefied, petrified, corporalized, and materialized.

In addition to representative elements another element is needed which would be a living and synthetic activity. Or rather, *besides* all the elements a living atmosphere is needed, that is to say a *unifying and transparent atmosphere*. This is what is called spirit. <???>. The apperception of the mind, that is to say of this diaphanous duality, which can be described but not defined, is not a deduced and proven affirmation. It is a fact of experience, it is the life of consciousness itself, it is what is given. What is in question is the legitimacy of the conception of the mind as a being that subsists. Some only see agnosticism or, even better, a *nothingness of idea* in the conception founded on the [582] negation of all corporeal note. Others do not dispute that the above mentioned conception is internally coherent, but deny the legitimacy of applying this conception to the subject who *apperceives himself* in the flux of phenomenal intellections.

Against both of these thinkers, I make a case for the intellectual fact of apperceptive synthesis and in such a manner that the very mechanism of its operation, that is to say the genesis of the idea of soul, demonstrates how necessary it is to apply it to the subject whose phenomenal activity is perceived. Yet I need to show, against the first view, the possibility for the conceiving mind to criticize concepts, as well as, against the second view, that the category of *object* with regard to its elements which can be purified through such a critique, can and must be applied even to the *subject*. But in order to do that, against both camps I have to show apperceptive synthesis at work when it is applied to "external objects," to objects of experience, and to discern in the most coarse of conceptions an element of palpitating infinity.

III

In his *Logic*[7] Hegel makes an excellent remark which is well suited to shed light on the notion of infinity Aquinas grants to all spirits and even to the human soul, by contrast with the restrictive [?] limitation of bodies. Hegel says that if we consider two fractions, one complete like 2/7, the other indefinite like 0.2857... which is equal to 2/7 or rather tries to be equal with it, the one that should be called infinite, if one wants to talk like a philosopher, is not the one that is never completed and constantly produces out of itself new terms without ever being able to be equal to its immanent principle of impetus [*impulsion*]; the infinite one is the one wherein this principle of impetus finds itself, so to speak, is added to itself, is in communion with itself, and purifies itself from movement by making its total value equal to its principle, its reality equal to its law. Above this false infinity of the quantitative indefiniteness and below Infinity properly said, which is the Infinity of pure Act, of God, there is room according to Aquinas for created and subjected infinities which are infinities in their domain [*ligne*], infinities in [583] their idea. For the fraction 2/7 is infinite with regard to 0.2857, is infinite in the domain, in the notion of 2/7, but is finite as fraction <and as number (since there are apart from it other fractions and other numbers and since it thus does not exhaust the idea of fraction nor the idea of number)> (because it does not exhaust the idea of fraction, there are apart from it fractions which fulfill another idea of fraction, like 3/7 or 1/8), and even more, finite as a number. Similarly, Aquinas says, beings that are free from space, pure spirits limited by their <(??)> Idea, are infinite with regard to the Idea. They fulfill it, they exhaust it, and one cannot conceive besides them another exemplar of the same idea. Aquinas calls this perfection of consciousness, of unicity and intelligibility subsequent to being freed from space, an infinity. Angels are, he says,

---

7 Lasson, I, 248, Buch I, Abschnitt 2, Kap. 2, C, (c) Anm. 1. Note of the French editor.

"finiti superius, infiniti inferius" [superior to the finite, inferior to the infinite] (these terms come from the Arabs?).[8]

We, human beings, do not possess this infinity, the infinity with regard to our proper nature; we do not encompass our consciousness by a clear intuition and there are several human beings as there are several oaks and several lions. Bodies individuate souls. But the human soul is infinite with regard to corporeal essences, with regard to everything that is a quantity, number, space. And this infinity filters through and is affirmed in all our conscious life, whether we consider the happy, natural, and undifferentiated state we described at [584]

---

8 Aquinas's principle, "There is only one angel by species" (or "if separated whiteness existed, there could only be one") is formulated in the theory of knowledge as follows: the category of number is correlative of the human mode of knowing with image, spatialized representation (To examine at the end of the article which one of these two formulations is the most philosophical). This principle, as we know, is not Aquinas's own. It can already be found quite clearly formulated if not by Plato (*Republic* X), at least in Aristotle: ὅσα ἀριθμῷ πολλά, ὕλην ἔχει [all things that are many in number have matter (1074a33)]. Leibniz and Kant also accepted it (see the *Critique of Pure Reason*) and the readers of the *Revue de Philosophie* recall the subtle article in which Moisant compared Aquinas's and Bergon's metaphysics on this point. Although this principle, which seems of capital importance to the most metaphysical minds, has been under violent attack today as well as in the Middle Ages (see Renouvier who expressly refers to Scotus: *Nouvelle Monadologie*), I leave to the Thomists, who have always acquitted themselves quite well, the task of proving this. In order to suggest the intuition, before providing the proof, I think the best approach is to succeed in drawing a distinction between the formal (spiritual) unity and material (numerical) unity of an object of art or a work of the mind. You have read the issue of yesterday's newspaper and you see two copies. You read: "Well it is the same." Analyze what is involved in the identity you have just affirmed.

But what matters here is taking note of the essential correlation between the fact of not being alone in one's nature, and the fact of not having the intuition of one's nature, of not intelligibly possessing the essence of one's ego [*moi*]. The common root of these two effects is the fact that matter is part of the human essence, that "my body is myself." The potential infinity of matter is not a problem or rather is only a problem (it is rather a definition) since the very essence of matter is the infinity of powerlessness. But this definition is contradictory (just as this problem would have been <would be> without solution) if one claims to explain matter without taking into account the superior infinite, the spirit.

the beginning of this article, whether we consider the conception of a corporeal essence, or whether we consider reflection.

If we wanted to follow the order the Scholastics would have liked and start from *priora naturae* [the prior in nature], one would have to say that this infinity has its root in the spirituality of the soul, and that through human action it is communicated to the human concept. But the converse order can be followed as well. We would first note that the general idea possesses the property of not being modeled exactly on the individual at which it aims, but of being able to fit successively or at the same time two, three, one hundred, one thousand, to an indefinite number of exemplars of the same species, without ever being worn out in this business, without the quantity having any direct influence on it: it transcends all quantitative order and in this sense possesses a certain infinity often highlighted by the Scholastics (Let us note according to the principles expounded above, that it is not the number of individuals subsumed under the general idea that confers infinity to the general idea: it is its transcendence above all the quantitative, that is to say its character of simplicity). This also holds true of ideas of specific essences: the idea of the tiger or the idea of the oak is also true of more general concepts such as those of body and substance, whose greater extension allows them to subsume under themselves a greater number of indefinite series of individuals. When we move to the concept of being, the infinity broadens even more and changes in character. It is no longer these or those objects of the mind that the concept of being expresses and encompasses: it is *the universal form of the objects of the mind* which retracts and shrinks in order to give its form to the most imperceptible elements, and which extends and expands so that it can be applied to the totality of things. The most feeble accident is conceived as being, and it is also as being that the "universe" is conceived. According to the felicitous expression of one of Aquinas's disciples, *being* [585] is "the inhabitable land of the human mind"; it is the atmosphere of the intelligent soul. One can even say that it is intelligence itself to the extent that intelligence becomes objects, to the extent that it is transparent, to the extent that it is like glass, πάντα πως. (All of this can be even better formulated by saying that being is *the word* [*verbe*] of the soul). In being then one no longer encounters only the infinity of inexhaustibility, the infinity of an everlasting receptacle (which to some extent suits space, imagination, the senses); one can also grasp in being an infinity of transparence, an infinity of spirituality. And at a closer look, *being* is what communicates to generic or specific concepts their characteristic diaphaneity. Being is immanent to them, it forms their ground [*fond*] and their substance; it illuminates and animates them. *Ens concretum quidditati substantiali* [A concrete being of substantial nature]: being is not only a *primo cognitum* [known from the first] in the sense of a temporal priority, it is also a *lumen (medium) in quo cognoscitur* [light (means) by which it is known], < see below, p.> [sic.—Translators' note] and being, with even better qualification than the phantasm, must be an essential part of intellection "non sicut transiens sed sicut permanens, tanquam quoddam fundamentum intellectualis operationis" [not as transient but as permanent, as though it were a certain foundation of intellectual operation]. This universal usage of *ens* [being] shows that one does not only grasp by *ens* [being] a concept, but also a *function* of the mind. But function means act, and so we are closer still to spiritual infinity.

When pressed to justify the distinction they made between *mode of conceiving* and *conceived* quality, few Scholastics believed they had to have recourse to the still very real and necessary distinction between conceiving action and conceptual residue. According to Aquinas conceiving action is not identical to the concept. Of course it would be absurd to imagine them as two physically and spatially separated entities: action is necessarily and constantly immanent in its result. Action is the act both productive and perceptive of the idea[9] <??>; the idea is the term perceived by the mind and the result of its productive activity. It is clear that the act is not only an external condition for the existence of the idea, it is its essential and necessary cause, it gives it its consistency, its unity, its being; it is its continued generation [?] and cannot be explicitly distinguished from it.[10]

---

9 McDermott (*loc. cit.*) reads and we concur: "la S. de l'Ap.": "the synthesis of apperception."—Editors' note.

10 See Aquinas, *De Ver.*, IV, a2 and C.G. 11ff Goudin. See Blondel, *L'illusion idéaliste* from whom I borrow the expression of conceptual residue. It goes without saying that this doctrine, which is intimately connected

[586] If I call the productive act the "synthesis of apperception" (here a note on the synthesis of apperception, Kant and Aristotle?) and the produced concept a "perceived synopsis," the synthesis, to use a Thomist comparison, is distinguished from the synopsis *tanquam floritio a flore* [as flowering from a flower]. Flowering lasts as long as the flower, flowering sustains the flower and when it ceases the flower falls since flowering is nothing else than the continued opening of the flower, the communication of vegetative life through the stem to the flower and thus what constitutes it as flower. And still, unless one falls in the illusion of the false commonsense of atomistic metaphysics,[11] one cannot say that flowering *is* the flower. Flowering is no more the flower than generation is the son, although the persistence of the causal influx in the former case and its momentary character in the latter case could tempt us into judging the distinction between the two terms differently.[12]

---

to the doctrine of the agent intellect, was the object of violent and repeated attacks in the School and was accused of leading to subjectivism.

11   The philosophy I am talking about only acknowledges as real what can be thought of spatially and statically. "There are, it says, only the tree and the flower." According to this philosophy, flowering is only a mental construction. This philosophy does not wonder whether, by affirming the isolated materiality of the flower and the tree, it does not yield to prejudices just as naive. In the same way, this view only recognizes ordered *things*... In short it constantly deceives itself in regard to the category of *thing*.

12   The son is begotten and then subsists separately. The flower lives in the tree *tanquam genitum conjunctum* [as a begotten connection]. However, it is still called a flower when it has fallen from the tree, and it can be clipped, planted, and thus can bring a new tree to life. Because of the immanence and the deeper personality of the spiritual life, the comparison with the flower only imperfectly expresses the relation between spiritual action and idea. In order to gain a solid knowledge of Aquinas's doctrine on this immanence of intellectual operation, see the passages in which he treats the generation of the eternal Word. Aquinas also writes: *intelligere ... ita se habet ad intellectum in actu, sicut esse ad ens in actu* [thus the understanding ... is related to intellect in act, as existence is related to being in act]. *Summa theologiae* I, q. 34 a. 1. We thus have:

floritio	*florere*	*flos*
[flowering]	[flowering]	[flower]
intellectio	*intelligere*	*verbum* (*intellectum*)
[intellection]	[understanding]	[word (understood)]

This being said, it is clear that infinity comes to the idea of being from the action of the spiritual act. What is finite, what is limiting in human conception are the corporeal notes which set its limit and determine it. What is infinite (in the sense specified above) is the influx of spiritual life, the communication of soul which is imparted to it through the very fact of its constitution, its generation, and its production.

However, now that we understand the distinction between act and term, it is important to come back to their physical union, to their living indissolubility.

To overlook the act is, as we saw, to stifle oneself in agnosticism in the most material and fullest sense of the term, for it amounts to killing all possibility of knowledge.

[587] But to forget or to overlook the solidarity, the reciprocal immanence of the act and its term is to reach the same goal through another way. For those who distinguish synthesizing activity from the representative and synthesized multiple and consider one *apart* from the other may well have the idea of a subject opposed to an object (and for this reason it is tempting to call it immaterial); but they have no right to transform this subject into an object and to apply to it any positive predicate, since all these predicates are taken from the world of objects (and as the subject is simply: non-object). Such people might well have the idea of a source of categories that nothing warrants being placed into categories; but precisely because nothing warrants placing the source of categories under categories, they will have no right to affirm this source as a substance. The apperception of the phenomenal ego will be recognized as a fact, but the assertion of the permanent ego will remain problematic and unjustified. By affirming the permanent ego one will fall precisely into what Kant

---

The act indivisibly belongs to the two components of essence (matter and form, intelligence and idea). The act is both *florere* [flowering] and *florēri* [being flowered], *intelligere* [understanding] and *intelligi* [being understood]. The *esse* [existence], the life of the flower is not distinct from the life of the tree. This is why in the moment of *perception* an essence is directly grasped through its *esse* [existence], under and in its *esse* [existence], which means: as the essence is (Τῷ νοεῖν καταλαμβάνεται τὸ νοούμενον): in prospection or perception, the object ??, approaching it *per viam suae infinitatis* [by way of its infinity]. [McDermott (*loc. cit.*) reads and we concur: "dans la prospection on *hebt* l'object *auf*"]—Editors' note.

calls *fallacia apperceptionis substantiatae* [the fallacy of the apperception of the substance] <*die Subreption des hypostasierten Bewusstseins* (*aperceptionis substantiatae* [of the apperception of the substance]) K.d.r.V. A 402—note of the French editor.>

The situation is different when the act and its term are considered in their natural unity, if we attempt to encompass the synthesis of apperception in its total reality. *Ens* [*being*], this infinity of objective representation, must not be considered as already done, but as in the making, in the process of being made (since its very reality is identical to its *generari* [being generated]).[13] This mirror of the soul, this *word* of the soul, will be grasped as a negative infinite, derived and relative if it is grasped [588] in its derivation and very reference, in the very formality of its negation. It must be caught in the act, so to speak, both deriving and actualizing, determining and negating, in short: relating. *Ens* [being] is then conceived as a transcendental relation to the soul. If this is recognized as its true nature, then its whole use, transcendental as well as phenomenal, has found justification. One can now see that, since being has the cause of its infinity in the soul itself, it also has along with the source of its *unity* the reason of its *objectivity,* of its *reality*. One can see that the apperception of the phenomenal ego cannot be recognized as a *fact* without at the same time having the universal application of the category of being implicitly justified, even outside the objective conditions of categori-

---

13 Aquinas, Op. 13, c. l, fin. "Verbum enim nostrum semper est in continuo fieri, quia perfectum esse suum est in fieri; sed hoc non est imperfectum, quasi totum simul non existens... nihilominus esse ejus perfectum servatur eodem modo quo gignebatur. Non enim transit formatio verbi ipso formato, sed cum actu intelligitur, continuo formatur verbum, quia semper est ut in fieri, et ut in egrediendo ab aliquo, scilicet a dicente" [For our word is always continually in a state of coming to be because its being is perfect in coming to be. But this is not imperfect, as it is not existing complete at once ... nevertheless its being is kept perfect in the same way in which it was begotten. For the formation of the word is not altered by that which is formed, but the word is understood with the act and continually formed, as it is always as it were in a state of coming to be, and as it were in a state of going forth from something, namely from the speaking] (Ed. Fretté, vol. 27, p. 270). This whole passage is of course about the mental word.

zation.[14] One can see that *ens* [being] is nothing other than the *back side* [*envers*] of the soul, the *other* of the soul, the *object* of the soul, *that it is precisely for this reason that ens* [being] *is affirmed as real*[15] (in the full and legitimate sense in which one affirms human spontaneity before the antinomies of reflection). Now we cannot know nor affirm a back side as back side and another as other without knowing or affirming *first and foremost* a first being and a front side. Thus as a consequence, since reality, affirmability, the right to existence of *ens* [being], comes to it from its infinity and not from its finitude and negation, one cannot affirm any object whatsoever[16] without also affirming—albeit implicitly [589], but *also first and foremost*—the soul to which this object is related. *All affirmation of an object implicitly contains an affirmation of the thinking soul on which this affirmation is essentially founded, as on its intrinsic and necessary condition.* One now grasps the meaning of the Scholastic distinction between *positive* and *negative* perfections. Everything that is positive (i.e., infinite) in what is perceived can and must be affirmed of the soul, not only with equal right, but *a fortiori*. Everything that is finite or negative must be denied of the soul. When they moved from the solidity of things to the substantiality of the soul, the ancient Scholastics were

---

14   This is precisely where Kant's mistake lies because of his ignorance of the category of being.

15   Here a note on sacramental conception.

16   But can any object whatsoever be affirmed? I believe that this question must be answered positively. I thus do not deny that this question is meaningful and I even believe that it is the starting point for a new deepening of the truths here examined. Hence I shall come back to it below. I content myself here with pointing out that being, because it is first given to external things, suits those things if it ever suits anything. The preceding pages lead us to the conclusion that any coherence whatsoever of mental life forces us to affirm the reality of the soul, that we thus have no other choice where we stand than a choice between the affirmation of the soul and absolute illusionism.

The doctrine of the sentiment of presence on which I rely (see the work cited) already shows that, if mental life has a meaning, if something has a meaning, the affirmation of reality is justified in the human mental life thus characterized, which is wholly informed by *ens* [being]. For *ens* [being] in its primitive, natural, and pure form, grasped at its source, is indistinct from its affirmation. The dissociation is a *derived form*.

right to apply the old adage: "propter quod unum quodque tale, ipsum magis!" [that on account of which anything is such is itself more (such)] <?? of Aquinas, *De Ver.* 10-8>. When deepened, unified, and spiritualized, their proofs for the soul hold good. In my view, they even take on a less extrinsic and more direct efficacy, a more clear and certain meaning (see below). Is the object real? Is the object substantial? Does the object last? Then the same holds true for the soul, even more so for the soul, *ipsum magis* [itself more (such)]. However, in order to have the right to make such an affirmation, one should not let one's own intelligence be seduced by the conceptual residue, by the conceived taken in isolation. One has to envisage the integrity of what is perceived, to throw oneself back into this sea of intelligibility, where the soul and things coincide, πάντα πως, where the soul communicates its transparent infinity to things after letting them drop their forms in the atmosphere of the soul, and where the soul goes back to that moment of [?] the ceaseless palpitation of the intelligible becoming, and where, in accordance with the law of its nature, the soul bathes them in the cloudless light of *affirmation.*

The rigorous coincidence of the doctrine I just expounded with the old theses of noetics imposed by experience would not appear clearly enough if I did not add some important developments on apperceptive synthesis, on the knowledge Aquinas calls *by way of nature* and which can also be called *by way of love,* and on the knowledge of analogy.

IV

It is clear that the thesis I defend, far from marvelously fitting into the noetic doctrines of the School, would on the contrary represent the most formal objection to them, if the knowledge of the soul we somehow assume [590] to lie at the basis of the knowledge of things were temporally prior to the knowledge of them; and this would be the case if this knowledge of the soul was conceptual, if the soul was its first object. But this approach does not seem to me to conform to experience. I believe that the soul first knows things and then itself (conceptually, not intuitively) through a reflection upon its act. I agree with Aquinas: "Mens nostra... ex hoc quod apprehendit alia, devenit in suam cognitionem" [Our mind ... from the fact that it apprehends other objects, arrives at its knowledge of itself], and I subscribe to what he adds: "alius est actus, quo homo intelligit lapidem, et alius quo intelligit se intelligere" [one act is the act by which the human understands the stone, and another the act by which the human understands itself understanding this] (Ver., 10, 8).[17]

It is thus in the knowledge itself of the object, prior to all reflection on the act and on the soul, that I seek this apperception of oneself which I claim accomplishes the synthesis of the intellectual conception, and even better, of all mental content. Because affirmation is in this apperception not distinct from perception itself, this apperception bears in itself the justification of the realist instinct which leads one to affirm objects and shows that this realist instinct is just an expression of the deeper and still better justified instinct which leads one to affirm oneself.

While it is Kant's merit to have clearly seen in the synthesis of apperception the central point of the study of intelligence, the principle was no less latent in the Peripatetic noetics. When Aristotle says that the soul becomes intelligible to the extent that it thinks an object, this fundamental proposition has two sides. First, it means that the soul only becomes aware of itself by becoming aware of a corporeal object; Scholastics commonly put emphasis upon this truth of experience. But, second, Aristotle's principle suggests further that this act of unifying the thinking and the thought, i.e., the intellectual conception, essentially and necessarily entails a certain apperception of the ego.[18] *Every human gaze at an object is also by definition a gaze at the soul.* Or if one prefers a more Scholastic formulation, actual self-perception [*la perception du moi actuel*] and conception of an object are one and the same act. "Ipsa perceptio mei, ipsa est conceptio rei" [The very perception of myself is the very conception of a thing].[19]

17　While the first portion of the quote from Aquinas is indeed from Ver., 10, 8, the second part of the quote is seemingly from *Summa theologiae* I q. 87 a. 3 ad 2 (though Rousselot substitutes *homo* for *intellectus*).—Translators' note.

18　I am fully aware that Aristotle wrote: … παρεμφαινόμενον …, but he only considers in this whole chapter *conceptual* knowledge and—what is its correlate—*material* essence.

19　See *L'intellectualisme de St. Thomas*, p. [sic.—Translators' note], and the texts quoted there. The phenomenal of the soul corresponds to the noume-

[591] It is clearly understood that this apperception should not be conceived as a perception of the proposition "I think!" It is not the conception of the soul as an object either. This is not strictly essential to psychological life, and this only comes later. This apperception is also even less an intelligible possession, a calm and clear intuition of the very essence of the thinking principle, as one can imagine it in pure spirits. *It is a fleeing apperception of a reality that is strictly indefinable, absolutely unfixable and indescribable in terms of the concept,* precisely because the concept is the form of its back side, of its word, of its other, of that which it has the task to isolate. It can thus be made known through things, but with the qualification that it is the other of things (τῷ πάντα γενέσθαι); that is to say, we are putting it in opposition to things at the very moment we unify it with things. For its relation to things consists precisely in a union which is identically an opposition. We would thus make the soul unintelligible if we were to apply to it spatial categories which suit the objects of concepts with their laws of equivalence, exclusion, and inclusion. The being of the soul consists in mingling itself with things, fusing itself with them, flowing into them, embracing them in darkness and fleeing from itself, hurrying out of itself (*to dispatch itself beyond itself* [in English in the text.—Translators' note]) (forgive me for the translation which adds a touch of velocity to the original). In short, the (empirical) soul in apperception is the other of the conceived things, since it is what generates the concept in itself and what remains itself by becoming things conceptually. We kill the soul if we seek for more than that. This is what is important to have understood.

When we bring this kind of descriptive suggestion or reminder of experience in connection with what was said above about the conception of the object that is identical to the production of the word, it shows that the apperception in question is a knowledge that is not *expressed*; it is a knowledge engaged in action, indissoluble from action, all vitality, all living, without conceptual residue, lastly: one

---

nal of the things, the intuition [?] of the soul to the *aevum* [eternity] [?] of things (just as "essences" are eternal). The life of a pure spirit is such that its objects are its moments. For humanity, which is stretched in space and co-existing with the other corporeal species, these other essences can also be called its moments to the extent that they delineate humanity, imitate it, attempt to integrate it into a harmonious progression.

of those [592] Aquinas calls *cognitio per modum naturae* [knowledge by way of nature].[20] We can know, he explains, chastity because we have followed a course of morality and we can know chastity because we are chaste. Let us suppose that the question arises whether this or that behavior hurts the perfection of chastity. The answer will be gained in a quite different way whether one possesses one or the other knowledge of chastity. Those who know theoretical morality will seek a general principle under which they will attempt to subsume the case in discussion. Those who possess in themselves the habit of chastity (as long as this habit is somewhat developed and somewhat exquisite and has penetrated the organism) will feel a reaction of an affective order—attraction or repugnance—which will warn them, as we say, instinctively, that the course of the considered behavior is inoffensive to virtue or hurts virtue. In everyday life we can observe at every step the exercise of such faculties of knowledge. I have seen a player at a loss when asked about a particular point regarding the rule of the game. "I will answer later," he said, and as soon as a concrete case occurred, he played according to the rule and then answered the question. Someone pointed out to me that this is often the case with questions asked about pronunciation or orthography. One pronounces or writes as mechanically as possible, and it is only afterwards that one can answer. What is to be noted in these examples is, first, that a true knowledge preexisted, as we said, immanent in the action itself (or in habit or nature), which should not be confused with the theoretical extraction one can give of this knowledge when posed a question. This knowledge is independent of the extraction, since it precedes its extraction; and this knowledge could subsist without its expression. According to Aquinas's principles, such knowledge should not be said to be *less* intellectual, but intellectual *otherwise* than abstract knowledge. This knowledge even has the advantage over abstract knowledge of reaching being more directly. If seen from below such knowledge seems to be in continuation with the instinctive knowledge of beasts, when seen from above it also offers an image of the knowledge proper to pure spirits, which

---

20   Allow me to refer again to *L'intellectualisme de saint Thomas*, p. 74ff; English translation, *Intelligence*, p. 65ff. But it is far more instructive to study what Blondel says about the knowledge he calls prospection (Le point de départ de la recherche philosophique, *Annales de Philosophie Chrétienne*).

is always essential, concrete, and sympathetic. [593] Let us note in addition that the two kinds of knowledge do not exclude each other (a man can know chastity both through abstract principles and because he is chaste) and, lastly, that the mode of acquisition of those two kinds of knowledge varies depending on the different examples: one can find at the foundation [*fond*] a natural disposition or an habit acquired willingly. One can find at the origin a theoretical teaching, but then that the content has become naturalized through habit. One can lastly, and this more curious case will be more useful, be in the presence of a desire, of an obscure love, although real and strong, which most people would simply call *unconscious* because they have never *expressed* it to themselves.

In all knowledge *per modum naturae* [by way of nature], in the same way as it is shown by the conceptual extractions that we operate on this knowledge, a judgment is made about the object through the act (or in a Scholastic formulation: about the specification through exercise). The judicative <conceptual> application could lack support (one could have acquired the habit of a spelling mistake), but the knowledge through habit itself will be infallible, since knowledge cannot be really distinguished from habit, since a habit is human only insofar as it is known in this manner. When one takes pleasure in a certain poet, one can sincerely be mistaken about the poet's importance in literary history, but one is not mistaken about the pleasure one takes from the poet, about one's dependence in regard to the poet. Similarly, when one loves somebody the lover infallibly knows the loved object insofar as he depends on it, *insofar as the object is beautiful to him.* Thus, the judicative response, the conceptual definition, only has value through its essential dependence on a good habit or a true feeling. Expressed knowledge holds through its continuity with unexpressed knowledge which it presupposes and proclaims (externalizes).

Let us now apply those principles to the knowledge the soul has of itself (of the actual acting ego) in apperceptive synthesis. The reader already no doubt surmises the general direction of my thought. Being is for me the expression of the soul, its mirror, as I have repeatedly said, its word. I want to get the reader to see in this word an essential and permanent relativity along with an undeniable objectivity. I want to show the following: although what first falls under expressed consciousness is not the soul, but the object, since we need to be excited by things from the outside, still the [594] natural and invincible affirmation of being contains in its core an even more natural and stronger affirmation, albeit unexpressed: the affirmation of the soul, which can and should be translated into terms borrowed from objects and manipulated by "negation" and "eminence."

One of the most competent scholars[21] criticized me for putting under analogical knowledge not only the ideas we form of the soul and pure spirits, but even our notions of material essences. The objection was: "If all abstract knowledge is *improper,* the formation of the *analogical* concept is inexplicable, for the latter *presupposes* the former." I indeed believe that every abstract idea is improper, or as I put it in the passage criticized: "every general idea of substances is necessarily an analogical idea." I make no exception for the general idea of body, nor for the idea of substance, nor even for the idea of being. I also deny that whoever wants to affirm the solidity of our affirmations about the world, the objectivity of concepts, must find at the basis of our conceptual pyramid *one* pure and proper idea of *one* substantial being that is external to us. This demand lies in my view on the very illusion I fought at the beginning and which consists in taking as (the norm and) the exclusive type of knowledge the isolating, exclusive, limited concept. Kant asks: "How can it be intelligible to us that a human being moves from the very affirmation of one thing to the affirmation of another?" As Caird rightly said, one has to reply to this question that this alone is intelligible to us: what would be unintelligible would be the conception of a thing from which all the relationships with the rest would have been cut off (the conception of a thing, I may add, which would satisfy the definition of substance that I find in a course on Scholastic theology: "substantia est ens absolutum" [the substance is absolute being]. Here a quote from Palmieri, th. XVII and Billot?).

I said "conception," since we are dealing with human cognition which always relies on an image. If we dealt with a pure spirit which by definition does not know things through *conception* but through

---

21 De Wulf, *Revue néo-Scolastique,* vol. 61, Feb. 1909, pp. 140-41. The same criticism was made by [Incomplete sentence.—Translators' note].

intuitions, [22] the only way we could represent the content of [595] consciousness such a pure spirit has is to believe that its intelligible essence is clearly and constantly present to itself: as I show below, the pure spirit does not bring about the synthesis of apperception in the intuition of its phenomenal ego, but in the intuition of its noumenal ego. All the objects thus appear to the pure spirit as referring back to itself (except for God: it perceives itself on the contrary as being referred to God). Hence in this hypothetical case, which is even more clear than in the case of human beings, one can see that in the first intellectual apprehension the universal *noumenal affinity* is not deduced, but rather present, implied, given. Relation then, which is the very expression of this apprehension, pertains to the essence of spiritual life and is superior to spatial categories. *Ens* [being] as soon as it is posited is in us the affirmation of the *affinitas noumenon* [noumenal affinity]. Let us again note in this the coherence of the doctrine and the new problem we encounter if, contrary to the experience of the vital flux, one presupposes the knowledge of *one* thing which entirely occupies the field (even representative) of consciousness: this amounts to canceling the sensible image, supposing that one *envisages* the object, and putting the subject in *aevum* [eternity].

Thus, the idea of being, the very general idea of *thing*, is known analogically, that is to say: it is known as entailing another, as relating to the *other* of itself. What is this other? It is the soul. Being, thing, object, all this means: object for the soul, being *for the soul*. It would be the formula of subjectivism if one meant by this that the being of things is reduced to what is actually perceived of them. But being is abstract, that is to say potential (*universum generalitatis* [a universal of generality], not *totalitatis* [of totality], full). We thus only have here the affirmation of the universal *noumenal affinity*, identical to the Thomist principle that intelligence is in potency (at least obediential potency) of anything that can exist, identical to the Aristotelian principle: ψυχὴ τόπος εἴδων.

Being entails the soul as certainly (if not as expressly) as the notion of son entails the notion of father, as right entails left and selling

---

22 The French original ends the conditional with a period, leaving the sentence incomplete. We understand the following sentence, *La seule façon* ("the only way…") as the main clause.—Translators' note.

entails buying. This transcendental relation (unequally reciprocal) does not cancel the identity of the two terms any more than the previously mentioned examples do. But a fogginess always remains in the mind which still believes it can discern in rational psychology the *fallacia aperceptionis substantiatae* [fallacy of the apperception of a substance]. On what basis, it is asked, can we attribute substantial permanence, duration, to this soul [596] which certainly exists? Is this not to treat it unduly as an object?

Here is the answer. If this objection holds, one has to go further back and deny that the soul even exists. Now one cannot deny that the soul exists if it is true that a thing is *said*[23] to exist only through its relationship (actual or possible, experienced or represented) with the soul. Thus, this objection does not hold <(Change the order of these two propositions.)>

Proof of the Major

Identity between the affirmation of "substantial duration" and the affirmation of "existence." In a true sense we have to say of the soul (as of God) that we know of it not its essence, but its existence, not *quid est* [what it is] but only *quia est* [that it is]. I do not thereby deny the legitimacy of another manner of speaking according to which the knowledge *quia est* [that it is] would be attributed to direct consciousness and the subsequent conceptual construction would be designated as *quid est* [what it is]. These different manners of speaking in fact presuppose a single truth. I do not claim against Kant (this would certainly be an expeditious and tempting manner of escaping the problem) that it is enough to consider, to establish the <???> synthesis of apperception as undifferentiated from the per-

---

23   I do not claim that a thing *is* existing only through its actual relation to the soul, but that this relation (represented as possible) is found at the ground of the affirmation of the being or the possibility of a "thing." (Thing = object for me, unifying my consciousness, potentiality [?] of unifying me, potentiality [?] of entering in the synthesis of my apperception). We can certainly say the following: I can well imagine "a being who could not unify my knowledge;" but this chimera is as self-contradictory as the one of an absolute evil. There is a contradiction in thinking an unthinkable being. The absolute Unknowable is absolutely repugnant. But can any being that is *thought, represented* be *envisaged*? Can any object of representation be the object of intuition or grasp?

ceived synopsis in order to *envisage* the essence of the soul (not even in order to perceive as such the attributes that have, against Kant, to be justified). This is what I claim: first, we perceive the nature of the idea of being (the "transcendental relation" to intelligent soul) and then this idea is applied to the soul as to the principal correlate, to the *analogum princeps* [first analogue] of this pair extracted from the undifferentiated unity of "life." Once this has been done, I claim, all the determinations that can be applied to the idea of soul will only be determinations (negative for us, positive in themselves) (*explanations*) of the primitive idea of being. That is to say, the explanation [597] of this "more legitimate," of this *ipsum magis* [itself more] immanent to the first application of this idea that is made to the soul and the only legitimate use of this *infinity,* in which "life" floated at the moment of primitive transparency and which remains useless as soon as the concept has been attached [*fixé*] to the "thing." The discussed predicates can be reduced to three: immateriality, substantiality, immortality. Of each of them I shall say something, but they are not what first needs to be considered. The first *transitus* [transition] that has to be imagined in order to find out whether it is legitimate, is the one in which one moves from vital and unexpressed knowledge to the affirmation: the soul exists. What seems debatable in this passage is that one finds already in it, it seems, a *quid est* [what it is] *subintroduced.* There is a quiddity (for one cannot answer the question *an est* [whether it is] without already having some conception, some representation which would answer the question *quid est* [what it is]); or, to formulate it in a Scholastic way, the soul is already submitted to the category of essence and *esse* [*existence*], that is to say: to this dualist function of the mind, which makes it take leave of the primitive affirmation and conceive the difference between the possible and the real.[24] What is the nature of this first *quid est* [what

---

24 Nothing lets us feel the solidity of the Thomist metaphysics better than to see how much light these distinctions between essence and *esse* [existence], nature and hypostasis, shed on the problems of knowledge, which holds the key to the problem of being. A detailed comparison with Hegel's *Logic* would be necessary to get us to see the latent wealth of Thomist metaphysics in its most arid articles; and with some sense of the complexity of life, we manage [?] to see that it is replete with being and reality. (Those arid rocks exude reality). On the distinction between nature and supposit

it is] prior to *quia est* [that it is] and necessary for it to have a meaning? (Aquinas describes it thusly "eo non dicitur quid res sit in se, sed quid nomine rei significetur" [by this is not meant what a thing is in itself, but what is signified by the name of the thing]). This first *quid est* [what it is], which is organically implied in the affirmation "the soul exists," simply means that the soul is *being*, that is to say: the soul is object of the soul, the soul is intelligible or at the very least representable. I was thus right to say that it is at this first step, if ever, that the soul is transformed in *object*. But if I am granted this first step (as the minor shows that I should be), I say that I have been granted all I want. This is what I want, nothing less, and you yourself grant me that it is legitimate. Nothing more, [598] for one cannot go one step further without submitting the soul to spatial categorization, without turning the soul into a corporeal object.[25] All our rational psychology is contained in this formula: the soul is for me a being such that for it the distinction between essence and existence holds, but not the distinction between nature and supposit [*suppôt*][26] (the distinction between nature and supposit is equivalent to that of form and matter (see note 6, pp. 71-72), which it precisely translates for the human mind). Corporeal beings composed of matter and form are known by human beings, as experience shows, as soon as they are set in their *unity*, through a concept which is necessarily supported by a sensible image. As soon as human beings in self-reflection isolate "intellectual knowledge" and "sensation" from primitive transparency, they can form the idea of a being that would be the object of intellectual knowledge without being the object of sensation, the idea of a "noumenon" in the proper sense. This physical potentiality is not in question. What is in question is the legitimacy, the value of this idea of the soul: one wonders whether it has more value than the pseudo-idea, for example, of an absolute evil.

[*suppôt*], which is the heart of all knowledge of sensible things, see Bilfort Bax (*Roots of Religion*. Note of the French editor).

25   It cannot be denied that a host of psychologists and metaphysicians fail this rule and encumber their idea of the soul with a slew of spatial dross. But too bad for them. See above on the implicit criticism.

26   Or, to express this in terms more intelligible to moderns: a being that is not a *thing* (See category 1). The body is what makes it the case that human individuals are not identical with their nature (See note 6, pp. 71-72).

And the previous deduction aims at relating this concept to an experience, at showing that existence is legitimately attributed to this quiddity. For the judgment "The soul exists," although temporally posterior to the knowledge of the object, is nevertheless entailed in such knowledge and plunges its roots in an ultra sensible experience which is prior to the "sensation"; which, with "conception," is dissociated from primitive transparency.[27] The first word of the soul is neither *Cogito* [I think] nor *Sum* [I am] but *Est* [it is]. But this *Est* [it is] has no meaning if *Sum* [I am] cannot [599] come out of it and there is no truth in this *Est* [it is] if there is no truth in *Sum* [I am]. This is the true way of raising the question and it dissipates the last objection that could be made, which would consist in saying that we contradict ourselves since we call the soul a being for which the distinction between nature and supposit does not hold, and since in our idea of being the notion of nature and support is included. This contradiction does not exist since the link to ultrasensible experience legitimates the self-critique that I carry out on my concept, denying, as I said elsewhere, "a subjective condition, which for me is really inseparable from expressed knowledge, and proclaiming the necessity of the soul, which causes what remains forever divergent and double in our thought to become one in its being." It is useless to attempt to integrate in this formulation all the predicates we attribute to the soul in rational psychology. Through the very statement itself one can see that it is immediately convertible with *immateriality*. *Immortality* applies in the same way by definition, since death is nothing else but the separation of matter and form.[28] *Substantiality* also applies, since besides permanence it only expresses the fact of being subject to

---

27   Kant raises objections of which he himself grasps the extrinsic character, since these are mere suppositions, possibilities that he would not regard as serious, but to which he believes metaphysical psychology is unable to reply, and which indeed sometimes continue to tease imagination even after reason has been convinced. Kant for example asks whether the soul, which is in one respect thinking, cannot be in another respect corporeal.

28   The distinction of form and matter is indeed drawn from the fact of substantial mutation (which means death for the living). Some being departs, some being remains. A *hoc aliquid* [this something] ceases to have this or that nature. Thus material being is composed of two components, of two entities (*entia quibus*) [entities by which].

accidental determinations; substantiality also expresses the fact that spiritual experience, from which one extracts as its natural expression the notion of the soul, leads us to the following conclusion: the soul persists under the flux of the provisional states of consciousness, it fuses with each thing and, being opposed to all, it hurries outside the forms of the different objects.

The problem can also be tackled from another angle: one can say that these three negative predicates, as well as all those which could legitimately be added to them, express a surplus of intensity of being: in the undifferentiated unity of primitive transparency they are due to infinity and thus have to be attributed to the soul. This manner of speaking has the advantage of showing that everything that is submitted to the category of nature and supposit, matter and form, although positively known thanks to sensible intuitions, is, however, an imperfection, a lesser being, a negative, when compared to the [600] perfection of psychological *infinity*.

Proof of the Minor

The right, if existence is affirmed of the object, to affirm the existence of the soul even more. This proof, the elements of which have been disseminated in all the previous pages, amount in fact to this. Things are conceived and affirmed as beings (that is to say: are conceived and affirmed *simpliciter*) only to the extent that they are conceived and affirmed as transcendent relations to the soul.[29] Now, this cannot be if the soul is not more being than things. Thus …

To say that a thing is, is to say that it is for the soul. Although this formula is accurate, it should not be taken in the sense of subjectivism (which I fight). It must be taken as a whole and without canceling the phrase *to say*. It does not mean that things are only as far as they are the actual object of the perceptions of the soul (which is false), but rather that to affirm the reality, the *entity* of a thing, is to affirm, whether one wants to or not, the possibility that this thing enters in combination with the synthesis of intellectual apperception. (One may try to isolate the concept, to criticize the conception *qua talis* [as such] when we abstract from apperception: still it is always under

---

29 The French sentence says: "les choses ne sont pas conçues… comme être… qu'en tant qu'elles sont…" The word "pas" must be a typo and the sentence expresses not a negation, but a restriction.—Translators' note.

the concept itself, which shows the illusion of this attempt). To say a thing (to say in the Thomist sense: *dicere* [to say] = to think) is not to have said, but to have apperceived the soul under the thing, the soul supporting the thing, the soul informed by the thing, and as it were the material cause with regard to the essence of the thing.[30] (Aquinas: "Illa similitudo est forma ejus" [That similitude is its form]). All this is in intellection, because the soul, which says being, is perceived at the same time as generating, as constituting its word, which is being, and as generating it in a way from its proper substance, generating it without expressing it outside, finding itself in it and *being* it in a certain manner. In intellection the soul is both efficient and material [601] cause (see possible intellect and agent intellect). When it says being, the soul thus hides itself under it without knowing it through a kind of innocent and unconscious ruse. Thus, if the soul imagines the possibility of possessing an absolutely *unthinkable being*, it innocently falls into the same mistake one makes when asking: "Were the flowers of the desert island blue and the leaves green before Robinson came ashore?" The one who asks this question, through the very fact that he asks it, that is to say, that he speaks of *color,* substitutes, hides in the question itself an eye, a potentiality of vision. In the same way someone who imagines an unthinkable being thinks something thinkable which would be unthinkable, something representable which could not be represented. Whether we want to or not, when we conceive any being whatsoever, we conceive it as combinable with the mind, as knowable. Whether we want to or not, when we affirm any entity, we affirm universal *noumenal affinity*; or in the language of Aquinas, we affirm, we have affirmed, that intelligence is a potentiality of being, that intelligence is in potentiality to living ideally, πως, through transparent duality, everything that exists or can ex-

---

30 And to consider a thing said is to re-say it (*In Verbo = esse = dici = considerari = generari* [In the Word = to be = to be said = to be considered = to be generated]).

We can see here the difference between the soul, on the one hand, and God and Angels, on the other: with regard to conceived quiddity the soul is both efficient and material cause. God and Angels are only active. They do not become the thing, *intelligere iis non est quoddam pati* [understanding for them is not a kind of undergoing]. This is why, as more *separated* [*détachés*] from things, they know things more originally, more naively, they are less entangled with things.

ist. This is the meaning of the formula: *to say that a thing is, is to see that it is for the soul.* The considerations I have just made allow us, moreover, to transform this formula into another one: *to say that a thing is for the soul, is to say that the thing is.* This is just another form of the principle that the soul is a faculty of being, of the principle of universal intelligibility.

Now that this first proposition has been admitted, how does it follow that the soul is *more* being than these material objects which are beings *for* it? <(We have not yet proven this further assertion: *to say that a thing is for the soul, is to say first that the soul is*).> Here is how this can be demonstrated. Three kinds of intellectual apprehensions can be distinguished: grasping, intuition, representation. There is grasping if the intelligible Reality is identical with the very idea one has of it: if God exists, this is how He knows Himself. Physically there is intuition if there is no objective intermediary between the idea and the object, even though the idea is not the same physical reality as the object itself (J. Maréchal, *loc. cit.* Aquinas). (Neither in intuition nor in grasping does the possible exceed the real.) There is representation when intelligence fabricates in itself an [602] image of the object to be contemplated and considers its object *in* this image (*medium in quo* [means by which]). Representation does not reach *what* is real.

According to what was said above, human conceptual knowledge belongs to this third group: it is *representation* because it is in its word, being, that the soul contemplates the thing it wants to consider (see above the Thomist theory of the word as *medium in quo* [a means by which], and of the "speculum non excedens id quod in eo cernitur" [mirror not exceeding that which is grasped in it]), (not in such a way that the gaze of the soul would stop at the mirror as such, but in such a way that the gaze reaches the mirror only as an image, and that the movement of the soul goes entirely into affirming the *thing* represented). This being granted, I submit that *representation* is knowledge that is essentially mediating, passing, and potential, and only has meaning to the extent that it is a means to a future intuition. This means in this particular case that *objects* are objects of *representation* only if the soul is an object of *intuition,* and that the objects are *conceivable* only if the soul is *intelligible,* thus is more intelligible than the objects, thus is more being than the objects. <(Does representation only have meaning to the extent that it presupposes the possibility of an intuition or to the extent that it [??][31] so intuition would be in it "sicut terminus motus est in motu" [as the end of motion is in motion]? This makes two things).

The mediating nature of representation as intellectual knowledge is proven through its imperfect nature, through its infinity of infirmity.[32]

The infinity of the conceived essence is twofold: it is a generality in the concept and it is an inexhaustibility in the conceived thing. As was shown above, and as the comparison with sensible intuitions indicates, this twofold infinity is precisely what is communicated to it [603] by the idea of being, that is to say by its entrance in the synthesis of apperception of the "soul," by the communication the soul makes to it of its spiritual life, or rather, if you want, of its life itself

---

31 McDermott (*loc. cit.*) reads and we concur: "qu'elle moyenne": "that it mediates."—Editors' note.

32 Sensible intuition is finite, τελάως, compared to the concept. Perception is exhausting; it is *tota simul* [all at once]: the whole white, for example, is given at once, and *in the domain of vision* there remains nothing more to do. Whiteness as such is everything to the seeing being: it is its good, its thing, its captive, and the seeing being knows it fully. By contrast, conception is essentially inexhausting; it is an effort to synthesize multiple possibilities of perception, which it can never manage to conquer, to subsume, to absorb completely in itself (*aufheben*). The lion or the oak, or any other substantial object that is conceived, does not belong entirely to the conceiving being: the conceiving being is aware of the imperfection of its act and feels in its object a mysterious remnant that escapes it. The synthesis of white in each perception is perfect, but the synthesis of the lion is never finished

Now, if this infinity of imperfection of the conceived comes to it from the spiritual acting infinity that I described in the first part, if it is as it were the trace of the conjunction of the sensible thing with the mind which acts, which endeavors, this infinity can only be its embossed image. The object of sensible perception *as such* (a) is a given ?? an actual intuition [?], but the object of conception represents a task to which there correspond mediately a future intuition and immediately a progress. Thus conception is only meaningful if it is an instrument for *the action of spiritualizing oneself.*

(a) <Meaning is by definition what knows white as such. But the mind also can apply itself to the white and know it as being. And consequently white no longer finds its explanation, its justification, in the intuition that exhausted it.>

(*spiritual* again being only a label). Thus, if we say that a thing is, we also say that it is for the soul; if we say that it is for the soul, we say that it is; it follows that a thing is for the soul insofar as it is infinite, i.e., inexhaustible and incomplete. To affirm the thing insofar as it is *being* is thus to affirm it insofar as it is inexhaustible and incomplete. The being that is conceived thus has these two characters. Everything that being is, it is such for something else; and it is inexhaustible, that is to say, exhaustible, but indefinitely.

Even better. What remains is to prove the following assertion: to say that a thing is for the soul is to say that the soul is. Here is how the proof goes: to say that the thing is (for the soul) is to say that it is infinite by imperfection or inexhaustible. Now, the affirmation of infinite being by imperfection or inexhaustible (or the conceivable or temporal) has no sense if it does not *presuppose* the will and the right to affirm more strongly (as a reality to which this being is suspended) the infinite being by intelligibility, which is exhaustible for a certain intellectual intuition and inhabits intensive duration (*aevum*) [eternity]. <The inexhausting or the exhausting, the being which endeavors to exhaust.>

Starting from this fact, one can reach the affirmation of the soul in two ways, one more extrinsic and the other more intrinsic. The extrinsic way consists in saying that the infinity of inexhaustibility, in the conceived thing, has no sufficient reason if it does not derive from an infinity of spirituality which is immanent to the subject conceiving it: this reasoning presupposes a transcendental usage of the principle of causality ("anima est causa intelligibilitatis in objecto, seu facit [604] illud esse intelligible actu. Aqui [sic. Atqui.—Translators' note] propter quod... Ergo anima est intelligibilis, ergo est ens") [the soul is the cause of intelligibility in an object, or it makes that object be intelligible in act ... However, on account of which ... Therefore the soul is intelligible, therefore it is being].

The intrinsic way consists in showing that the *affirmation* of a being which is infinite by inexhaustibility is absolutely incoherent and *nonsensical* (deprived of meaning), if such an affirmation does not implicitly rely on a deeper affirmation of a being that is infinite by spirituality. Since *being* means *knowable* (pp. 96-97), I claim that the affirmation of a represented knowable has in fact only one meaning, namely: a means for reaching an intelligible possession, which can only be the intuition of oneself. Now this is the case if the idea of being is with the soul in a relationship that is called in the Scholastics the *analogy of attribution*. For if this is the case here, one does not need an extrinsic application of the principle of causality, rather one only has, so to speak, to open the concept of being and one will find the soul implied in it, this concept being wholly of itself relativity. If the *remedy* were fully known, not insofar as it is this plant or that drink, but insofar as it is a *remedy*, one would see that the one who would affirm it as remedy would at the same time affirm the legitimacy of the idea of health. In the same way, if *being* is examined in its natural naivety, we will see that the soul is internally affirmed in it, not simply as being, but as more being than the essence of bodies.

There is a certain inaccuracy in saying that the soul is affirmed as being, or even in saying that the soul is affirmed, before the knowledge of being. For, *affirmation* means *judgment* and *judgment* means *concept*. It is only after conceiving the material object, after conceiving being, that the soul is also conceived as being. Strictly speaking, one has to say that the soul is known in the apperception of a certain inexpressible knowledge, and that when one wants to express it after conception and reflection, one can only (of subjective necessity) express it through the idea of being, a necessary form of all our concepts. But either this concept is illegitimate, or it contains an internal correction (or self-critique) (which consists in negating the distinction between matter and form, nature and supposit). It is at this price only that the application of the note of *ens* [being] to the soul is legitimate. But once this is made, one obtains the whole rational psychology. One then needs to go on to show that it is *per modum amoris, cupiditatis* [by way of love, of cupidity] [??] that apperception is not a declaration of experience [?] but a *motus* [movement].>

[605] If one considers the being which is solidified and isolated in the conception already made, all this will only make sense through a juxtaposition of distinct notions, through a transcendental usage of the principle of causality. But if one starts from the transparent and primitive continuity, of which the concept of being is, *as* we saw, only a partial expression, *if one sees it in its fluency [fluence] which is its being* (ipsum generari verbi est ejus esse [the being generated

of the word is its very existence]), *if one manages despite the tyranny of custom to realize that, as being, as word, it is only a relationship, it is only* πρός τι, *then one realizes that the relation, the* πρός τι, *the solidarity is given even prior to being;* there is thus no need to speak of an illegitimate usage of the principle *propter quod ununquodque tale, ipsum magis* [that on account of which anything is such, is itself more such], since the *intuition* expressed by this principle is even more presupposed by the notion of being than the notion of being is presupposed by it. *One has said nothing before saying: being exists, but one has apperceived the soul before saying of being: it is.* Thus, the primitive and transparent continuity which is represented in the intellectual operation through the moment of apperception, which is thus prior to the moment of conception and thus more natural than the moment of conception, shows that the desire of the soul (lived knowledge) is what generates the affirmation of being (conceptual knowledge). The synthesis of human intellection is a kind of τίκτειν ἐν καλῷ wherein the word is generated only through the effect of the passionate gaze that has been thrust upon the soul.

In other words, the only sufficient reason, the only interior motor of all of our mental life, and what gives a meaning to each of our conceptions, is the love of this ideal goal: the intuition of the soul by itself, the intelligible grasp, intellectual [?] of our proper essence.

It seems that we can summarize everything in this way: if one takes the ready-made conception, one cannot escape the problem without a transcendental usage of the principle of causality (applied to *some* categorized things, and indeed one presupposes the proof given). But if one takes conception while it is in the process of being made (and it has to be taken in this way, since, as we can readily see, "ipsum ejus esse est generari" [its very existence lies in being generated]), then we realize that the affirmation of being is essentially bound up with an apperception of the soul, that it draws from it all its superior (intelligible) value which characterizes the "entity," and thus, if being has a meaning, a value, a solidity, a right to be intellectually affirmed, to signify [606] something to human beings, the soul—I do not say must have or will have—but, had, *possesses* such a meaning, value, solidity, and right, even more so.

Compared with this result, it is a rather frivolous question to ask whether it is proper to apply to the soul precisely the same word (being) one has *said* of objects. A question about words cannot be of capital importance; whether one says *being* or, if one pleases, *hyperbeing*, the result remains that being and the soul are only known through an analogy of one with the other. The soul is said (thought) only after being has been said, and being is said (thought) only after the soul has been apperceived, known through a concrete knowledge *per modum naturae* [by way of nature], by way of love.

By starting with the primitive transparency of "life," one finds oneself here at the head of two series of analogicals: *acts* (forms) and *things*, and we should not let ourselves repeat against Kantian reasonings that *things* are not less known according to *acts* than acts are expressed according to things.

> Excerpt from a letter to Blondel of January 29, 1914 [—Translators' note].

... It has appeared certain to me and for a long time that (1) under all knowledge *per notionem* [through a notion] there is a certain knowledge *per connaturalitatem* [through connaturality]: this is the *a priori* condition of true knowledge; (2) all knowledge *per notionem* [through a notion] anticipates and ?? a more fundamental knowledge *per connaturalitatem* [through connaturality]. It is a universal law ... I think I indicated this several times, probably in too elliptic a manner, as in the note where I was taken to reduce all knowledge to perception of the beautiful ("Les yeux de la foi," 3rd article, p. 32), and where I suggested that Kant's "reflective" judgments, which cause a sympathetic vibration with the object, should have brought him back to an express realism. Our friend Auguste Valensin was the first to draw my attention to the links between the *Critique of Judgment* and the Thomist theory of sympathetic knowledge. This connection at first seemed merely ingenious to me, but now I find it very fruitful. These problems have been the object of almost all of my reflections for the last three or four years. I would like to offer a [607] public explanation about them. Unfortunately I have little time and above all, I have to confess, some points are not yet clear enough to me such that I could be satisfied in writing about them now. But I hold as a certain thesis that it is not just grace which introduces a voluntary element into our knowledge, in order to render it perfect and a grasper [*preneuse*] of being.

I wholeheartedly also grant you that I have exaggerated the irrealism of conceptual knowledge in my book on Aquinas. It seems to me that I should maintain what I said about the idea the holy Doctor had of *definition*, but that I was mistaken about the spontaneous *concept*. I cannot find the time to prepare a 2nd edition and at the moment other works appear to me more urgent. Yet if God pleases, I will correct this chapter. Allow me, however, to express my astonishment at the interpretation Fr. Laberthonnière and several others after him (among them de Sailly) specifically gave of my word ("unfelicitous" also, I acknowledge) of "simulacrum" (or "imitation"). In the *Annales* of 1910 (vol. IX, pp. 395 and 525) I explained that the expressions "to feign the grasp of being," "to imitate intellection" precisely mean for me that the whole truth of our conceptual representations comes from the effort toward complete vision, from the appetition of the supreme truth which animates them … The excess of irrealism of which I have been accused is real, but it is circumscribed, and it is difficult for me to understand how one could have understood the general thrust of my thesis in a sense so different from mine.

[225] SPIRITUAL LOVE AND APPERCEPTIVE SYNTHESIS

The most intellectualist of Scholastic metaphysics culminates in these two affirmations: *The perfect intelligible is living spirit; perfect knowledge is identical with love.* I have no intention of trying to show in these few pages either the entire coherence of these two theses with traditional intellectualism or the necessary insufficiency of that intellectualism insofar as it has not reached that coherence. I propose only to present some insights that will perhaps clarify the second of these two propositions.

I

Passion blurs the clarity of intelligence's gaze. Love blinds.—Affection gives eyes in order to know. Love makes us see. These two truisms, while apparent opposites, in reality only express two sides of a single truth, one of considerable philosophical importance, and one we could formulate in these terms: *every knowing [connaissance] is defined by a love.*[1]

We get stuck inside a very narrow and superficial view of things if we conceive all influence of appetite on knowledge on the model of a "commandment" made to "intelligence" by "will." Psychology—the psychology of philosophers, of literary figures, and of common sense—has for a long time shed light on another form of the same influence, subtler, more interesting, and more delicate. This psychology has shown that it happens that appetite rules knowledge *from the inside,* so that it not only makes us adopt this or [226] that proposition, but also *makes us see* things in this or that color, under this or that aspect. Intelligence is not determined by the sole sway of willing, without anything presenting itself to intelligence, but love, which renders the subject *such,* makes the object appear *such.*

There is no need to pile up examples of so well known a phenomenon. All the "passions," loves, hates, pleasures, all the "emotions," angers, sadnesses, etc., could supply as many examples as one could

---

1 Love is taken here in the metaphysical sense of *appetite* in general.

wish, and these affective presuppositions pertain to the commonplace. The only point worth insisting on is this: the more the love involved is absolute and dominant, the more the vision it commands and defines seems to impose itself with evidence. The more an affective bias passes into nature and becomes unconscious, the less sensitive one is to contrary reasons. The more one is carried away by a passion, the more non-existent and null seem the arguments that contradict it. *The blinder you are, the better you see.* The two truisms overlap.

This concordance of blindness and evidence, when we reflect on it carefully, can transform a truth of banal experience into a very fruitful principle for the general theory of knowledge. Love only blinds by giving new eyes. Love does not make us judge falsely objects first seen in clear light; it colors the very light or the very atmosphere, in which we see objects. It makes us draw forth, as by nature, a new term of knowledge. I would say, in Scholastic terms, that *it elicits a new faculty of abstracting and prescribes for the knowing subject a new formal object.* And this claim of an accidental perversion of knowledge allows us to understand better what a "faculty of abstracting" is and what a "formal object" is.

Contemporary philosophy has very fortunately cast light upon the appetitive and practical [*utilitaire*] nature of the faculties of abstraction, and clarified how their interplay resembles that of natural powers. Henri Bergson has shown, in some pages of great penetration, how "grass *in general* attracts the herbivore: the color and odor of the grass, sensed and endured as forces ... are the sole immediate data of its [227] external perception."[2] As an acid draws its base solely from

---

2 *Matière et Mémoire*, pp. 172-74. Bergson does not agree that there is an *abstraction* here. "Things and beings," he writes, "grasp in their surroundings what attracts them, what is of practical interest to them, without a need to abstract, simply because the rest of their surroundings has no hold on them." He is right, if *abstraction* is understood as an operation preceded by a comparison: clearly this supposition would prevent us from explaining the genesis of general ideas. But I see no reason not to follow the age-old way of using these words. As we know, for Aquinas intellectual "abstraction" of *being*—the basis of general human ideas—is quite similar to the "abstraction" of color by sight and of odor by our sense of smell: these diverse operations are also made *per modum naturae* [by way of nature], not *per modum collationis* [by way of collection].

a salt, *abstracts*, so to speak, its base from a salt, so too the eye, we can say, focuses on color in things, *abstracts* color from things, because, as the Scholastics quite rightly say, the eye *is moved* by color. So also, an animal of prey knows its victim by a natural, irresistible, instinctive sympathy—insofar as it is good, appropriate, tasty: it abstracts from the victim the aspect that matters to it.

So we represent beings that only have sense knowledge as "charmed," as "enchanted," as "bewitched" by their species's good. And passionate persons are led in the same way by their love, if we take *love* in the general sense of a powerfully rooted affective disposition. Now we see what was meant when we spoke of *faculty of abstraction* and *formal object*. Optimists *see* everything through rose-tinted glasses: their formal object, insofar as it is such, is the smiling aspect of things. Pessimists see the dark side of everything: they are like Shakespeare's Jaques who "sucks melancholy out of a song" with the instinct of an animal;[3] pessimists suck naturally and irresistibly the melancholy out of things: they extract the funereal aspect of things, which dominates them, subjugates them, *imposes itself upon them.* In the same way, ardent love for people can so well take hold of their entire mental life that they can only consider objects through the eyes of such a love, or as means of pleasing it. And in all these cases the more the inclination has passed into habit and, as it were, into nature, the more powerfully it imposes [228] its manner of seeing. You are "charmed," which says it all: you are another being. *Qualis unusquisque est secundum appetitum, talis res videntur ei* [Whatever manner anyone is in according to the appetite, such is how things are seen by that person].

The proliferating modern affirmations of the priority of the affective over the cognitive, along with considerations of the sort just made, often leave the friends of logic and intelligence with a very understandable uneasiness. As partisans of the old intellectualisms or independent thinkers, many philosophers refuse to see in the directions imposed by appetite on knowledge anything but distortions or corruptions. The more affective influence there is, they say, the less intellectuality, the less *reason* itself there is. Neither the good nor the

---

3 "I can suck melancholy out of a song, as a weasel sucks eggs" (*As You Like It*, II, 5).

agreeable should be the measure of being and the true: rather the good is essentially measured by being and the true, i.e., it is "good" only in the measure it conforms to them. It is strictly immoral, they also say, and even the supreme immorality, to allow one's reason to be dominated by a superadded appetite, to impregnate this divine portion of ourselves with an appetitive color, to impose on it a practical restriction. "Keep the inner daimon pure," rightly says stoicism: this precept demands the assent of all reasonable people. Speculative reason appears naturally to human beings as the light that ought to lead them. "But if the light within you is darkness, what will darkness itself be?"

Nothing appears to us more natural than these fears, nor more evident than these reflections. But push the logic to its conclusion—nothing less should be expected from very firm partisans of reason—and abruptly we see the doctrine of the primacy of the affective life reverse itself. If we push *appetitivism* to its final consequences and take it to its limits, we find instantly confirmed and justified, at the same time as it is explained and transcended, the most delicate, most receptive, the most rightly uncompromising *intellectualism*. For given the absolutely dominant, imperious, intransigent character of the demands of intellectual inclination, this inclination cannot be taken as an entirely natural appetite without the necessary inference that its speculative claims are legitimate [229] and even that the good that attracts, commands, and can alone satisfy it is real: Pure Truth exists.

Human persons, enamored by a love that blinds them, are imperiously dominated by it all the way to the depths of their faculties of knowing and see according to this love with all the more evidence as they are more bewitched. Similarly, a faculty of sense apprehension is entirely, irrevocably enslaved by the charm of its formal object, however narrow and relative it may be, and so also human intelligence is attracted by being and by the true, as the sole object that charms it, only because its very nature is to be an inclination toward infinite Being insofar as it is the Good of intelligent beings, i.e., insofar as it is supreme Truth. Here as elsewhere the formal object is commanded by a propensity, knowledge is defined by a love. Just as an earthly and carnal love creates in its image a deceiving and abasing evidence, so also the movement of intelligence, which is just a certain natural inclination toward God,[4] arouses in the soul the pure and legitimate intellectual evidence.

I have elsewhere proposed to sum up the principle of Thomist intellectualism in these words: "Intelligence is the sense of the real because it is the sense of the divine." The foregoing developments will perhaps clarify this formula and the formula itself can serve to make the meaning of those developments more precise. Making our own an expression of an ascetical writer one can also say that *being* and the *true*, which the soul grasps in objects, is the perfume of God, the "odor of the divine hands." So desire for God is the dynamic and active element of knowledge: *we understand things only insofar as we desire God.*[5]

---

4 Please understand that it is not a matter here of one of those inclinations the Scholastics call *appetitive faculties*, but of a *cognitive faculty*, identical with a natural inclination by reason of its potentiality. Every faculty that is a power [*en puissance*], that is not its act, is nothing other than an inclination toward its object. Thomas notes the difference between these natural inclinations and appetites in the strict sense in the *Quaestiones disputatae, De Anima*, a. 13, ad 11.

5 Not, it is clear, by a conscious, voluntarily personal desire but by that natural desire that is intelligence, i.e., the innate inclination of the soul toward God, according to the sense of the preceding note. It is not difficult to see what difference separates this doctrine from the ontologist opinion according to which we judge things only insofar as we measure them against the Infinite, measure them by God *previously known*. My doctrine is completely different. To borrow yet another of Aquinas's expressions, we can say that God is in intelligence "sicut terminus motus in principio motivo proportionato per convenientiam et proportionem quam habet ad ipsum ..., ut inclinans et quodam modo impellens intrinsecus amantem in rem amatum" [as the term of a movement is in its proportionate motive principle by the suitability and proportion that it has for it ..., as inclining and in some way internally impelling the lover toward the thing loved] (*Contra Gentiles*, IV, 19). Thomas speaks here of the presence of the beloved in *voluntate amantis* [in the will of the lover], and distinguishes it from its presence *in intellectu* [in the intellect], where it is *secundum similitudinem suae speciei* [according to a likeness of its species]. But these words can serve to make intelligible what the presence of God is in intelligence insofar as it is potential and insofar as it is an inclination. It is precisely because of this *natural* appetition of God, which constitutes the *mens* [mind], that there is no need, it seems to me, for *personal* moral action in order to render us capable of perceiving the value of the philosophical proofs for God's existence. This appetition is

[230] It would be a big mistake to find a taste of agnostic pragmatism in this theory. The absolute value of intellectual evidence is here legitimated, far from being denied; if *truth* is subordinated to spiritual *finality*, then, unless we make our soul the divine being and earthly intellection the final end, we must recognize in our conceptual knowledge a *ratio medii* [nature of a medium], an imperfect, mediating, transitory character—and not only as to its *exercise* but also as to its *specification*.

Besides, it would be surprising that the subordination of all truth as such to subsisting and divine Truth compromises, in the eyes of believers, traditional intellectualism, the support of necessary dogmatism. The doctrine I propose here is nothing other than a stricter and more rigorous interpretation of the Augustinian notion: *Fecisti nos* AD TE, *Domine* [You have made us FOR YOURSELF Lord]. Creatures, whatever they may be, are only, we might say, inclinations toward the Divine Essence, as Aquinas has explained in some immortal chapters. But corporeal essences can only be brought back or "reduced" to God, to use the archaic term, by the intermediary of humanity; spiritual creatures, on the contrary, whose nature is defined by their appetite for the known God, are in some way pure inclinations toward the first truth, and are as it were "transcendental relations" to God. Their end is divine contemplation and their progressive potentiality is entirely regulated by the attraction to this end.

[231] If the philosophy of past centuries has not clearly discerned this profound dynamism of natural intellection, at least the greatest thinkers of Catholicism have plainly recognized this essential penetration and animation of intelligence by love in supernatural knowledge. It was more apparent there, besides, because of the freedom of this knowledge and because of its more intimate sweetness. Among so many passages and authors I only want to recall this famous sermon where Augustine comments on Christ's word: *Nemo venit, nisi Pater traxerit* [No one comes unless the Father has drawn one], and compares it to Virgil's word: *trahit sua quemque voluptas* [one's own pleasure attracts everyone]. "Revelation," he says, "is attraction it-

---

what legitimates, justifies the metaphysical value of the idea of being, as I show below.

self." *Ista revelatio, ipsa est attractio.* "You show a green branch to a sheep: you draw it to you. You show nuts to a child: you draw the child to you; the child runs, and nevertheless the child is drawn on, driven by love …. Each of us then is driven by our pleasure. But what does the soul desire more than truth?"[6]

One will find these expressions and the philosophy they imply simple and natural if one is familiar with this classical idea that God is not a true thing, a true being, but Truth itself, subsistent truth, pure, substantial, infinite Truth.[7] But I admit that this principle always sounds a bit strange to the ears of those who conceive all truth and all knowledge in the manner of a *representation* painted in the spirit.[8]

II

Intelligence, we said, is the sense of the real because it is the sense of the divine. This formula is not complete, and we must [232] insert between these two terms *the sense of the self.* What is indeed proper to intellectual beings, what is the nobility of spirits, is that since they

---

6 Augustine: *In Joannem*, tr. 26, n. 5. Migne, 35, 1609.

7 Thomas: *Contra Gentiles*, I, 60, 61, 62.

8 One can still give a plain and complete idea of the principle I have tried to present by referring to the passage where Thomas explains that vision will be, in heaven, commensurate with love, and that this concordance is in no way accidental but results from an essential relation. It is explained thus: "Intellectus plus participans de lumine gloriae perfectius Deum videbit. Plus autem participat de lumine gloriae qui plus habet de caritate; quia ubi est maior caritas, maius est desiderium; et desiderium quodammodo facit desiderantem aptum et paratum ad susceptionem desiderati. Unde qui plus habebit de caritate, perfectius Deum videbit, et beatior erit" [The intellect that is participating more in the light of glory will see God more perfectly. Now one participates more in the light of glory who has more of charity, because where there is greater charity there is more desire and desire in a certain way makes the one desiring apt and prepared for the reception of what is desired. Hence, the more charity one will have, the more perfectly one will see God and will be happier] (*Summa theologiae* 1 q. 12 a. 6). The "light of glory," as we know, is conceived by Thomas in the manner of a faculty: "facultas seu virtus ad videndum Deum" [the faculty or power of seeing God]. Let one apply the principle here enunciated to the innate appetite for God (of which Aquinas speaks so often) and to natural intelligence, and one will admit precisely what I am saying.

are essentially "capable of God," according to the Augustinian expression, they are also "capable of themselves." These two properties have only one root, or rather are only one property, and the sense of the divine is necessarily the capacity of conscious transparency, the capacity of clear self-possession [*jouissance de soi*]. The created spirit "finds" itself to the extent that it "finds" God.

But the spirit who has found itself, who is spirit alone, enjoys the love of God that constitutes its nature. It sees itself entirely from God and for God, *ex Deo, ad Deum*. And it is no doubt in this love concretely perceived, in this ardent and as it were liquefying knowledge that its natural beatitude must consist.

To say, on the contrary, that a spirit is still tied down to the laws of a body is to say that it is not all spirit, that it does not possess itself fully. The human soul has not found itself, it searches for itself; this sort of absence from itself outside of itself is the essential feature which characterizes the state of wayfaring [*voie*], in any case, and which hides from the soul its profound tendency toward God.

The object that definitively attracts the soul and of which love is the last word of its nature, is God, as I have said. But if it is only in order to gain God that the soul wants to gain itself,[9] it is only in order to gain itself and not an external object that our soul exercises itself and multiplies itself in its pursuit of being here below. One can therefore say rightly that the unknown and most loved goal whose discovery—or better whose *finding* [*invention*]—accounts for our entire mental dynamism, is the subsistent noumenon that we are, that we will be.[10] [233] The soul itself exhales the perfume that charms it.[11] It is not a matter, as we know well, of obtaining an idea

---

9 See Aquinas: *Contra Gentiles*, III, 24. "Propter hoc tendit ad proprium bonum, quia tendit ad divinam similitudinem, non e converso" [On account of this it (a thing) tends to its own good because it tends to the divine likeness and not conversely].

10 See Blondel's fine article, "L'Illusion idéaliste," in the *Revue de métaphysique et de morale*, Nov. 1898: "Thought is to itself its own unknown …. The truth to be acquired is not an external abstract thing but is an internal and concrete thing" (p. 12), etc. See also the "Point de départ," in the *Annales de Philosophie chrétienne*, June 1906, p. 233.

11 The Mediaeval Arabic or Latin writers sometimes compare the pursuit of the true, which is the life of intelligence, with the course run by a hunting

of self, a definition of self in the manner of a conceptual representation. It is a matter of this grasp of self by fusion of subject and object, which is the ideal of all conscious life, of this "winning [*gain*] of self," where perfect intellection and full freedom coincide: we cannot miss this grasp of self without having, at the same stroke, lost everything.

A pure spirit, naturally having consciousness of its own essence, would see itself simply dependent on[12] and suspended from God; similarly, the soul, naturally having consciousness of material essences, vaguely has consciousness also of searching for something other than them and lives, so to speak, with this unrest [*inquiétude*]. As long as the soul is not delivered from its material potentiality, as long as it is not equal to its nature, this anxiety persists and moves it in its core. It is the desire of self, whose disturbing restriction keeps, so to speak, the pure desire of God captive.

"The body," Bergson says, "has for its essential function to limit the life of the spirit for the sake of action."[13] "The inadequation between what we know of ourselves and what we are," Blondel says, "is not an accessory and provisional fact but the essential law of life and the first truth of philosophy."[14] Human individuals, Aquinas says, are not identical with their nature,[15] in other words: *they do not fill [remplir] their essence*. Drawn up according to very different philosophical mentalities, these formulas nevertheless have the same truth in view. It could be expressed in these terms: human beings are not placed right from the start in their natural attitude toward the Supreme Being; they must gain and constitute this attitude by a free effort. For that reason their speculation here [234] below, directed not only by the desire for God, but also by desire for their own essence, does not allow them to conquer being directly but only makes them prepared to do so.[16]

---

dog in avid quest of its prey.

12 Compare the definition Schleiermacher gives of religion, forgetting, as Protestantism ordinarily does, that we are not purely spirits.

13 *Matière et mémoire*, p. 197.

14 "L'Illusion idéaliste," loc cit., p. 13.

15 "Socrates non est sua humanitas, sed angelus est sua natura" [Socrates is not his humanity, but the angel is its nature].

16 I do not deal with the supernatural order in this article.

III

The love of God is what drives us, and we are not conscious of it. We ceaselessly pursue the First Truth, and we do not know it. Love for God is solidified in us, as it were, in *unconscious* nature. This is what gives our intellectual certainties their character of impersonal coldness and of *imposed evidence*. Our blindness is what makes us see thus.

If our spiritual nature were for us an object of intuition, if instead of searching for ourselves we possessed ourselves, then knowing everything else only through our intuited [*vue*] essence and by our *connaturality* with our essence, we would know everything sympathetically. We would be conscious of the love that guides us, we would see, so to speak, emanate from ourselves the law that defines our knowledge, and we would feel the kinship of our object with ourselves.

We can form a certain conception of this ideal thanks to æsthetic knowledge. As Kant so rightly observed, the pleasure that characterizes æsthetic knowledge does not depend on some new note perceived in the object: for æsthetic perception as such adds no new note. It consists in an at least implicit consciousness of the harmonious play of our faculties, which make us vibrate, as it were, in unison with the object and installs us, so to speak, in its essence. We can see this especially in the case of the knowledge artists—for example, poets—have of their own work. Poets in a certain way exhaust the intelligibility of their works, because they know them from inside [*par l'intérieur*]. Their knowledge being creative, the object is *in itself* what it is *for them*; their works do not present for them the character of being *infinite by reason of inexhaustibility* which is the essential defect [235] of our conceptual knowledge.[17] The spirit who knows

---

17　In comparison with other humans, who know art works only from outside [*par l'extérieur*], *a posteriori*, this character of "infinite by reason of imperfection" persists. Critics will *never be done* with analyzing the characters of Andromache, Polyeuctus, or Bajazet. In contrast, Racine's knowledge of Bajazet as a Racinian character is *mensurans non mensurata* [a measurer not a measured]. (If Racine then for fun conceptually cashed in his first intuition, he would no longer know his characters as creator). This example can help make intelligible how the infinity, ἄπειρον, of our concepts—and primarily of our idea of being—will never be sublated [*supprimé*] (*aufgehoben*, in

the poem by inventing it exhausts it by that very fact, for the poem is what it is only insofar as it is created by the poet, insofar as the poet wills it, insofar as the poet loves it. For the æsthetes who take pleasure in others' works, they coincide all the better with these works when their supple souls coincide with the souls of the creators; to understand fully sixteenth-century art, for example, what matters is not so much to establish statistics and study meter and rhyme, but to arouse in oneself the frame of mind of a courtesan of the Valois. Just as then an art work is perfectly understood not in some "in itself" state or other, but in its relation with the psychological state that engendered it—and just as ordinary life is an uninterrupted intellectual feast for those who, knowing thoroughly their epoch and their descent [*race*], *understand* at every instant the reactions that things arouse in them—so would our entire world of objects be known to us by sympathetic intuition, if we possessed ourselves.

In God alone, as is clear, the ideal of sympathetic intellection, of creative knowledge, of perceiving love is realized fully. For God alone the "formal object" coincides fully with the "material object," because there is in being only what God is pleased to taste there. Beings are insofar as God sees them, and insofar as God loves them. *Scientia Dei est causa rerum. Amor Dei est profundens et causans bonitatem in rebus* [The knowledge of God is the cause of things. The love of God is pouring out and causing goodness in things]: these are only two aspects of one identical act. God knows things by their *esse* [existence], by what they *are.* This means that God knows them exhaustively; but it also means that God knows them by what is "deiform" in them.[18] *God knows them by loving himself in them.* God's knowledge is love.

[236] If there are pure spirits, i.e., spirits who intelligibly possess their nature, and who see every foreign being by its conjunction with their nature "as one sees," Aquinas says, "color by its conjunction

---

Hegelian language) by an exhaustive objective analysis, but would disappear in one stroke, cut at the root, if the soul possessed itself.

18   Saints are the true sages because they appreciate, because they taste things as God does. *Cui sapiunt omnia prout sunt, non ut dicuntur aut æstimantur, hic vere sapiens est* [The one to whom all things are known just as they are, not as they are said or estimated to be, such a one is truly wise], says *The Imitation of Christ* (II., 1, 7). In God alone is this saying verified absolutely.

with light,"[19] then one can represent their intellection only as belonging to the æsthetic type, and one can only say: *they see beings insofar as they are beautiful to them.* Indeed it is enough that they love their own essence for them to delight ceaselessly in the blossoming of its natural relations with objects. But as we have said, spiritual nature is but an inclination toward divine truth. So for pure spirits to live their nature is to feel a desire for God. They feel themselves flowing from divine hands and aspiring to the divine good. In a way they are subsistent poems[20] of the First Truth, with all their being *crying out to God* [*des cris vers Dieu*].[21] And since the entire *meaning* of their essence is found in this love—an essence that itself gives its *meaning* to all their objects—we have to admit that what finally illuminates their intellectual perfection is the appetite they have for God.

Intellection is all the more intuitive, all the more elevated above the low infinity of the concept, the more that it coincides with love of being and love of self.

[237] IV

Does Thomas know what ceaseless effort of spirit it takes to discover and gain oneself? When he discusses memory in the sense of the

---

19 "Sicut patet in visu: lumen enim est quo videtur color ... color et lumen sunt unum tantum visibile, et simul a visu videntur. Essentia autem angeli est ei ratio cognoscendi omne quod cognoscit ...." [As is seen with sight: for light is that by which color is seen ... color and light are one visible entity and are seen simultaneously by sight. Now the essence of an angel is its basis for knowing all that it knows] (*De Veritate*, q. 8 a. 14 ad 6). The entire critique Thomas makes of conceptual knowledge derives from his theory of angelic knowledge. The principles he presents there are, of course, independent of the real existence of angels, and one can make use of them as Kant makes use of the hypothesis of a perceptive intelligence in order to help comprehend what perfection he refuses the human spirit.

20 "Sicut si arca haberet intellectum, et per formam suam cognosceret artem a qua talis forma eius similitudo processit ...." [Just as if a box had an intellect and knew through its form the art from which such a form proceeded as a likeness of it ...] (*Contra Gentiles*, III, 49, "Quod substantiæ separatæ non vident Deum per essentiam ...." [That separated substances do not see God in his essence]).

21 Compare this conception of pure spirits with what mystics say about separated souls and about those whom contemplation frees partially from bodily ties (See especially Catherine of Genoa's *Treatise on Purgatory*).

ancients—*qua mens sui meminit* [that by which the mind remembers itself]—does he allude to the persistent activity, indistinctly conscious but internally illuminating, that animates the entire life of the spirit? Does he say that the desire the soul has for itself is what gives intellectual perception its certainty and clarity?

Whether he says it or not is a historical question whose interest is after all secondary. What is more important is that it seems we have to state the propositions above in order to give full meaning and import to an observation Aquinas has quite rightly made. I mean: the relation between the act of conceiving and the idea conceived.

The conceived idea, Thomas says, is not the act of conceiving, but its effect. *Ipsa enim conceptio est effectus actus intelligendi* [For this concept is an effect of the act of understanding].—We should not picture this distinction as that between two spatially separable *things*. To use a comparison he proposes elsewhere,[22] let us say that the active idea and the passive idea, the intellective act and the concept, differ from one another as do the "flowering" [*floraison*] (the act of flowering [*fleurir*]) and the flower. The flowering, of course, does not happen *without* the flower; flower and flowering go on together; when the flowering stops the flower falls since the flowering is nothing other than the flower's continued development [*éclosion*], the communication of the tree's life by the branch to the flower, and so is what constitutes the flower. And yet, unless we fall into the illusions of the false common sense of atomist pseudo-metaphysics, we cannot say that the flowering *is* the flower.[23] The same goes for the intellective act (*intellectio*) and the idea produced (*verbum mentis* [the mental word]). [238] The irreducibility of *act*, of *movement*, to its result, to its term (*fact* or *thing*) has been too often and too brilliantly stressed in recent years for me to judge it necessary to dwell on this distinction. The thinking thought [*pensée pensante*] is not identical to the thought thought [*pensée pensée*], nor is conceiving

---

22 *Summa theologiae* I q. 37 a. 2 corpus and ad 2.

23 The flowering *is* no more the flower, than the "begetting" (the act of begetting) *is* the son, even though, in the one case, the persistence of the causal act and, in the other, its fleeting character, can induce us at first glance to judge differently of the distinction between the two terms.

action to conceptual "residue."[24]—But the Thomist doctrine adds that the very act of *producing* the idea [*agir l'idée*] is what makes us know the object. *Dictio verbi* [The speaking of the word] (it is always a matter of the *mental* word [*verbe mental*]) *est ipsa cognitio rei* [is the very knowing of a thing]. Is this not to say: it is through the act that the thing appears; it is the act that illuminates the thing with intellectual light? Active consciousness, *the vital thrust* [*pousée vitale*] *of the idea directly brings the object to light.* It is as though the tree were to become conscious and know the flower by the flowering—not by the flowering already known but by the very act of flowering, insofar as it is its movement, its germination, the expression of its natural progress.[25]

In quantum dicit verbum, anima cognoscit obiectum [Insofar as it speaks the word, the soul knows the object]. I translate: what illuminates the object is the effort of the soul that wants to become in act. But what is the *meaning* of this effort, what appetite actualizes it, if not love of self and of God?

2

Kant saw very clearly that the central fact of intellectual knowledge is the "synthesis of apperception." The characteristic property of the intelligent soul is that it reduces the multiplicity of objects to the unity of a whole in consciousness *by the very fact that it apperceives itself.* The foregoing pages help us see what the true nature of apperceptive synthesis would be according to Thomist principles.

We have to maintain the very accurate and very fruitful Scholastic doctrine according to which the synthesis of all our representations is made within the idea of *being, the universal* OBJECTIVE *form of objects of the spirit.* The idea of being is, according to the [239] felicitous expression of one of Aquinas's disciples, the "inhabitable

---

24　Blondel writes ("L'Illusion idéaliste," p. 15): "If knowledge is the extract or the residue of a whole life that projects itself in knowing by concentrating itself therein, the act itself that performs this synthesis exceeds the abstract representation that results from the act."

25　For this doctrine of idea and act see Aquinas's *De Veritate*, q. 4 a. 2, and *Contra Gentiles*, IV, xi.—Goudin very clearly presents the equivalence of *dicere verbum=cognoscere objectum* [speaking the word=knowing the object] in *Philosophia*, vol. II, pp. 175-76 (the 1885 edition).

land" of human intelligence; it is its atmosphere; one could say, it is intelligence itself insofar as it is transparent, insofar as it becomes its objects, πάντα πως;[26] the idea of being plays for the human soul the same role as the idea of its own essence, in which it sees objects, plays for the angel. But this idea of being, the natural fruit of our spirit, is not the last word of our mental life. If this idea communicates to general concepts their characteristic universality (infinity of inexhaustibility), it owes its superiority over sensible life (infinity of transparence, of spirituality) to the fact that it has been produced by the soul. Objective synthesis is not thoroughly understood without subjective synthesis. We must take into account *apperceptive synthesis* and not stop at *conceived synopsis*.

Besides, we remain stuck at an insufficient notion of apperceptive synthesis, we identify it only by a derived property, when we explain it by saying that all intellectual representation can be accompanied and informed by the conception of the judgment: *I think.* If *every look at an object is also by definition a look at the soul,* the soul and the object are seen quite differently.

The object is represented, the soul is experienced, and these two aspects coincide in one same indivisible act because *the idea is enacted* [*agie*] (or, as Thomas said, the mental word is spoken). Perception of the *actual* I [*moi*] is conception of the *essential* object. The soul reacts to the presence of sensible reality because it is in search of itself; the soul expresses sensible reality spiritually because the soul is in search of God; the soul expresses sensible reality conceptually, in terms of being (*ens concretum quidditati materiali* [a concrete being of material nature]) because the soul desires God through human essence.

Love would therefore play a double role in intellectual knowledge. It would actuate intellectual knowledge, as the appetite for God actuates every passage from potency to act. It would specify intellectual knowledge by indicating its formal object for it. The love of God who is Truth [*Dieu Vérité*], naturally [240] imprinted on our essence, is what makes us see in every truth our good and actively operates the synthesis in us.

---

26 It is not a matter of the reflex idea, the fruit of skilful abstraction, but of the direct idea, the spirit's formal object.

Love of God and love of self: there we see what justifies the claims of our earthly speculation to give us full and serene certainty suitable to the state of hope. Lack [*indigence*] of God and lack of self: there we see what explains its defects and its incapacity to allow us here below to conquer being. Here is the double root of a correct appreciation of knowledge. One cannot stop at conceptual clarity: "light of being," "evidence of principles."[27] The cold consistency of the *perceived synopsis* only holds through the vital effort of the *apperceptive synthesis*; being hides spirit imperfectly; and when the soul believes itself lost in the object, it is before itself and before its God that it remains entranced [*extasiée*].

---

27   I do not mean that *metaphysical certainty is not valid* as long as one has not explicitly seen this: I am formally convinced of the contrary. I mean simply that the *question of knowledge is not exhausted*, as some imagine it to be sometimes. The question of knowledge is no more exhaustible than philosophy itself, and they are inexhaustible precisely because the soul has no intuition of itself.

[561] BEING AND SPIRIT[1]

To impregnate intellectual knowledge with appetite right to its core, is that not to compromise its objective value? To search, behind being as perceived evidently, for a force that accounts for this very evidence, is this not to give into a morbid curiosity, to an unreasonable caprice of the spirit? To appeal to the force of life [*effort vital*], to the desire that drives all of creation toward God, in order to explain intelligence, not only as to its exercise but even as to its specification, is this not to break with the Scholastic theory of "species"?—I think precisely the contrary. Let us begin with the last point.

❄

After spending several pages speaking of the "mental word," it is surprising to hear that I seem to despise "the old theory of species." For what in Aquinas is called *verbum mentis* [mental word] is precisely what later Scholastics named *species expressa* [the expressed species]. To distinguish this mental word, or idea, from the act that sustains and constantly engenders it[2] is unquestionably not to swamp the

---

1 This article is a sequel to the one that appeared in the *Revue de Philosophie* on 1 March under the title "Spiritual Love and Apperceptive Synthesis." (See chapter three, pp. 119-134, of this volume.)

2 "Differt (conceptio seu verbum) ab actione intellectus: quia prædicta conceptio consideratur ut terminus actionis, et quasi quoddam per ipsam constitutum" [It (the conception or word) differs from the action of the intellect: because the aforesaid conception is considered as the term of an action and as something constituted through it] (*De Potentia*, q. 8, a. 1). See *De Veritate*, q. 4, a. 2; *De Spiritualibus Creaturis*, a. 9 ad 6; *Quodlibetum* 5, a. 9.—Elsewhere one reads: verbum enim nostrum semper est in continuo fieri, quia perfectum esse suum est in fieri … esse eius perfectum servatur eodem modo quo gignebatur. Non enim transit formatio verbi ipso formato, sed cum actu intelligitur, continue formatur verbum, quia semper est ut in fieri, et ut in egrediendo ab aliquo, scilicet a dicente" [For our word is always continually in a state of coming to be because its being is perfect in coming to be … its being is kept perfect in the same way in which it was begotten. For the formation of the word is not transgressed from its being formed, but the word is understood with the act and continually formed,

representative species [562] in vital dynamism, since this is precisely to distinguish word from act without separating them.

But to say that the act illuminates the object, while identifying intellectual light with a natural love of the soul and of God, is that not to reject by that very fact some characteristic points of the Thomist noetic? Is that not to take up and dress up in modern terms the old Augustinian conception of divine illumination, which the most sensible authors agree in presenting as the historical and logical antithesis of the doctrines of the "impressed species" and of the "agent intellect"? This point deserves more serious consideration. I hope to make clear that between the classical theory of the "impressed species" and that of spiritual love, which I have sketched, far from there being an incompatibility, there is on the contrary an intimate affinity such that the one ushers in the other quite naturally.

The Scholastic theory of intelligence which, as it is presented in some manuals, appears so mechanical, so verbal, so unreal, would perhaps be rendered more intelligible to our contemporaries if we suggested it in these terms: there are two elements [*moments*] in human intellection, the *attitude* element and the *knowledge* element[3]—or again: the *sympathy* moment (*connaturalitas* [connaturality]) and the *representation* element.—Indeed intellection, as Thomas often says, requires, as does all knowledge, a certain identity, *connaturality* or resemblance of knower and known. There could in no way be knowledge if the soul did not express *itself* by expressing the object, and this or that object.[4] So intelligence must in the first stage be ren-

---

as it is always as it were in a state of coming to be, and as it were in a state of coming out of something, namely out of speaking] (*Opusc.* 13, c. 1, at the end.—Vivès edition, vol. XXVII, p. 270).—The opusculum is perhaps apocryphal; it is nonetheless very instructive.

3 See Bergson, *Matière et Mémoire*, p. 175. But the *attitude* of which we humans are conscious in the concept is not a simple organic attitude; in addition to the imaginative schema, which animals have as well, we keep also our permanent attitude of soul, which makes us conceive everything in terms of *being*. The idea of being is the proper reaction of the reasonable soul; it is no less essential to the general idea than to the imaginative schema.

4 Also certain extremist objectivists have accused the theory of the agent intellect of being genuinely and properly subjectivist and "Kantian." See

dered like the thing, be in communion, so to speak, with the nature of the thing (impressed [563] species) for it to be able, at a later stage, to express the thing, to know the thing, and as it were recognizing itself in the thing (expressed species). So the impressed species, if it is "a resemblance" to the thing, is not a resemblance thought or conceived, but is a certain configuration of intelligence to the thing *per modum naturae* [by way of nature]; by that configuration intelligence clothes itself with the form of the thing, vibrates in unison with the thing in order to be able to represent it. In this first stage, intelligence seems to forget itself and completely become the *other*, and this *seduction*, this enchantment, this fascination by a foreign essence is necessary for the specification of the concept, i.e., for the word [*verbe*], the idea, to represent this essence rather than some other one. In two words, the impressed species is an *illuminating sympathization*.

Now Aquinas has explicity remarked that if an intelligible form is immanent to intelligence, it matters little whether it be temporary or permanent, whether it be inherent in the manner of an accidental determination or be subsistent, constituting the very essence of the subject: in both cases the intelligible form will likewise cause intellection; in both cases it will determine the production of a word [*verbe*]. And in this way Thomas proves that created spirits directly know themselves.[5] Their nature is in them, one might say, as a sort of impressed species—*impressa non ab ullo obiecto, sed a Creatore* [impressed not by any object, but by the Creator]—which is always accompanied by its expressed species. Reflecting itself constantly in the mental word which makes up the core of their conscious life, their nature constitutes created spirits as intelligent in act and defines the intensity, or if you will, the nuance, of their intellection.[6]

Bernies in the *Revue de Philosophie*, vol. I, pp. 293, 296, and Isenkrahe in the *Philosophisches Jahrbuch*, vol. II, p. 357.

5 *Summa theologiae* I q. 56, a. 1.

6 "Mens angeli semper se actualiter intelligit ... Nec tamen cum mens angeli quodammodo se intelligit et aliquid aliud, intelligit simul multa nisi ut unum ... sicut patet in visu ... color et lumen sunt unum tantum visibile, et simul a visu videntur. Essentia autem angeli est ei ratio cognoscendi omne quod cognoscit, quamvis non perfecte" [The mind of an angel always actually understands itself ... But nevertheless although the mind of an angel in

But what is true, on the one hand, of the impressed form that specifies each of our kinds of knowledge, and what is true, on the other hand, of this subsistent form, of this living Intelligible which is [564] *the essence of pure spirit, cannot not be proportionally true of this substantial form that the human soul is and which participates in intelligibility to a lesser degree than the pure spirit, but to a greater degree than the corporeal essences we conceive.* The human soul is the end and ideal limit of earthly forms; it is also the last-born of subsistent forms. We humans are first among bodies and last among spirits. So what is verified of the two sorts of essences between which we find ourselves is verified also in us, in a manner that remains to be clarified. We can certainly say, *a priori*, that *rational nature is in us as an impressed species which defines the quality of our intellection.*

Now two properties linked together and known *a posteriori* by experience characterize this intellection. The first property consists in the fact that the objective and permanent light of our intelligence is the abstract idea of *being*, and not our intelligible essence concretely grasped. The second is that in our conceptual intellection the *attitude* element, or *sympathy* (action of the agent intellect, impressed species as such), does not fall directly under consciousness: we humans are conscious of the impressed species only in and by the produced word.

Furthermore, I agree that all acts of any potential being whatsoever are naturally directed toward its realization and produced by its appetite for self-realization. So all acts of a spirit still imperfectly conscious result from the appetite such a spirit has for its spiritual self-realization.

If then, as I have shown elsewhere, there corresponds to the concrete and substantial self-perception the concrete and sympathetic intuition of the *other*, then there corresponds to the indigence, to the unsatisfied desire of oneself, the conceptual abstraction, with its coldness and exteriority. *It belongs to spiritual being in search of itself, to the soul still absent from itself, to illuminate its way by the* ABSTRACT

---

some way understands itself and something else, it does not simultaneously understand many things unless they are one ... as is manifest in sight ... color and light are merely one visible thing, and are seen simultaneously by sight. For the essence of the angel is its basis for knowing all that it knows, albeit not perfectly] (*De Veritate*, q. 8, a. 14, ad 6).

idea of being. This connection is *given*; what remains is to elucidate it.

❄

[565] In order to formulate accurately the question let me stress the properties of conceptual knowledge.

I presuppose as granted that, according to the formula currently accepted today, our intelligence "renders abstract everything it touches"; or, in Scholastic terms, that it conceives the idea of the essence, but does not directly perceive the particular [*singulier*], the *hoc aliquid* [this something], the individual. Thomas had already perfectly seen that the categories of *nature* and *hypostasis* (*suppositum* [supposit], τόδε τι), are equally characteristic of the sensible world and of human intellection;[7] this distinction which, along with that of essence and *esse* [existence], grounds both the metaphysics and the critique of knowledge, is imposed by the facts.

---

7 "Intellectus noster, ex sensibilibus cognoscendi initium sumens, illum modum non transcendit, quem in rebus sensibilibus invenit, in quibus aliud est forma et habens formam, propter formæ et materiæ compositionem. Forma vero in his rebus invenitur quidem simplex, sed imperfecta, utpote non subsistens; habens vero formam invenitur quidem subsistens, sed non simplex, immo concretionem habens. Unde intellectus noster quicquid significat ut subsistens significat in concretione; quod vero ut simplex significat, non ut quod est, sed ut quo est; et sic in omni nomine a nobis dicto, quantum ad modum significandi, imperfectio invenitur ... ut patet in nomine bonitatis et boni. Nam *bonitas* significat ut non subsistens; *bonum* autem, ut concretum" [Our intellect, taking the origin of its understanding from the senses, does not transcend that mode which occurs in sensible things, in which the form and the possessor of the form are different on account of the composition of form and matter. Now a simple form is indeed found among those things but imperfect, inasmuch as is not subsisting; and though the subsisting possessor of the form is indeed found, it is not simple, but on the contrary a possessor of concretion. Whence whatever our intellect signifies as subsisting it signifies in concretion; indeed what it signifies as simple, it signifies not as that which is, but as that by which something is. And so insofar as the mode of signifying goes, in every name spoken by us there is found an imperfection ... as is evident with the name goodness and good. For *goodness* signifies as not subsisting; *good*, however, as concrete]. (*Contra Gentiles*, I. 30.—*Concretum* [concrete] means in Aquinas not *real* but *individual* in the strict sense, composed of matter and form.)

But *why* does our intelligence stop at the common essence? Would the material particular be absolutely unintelligible? Absolutely not, since it is the object of divine intellection and of that of pure spirits, since the material particular has being directly, since it is more real than specific nature in its indetermination, and since, besides, intelligence is nothing other than the sense of reality. So it is an infirmity of our intelligence not to penetrate the material particular, and this infirmity is Consequent upon our corporeal nature.—Will it suffice to say: "It is because I am a soul in a body that the proper and proportionate object of my intelligence is a nature in a body?"[8]—This is no doubt correct. But when this statement of a static order: *I am a soul in a body*, has been translated (with no loss of truth) [566] into the dynamic order: *I am an imperfectly spiritual spirit who desires self-possession* [*se posséder*], we must go deeper, in the same sense, into the relation between our substantial composition and our mode of intellection.

This is the purpose of the example of some kinds of intellectual knowledge where feeling mixes in: they hence give us some idea of what concrete knowledge by *conscious connaturality* can be. In ordinary conceptual knowledge the *sympathy* moment is unconscious. But in certain mental activities of a special type, when the sense powers find pleasure in their exercise by their harmony with their object, we experience a certain consciousness, thanks to this pleasure accompanying the free play of our faculties, not only of the object but of our *attitude* itself. We know that Kant made great capital of his observations on this type of knowledge in the *Critique of Judgment*; he could have made even better use than he did. For what concerns us here we must join to knowledges of the æsthetic type those of the affective type. Through what the two have in common we can understand how an inclination directs a knowledge and how, insofar

---

8 "Modus cognitionis sequitur modum naturæ rei cognoscentis. Anima autem nostra, quamdiu in hac vita vivimus, habet esse in materia corporali; unde naturaliter non cognoscit aliqua, nisi quæ habent formam in materia, vel quæ per huiusmodi cognosci possunt" [The mode of knowledge follows the mode of the nature of the knowing thing. But our soul, as long as we are living in this life, has its being in corporeal matter; hence naturally it cannot know anything other than what has a form in matter, or what can be known through such a form] (*Summa theologiae* I q. 12 a. 11).

as this inclination is unconscious, the knowledge it illuminates is necessarily affected by *abstraction.*

These considerations, applied to the whole of our intellectual life, insofar as it is specified by the *desire of self,* provide a small sketch of what could perhaps be called "the deduction of the category of being," understanding by *being* the abstract being that specifies our intellection.

Clearly such an attempt at "deduction" leaves absolutely intact the legitimacy of intellectual evidence, all the while bringing to light the imperfect nature of our ideas. To observe our intelligence at work does not mean to doubt our intelligence.

Let me point out again that I do not try to explain here the abstract idea insofar as it is actually general, i.e., applied to several subjects; for this explicit generality (of the "reflex universal") supposes the multiplicity of the sensible given. One can only deduce what is called "direct universality," i.e., that property of the abstract idea [567] of being indeterminate, of not attaining the intelligible in its particularity, of remaining half-way, presenting the object neither as one nor as many (*essentia absoluta* [absolute essence]). This is the property which I said has its root in *indigent* love, which the soul restrained in a body has for itself. And I propose the following *comparisons* to clarify it.

When a vague anxiety weighs on the spirit—when the semiconscious apprehension of a painful hour restrains the soul's freedom—when we know we have something important to do, and we forgot what it was, we cannot devote ourselves fully to our present occupation. We feel something between us and the objects. We do not abandon ourselves to them. The soul is somewhere else, it is as though separated from itself, it is distracted (*dis-tracta*). It is not the object that is more obscure, it is the soul that is less supple and less vigorous. This internal discomfort, this restriction, this semidarkness, this self-absence that resolves into a lack of affinity with objects, represents for us, as in a first sketch, the indetermnation, the powerlessness, the *impenetration* characteristic of the abstract idea.

Now, take the example of being in love and consciously abandoning ourselves to our passion. Not only does our love tint and dilute our judgments on things, but—in certain cases at least—we know it, we feel it, and we delight in it. If, in contrast, I begin to love and do not know it yet, I feel vaguely and as through a fog that I am seeing things otherwise than before. A certain strange quality is spread all over the objects like a light mist; why has the world changed? why is the world new? But what is new is myself; it is as though I have acquired a new category and it is because of it that I imperfectly penetrate my objects. When I become conscious of my attitude, i.e., of my love, the *meaning* of things will appear to me. I will see myself loving and take pleasure in it; everything will be clear to me, the object and the act, the object through the act. To the attitude, to the unconscious inclination there corresponds the imperfectly penetrated object; to the conscious inclination there corresponds the *possessed, understood,* concretely known object. To perceive my object without perceiving my attitude at the same time, to perceive only the *result,* the [568] *product* of my attitude—as the soul perceives the word, not the impressed species—this is still to abstract, not to have intuition.

These two comparisons, which perhaps help us understand how the soul's unconsciousness in part hides the object from it, suppose that a certain disturbance, a discomfort, a disquiet, is *felt.* Another comparison will perhaps help us understand better how abstract intellection is naturally accompanied by *imposed evidence.*

I have proposed as a hint of what intuitive knowledge is the example of those "who, knowing thorougly their epoch and their descent [*race*], *understand* at every instant the reactions that things arouse in them." "So," I added, "would our entire world of objects be known to us by sympathetic intuition, if we possessed ourselves." Suppose yourself to be an æsthete, passionate for our country, and in whom the study of history and national genius, as well as comparison with foreign civilizations, has exalted to the most extreme refinement your consciousness of what could be called the *French quality.* Not only would you feel, judge, and see *in the French way*—something you would have in common with the crowd, with the "man in the street"—but in addition you would feel, you would see that you see and feel in the French way. You are conscious of your descent acting in you, of seeing yourself think and react in the French way. The French attitude in you is all at once perceiving and perceived. Your knowledge of what is French is concrete: you can taste it [*savoureuse*]. It is also concrete because your affinity is totally with the French object, and none of its determinations escape you; you penetrate to the core of a song, a conversation, an anecdote, where the national genius comes to expression. You can taste it because you vibrate in unison with anything the least bit French, *recognizing yourself therein*: a mere hint, a gesture, an intonation, the banter of a child passing by, will suffice to move you profoundly with an emotion full of intelligence, to make you almost faint with joy in the keen perception of the French quality. The man-on-the-street, on the contrary, sees in the French way, but does not see himself, consciously, as French. Habituated as he is to French things, French customs and ways seem to him *obvious*, self-evident, and awaken [569] no such joyous vibrations in him. He does not see his attitude but merely sees the object in the way his unconscious attitude makes him see it. But the same unconsciousness which operates in him with cold evidence also operates without penetration. For he does not know the French object as French, but merely as object. He does not discern in the object the French quality. *And because he has not drawn himself into the light he cannot draw his object into the light.*

Such is the law of intelligence. A mind sharpened to *perfect attunement*, it has been said, would penetrate to the heart of the real.[9] "To the extent one has more spirit," Pascal says, "one sees that there are more originals," and, for pure spirit there are only originals. One who is all spirit is all affinity with beings, all *noumenal affinity*; all of the real is sympathetic to him; all quality of the real is "connatural" to him; to speak as a Hegelian he finds no *suchness* [*talité*] on which he stumbles, but he infiltrates and slips into an intimacy we cannot penetrate. Pure spirit, Aquinas says, knows the individual in its very particularity; the human soul abstracts from the particular the idea of the quiddity. Still absent from itself, how could the soul *apply itself* entirely to objects?

---

9 I borrow this expression from the article Pierre Charles devoted in the *Revue de Philosophie* (June 1909, p. 673) to Eucken's work.—If a little German be permitted in such a case, one can say that the man-in-the-street is French *an sich* [in himself] and not yet *an und für sich* [in and for himself].

Here we see in what sense one could, thanks to a notion of unconscious inclination, attempt a deduction of the category of abstract being. One shows in this way how the corporeal nature of humanity substitutes the common and indeterminate idea of being (univeral of generality) for the concrete apprehension of the unified whole that the world is (universal of totality). So being is deduced insofar as it is abstract, not insofar as it is being. To treat this last point we should no longer speak of the appetite the soul has for itself, but the appetite it has for God.[10] I [570] have said elsewhere how a fully self-conscious spirit would know itself only as a whole depending on God, caused, attracted, charmed by God. This relation to God would simplify and unify its knowledge of the world, just as (to return to the examples we just used) because lovers see themselves dependent on the objects of their love, totally ordered to them, they *recognize* in every object a new complexion; because those French, who are consummate and refined, know themselves concretely as effects of this cause and part of this whole that France is, they sympathetically know French things. From the moment when, freed from corporeal bonds, we would have gained our souls, we would feel this intense and total seduction of God. We do not feel it because we do not feel our whole soul. We are not completed spirits [*esprits achevés*]. We have not yet, so to speak, taken our immutable position toward God. We have not gained our definitive and fully natural attitude toward infinite truth.[11]

---

10   If we undertook here to dig more deeply into the category of being, and to distinguish its elements, we would experience once more the solidity of Thomist metaphysics. Just as the distinction between nature and supposit, characteristic of the being composed of matter and form, corresponds to human conceptual knowledge, so also the distinction between essence and existence, found in every creature, characterizes all created knowledge. Insofar as intellection aims at essences it betrays the inclination of a created nature toward itself. Insofar as it aims at *esse* [existence] it is appetition for God.

11   And it depends on our free effort whether this attitude (fixed at the moment when death introduces us into purely spiritual, i.e., fully real, life) is *aversion* or *conversion*.—Regarding a sentence where I pointed this out, I read in the *Annales de Philosophie chrétienne* (April 1910, p. 101, note): "How is it that Rousselot did not realize that in appealing to 'free effort' to constitute the soul's attitude which is necessary to 'gain God,' he reintroduces 'personal moral action,' which he had just declared useless?" But I ask

❈

But in the end, to subordinate intellectual knowledge to an appetition, even the appetition for divine truth, is that not pragmatism?

---

in turn: "how is it that Laberthonnière, thinking he had seen so glaring a contradiction in my position, did not for an instant doubt the rightness of his interpretation? Had he re-read me carefully he would have seen that he confuses two "attitudes" that it was one of the principal goals of my article to distinguish, the attitude toward being such as it is knowable to human reason by abstraction in this life, and the attitude of pure spirit toward God. The first of these attitudes, in my view, is naturally imprinted on the human soul by God and constitutes intelligence itself; I believe it is false to say that we *essentially* need a free effort to adopt the first attitude, or that we essentially need to have converted our hearts to God in order to know with certainty: these positions appear to me as prejudicial to true philosophy as they are contrary to the clear doctrine of the Vatican Council. The second of these attitudes consists in feeling God by the very fact that one knows one's own spiritual nature; so it is that Thomas represents the consciousness of pure spirits and, on earth, we have some image of this in the extraordinary states of mystical contemplation. If this state of ceaseless and passionate knowledge of God is natural to "separated substances" (whose freedom, according to Thomas, is beyond all lapse *in the natural order*), human souls only possess such a state in a stable manner in the future life: the imperfect freedom of human beings, and their ability to turn to evil, can make them lose their souls, and can constitute them forever in the attitude of aversion toward God.—Does Laberthonnière's theology permit him to distinguish these two attitudes? Does it force him essentially to subordinate all certain perception of being to the free conversion of the heart to God? This is not the place to examine that question. It remains, though, that when he criticizes Scholastic thought he fails to distinguish clearly human corporeal potentiality from the essential potentiality of all created spirit. This confusion is due to the fact that Laberthonnière forgot what in a preceding exchange of ideas with Laberthonnière I called the ABCs of Thomist metaphysics, viz., the double distinction of essence and existence, of nature and individual. For the same reason Laberthonnière imagines that, according to Scholastic doctrine, a created spirit "would grasp" God naturally if God had not been careful to shut the spirit in a body to keep that from happening. But it suffices that a creature be a creature; it is not necessary that its nature be restrained in it by the individuality of the body for this creature to be incapable of "invading" the Beatific Vision by the natural force of its spirit. Thomas explains this (*Summa theologiae* I q. 12 a. 4) in a very often cited article. It is regretful not to find a more accurate knowledge of Thomist doctrines in the able writer who has declared himself for a long time its indefatigable opponent and something like its appointed critic.

A doctrine is pragmatist to the extent it defines truth by relation to utility. So there is pragmatism and pragmatism, as there is utility and utility. There are low and dull pragmatisms, which take for their measure of truth service to an egoist self. There are pragmatisms that assume disinterested and noble appearances, as would be the one that would define truth by the utility of human society as a whole in space and time. As speculative philosophies all these pragmatisms are equally unjustified; they do not account for what intelligence *sees* when it declares: "It's true, it's absolutely true."

But if we wanted to call pragmatism every doctrine that in relation to the final divine End recognized a quality of utilitarianism intrinsic to earthly and conceptual intellection, then one should indeed say there is a noble and true pragmatism, one that imposes itself on anyone who believes in the soul and believes in God. For, either earthly intellection is the final end or, in relation to the final end, it is the means; there can be no middle position. So if earthly intellection is [572] not the final end, analysis ought to be able to discern in it a *ratio medii* [character of an intermediate], an aspect that will betray its imperfect, *mediating*, transitional character; and this not only as to its exercise but also as to its specification.

This conclusion is as evident as it is disastrous to claim to measure truth by a *particular* will, by a *particular* feeling, whatever it may be. Will in the strict sense (*appetitus rationalis* [the rational appetite], not *naturalis* [natural]) is essentially specified and commanded by intelligence; *a* willed good ought to be consequent upon an understood *being*. Of any theory that reverses this relation one must say with Leclère that it is the very negation of philosophy, and again "All pragmatism profanes thought." To be a pragmatist in this sense (which is, unfortunately, that of a great number) is to take, as he says elsewhere, "an idiosyncrasy for a philosophy."[12]

So when we subordinate vision of the real to the natural love of God, we are not saying in the least that we must "think with our hearts." This metaphor can hide a thousand mistakes, up to and including pure absurdity. Taken literally it is the battle cry of spiritual anarchy, sentimental barbarity's revenge taken against reason, the animal's rebellion against the angel: *hæc est iniquitas maxima* [this is

---

12 A. Leclère, *Pragmatisme, modernisme, protestantisme*, pp. 46, 267, 54.

the greatest injustice]. The invitation "to go to the truth with your whole soul" must be no less carefully distinguished. If what is meant is that once truth is known we must regulate all the soul's movements according to it, this is perfect. If what is meant is that all the soul's movements are equally suited to give us knowledge of the truth, this is a pernicious formula; it contains in abridged form an entire *Discourse on Method*, the bad method to which we owe modernism in religion, the current pragmatism in philosophy: it could still hold many other evils in store for us.

So if there is a philosophy that claims we can affirm things as *beings* only to the extent that we have constituted ourselves in being by a free effort, *and so much so that all the priority belongs to freedom over* [573] *intelligence*, this philosophy, by making our good pleasure the essential measure of being, quite simply puts the human in place of the divine. On this issue Aquinas formulated a profound and decisive point when he taught that to locate the Sovereign Good in practical reason is to deny that we humans have our final end in a Being other than ourselves.[13]

Ordinary pragmatism is absolutely irreconcilable with divine transcendence. But we must not, for all that, let ourselves be drawn into a blind reaction and forego certain precious truths that recent philosophy has uncovered.

We should remember that between some uses of freedom and some perceptions of being there can be a reciprocal priority, with intelligence legitimating the decision at the same time that will opens the doors to light.[14]

We should not ignore that although speculative truth is never the work of our freedom, nevertheless its perception can be hindered in the subject by some fatal accident, and that a perversion of spirit can combine with a vice of the heart. How will the light return? No doubt, *whether we like it or not, we will always start from perceived being.* But an effort of will may be necessary in order to remove an

---

13 *Summa theologiae* Iᵃ IIᵃᵉ, Q. 3, a. 5 ad 3.

14 Recently Fr. Garrigou-Lagrange nicely shed light on the doctrine of the reciprocal priority of causes of the spiritual act in his opusculum *Intellectualisme et liberté chez saint Thomas*, pp. 40-44.

obstacle on the way, *tanquam removens prohibens* [as though one were removing the hindering].[15]

Finally we must try always to know better the essential appetition that shows that we are not our own and that drives us toward the one who made us, an appetition which is deeper than all our free volitions.

[574] Intelligence is the expression of an appetition. But we do not account for its absolute value as long as we have not seen that this appetition aims at God Himself. Current forms of pragmatism destroy reason insofar as they make it the expression of physical instincts or of particular volitions: I call *particular* all appetition that does not aim at God.

Being, intelligence's formal object, is the perfume that altogether attracts and guides the soul in its search for subsistent Intelligibles, i.e., itself and God.

---

15 Many extra-intellectual determinations can render the subject more intelligent *in actu primo* [in its first act]. "Molles carne, bene apti sunt mente" [Those with soft flesh are very apt in mind], Thomas often says, after Aristotle. The same can hold true for voluntary effort but it is not the heart that judges formally nor should it finally dictate the judgment.—Even insofar as we are intelligent we must know how to acquire good habits; for this reason it is perfectly legitimate, after we have recognized its excellence, to abandon ourselves to an instinct that tradition has deposited in us "of the best endowed, the most sensitive, and the most rationalist of all people." To abandon ourselves in that way is still to possess ourselves again because it is to see that we ought to abandon ourselves in that way.

[476] THOMIST METAPHYSICS AND CRITIQUE OF KNOWLEDGE

There exists a striking parallel between, on the one hand, the most original and, as is sometimes said, the most "systematic" theses of Thomist metaphysics and, on the other, the results to which the modern critique of knowledge has led the most fashionable philosophers today.—The authors of whom we are speaking employ the better part of their activity to criticize the function which in their eyes is characteristic of human intelligence, a function whose two interdependent aspects are, as they say, the "parceling out" ["*morcelage*"] and the "solidification"; this function, in order to know, makes us transform reality, which is moving and flowing, into "things" juxtaposed in homogeneous space and into the "ready made" ["*tout fait*"]. The "spatial schema" is "turned into the general schema of abstraction":[1] to be brief, I call this property, or this defect, essential to human conception, the category of "thing."[2] The New Philosophy [477] is therefore above all a critique of the category of thing: all its representatives apply this category, with more or less ingenuity, measure, and

---

1 E. Le Roy in the *Revue de métaphysique et de morale*, 1899, p. 408.—Bergson has often condensed the critique of intelligence, which was already classic in his school, into clear and complete formulas: "Our intelligence, as it issues from nature's hands, has for its principal object the unorganized solid"; "Intelligence represents becoming as a series of states" (*L'évolution créatrice*, pp. 167 & 177), etc.

2 In Scholastic usage *res* [thing] has the same extension as *ens* [being]; they nevertheless differ by a nuance which indicates that *res* [thing] is taken rather from the potential element of being: "*Res* ... in hoc differt ad *ente*, secundum Avicennam in principio metaphysicae, quod *ens* sumitur ab actu essendi, sed nomen rei exprimit quidditatem sive essentiam entis" [*Thing* ... in this regard differs from *being*, according to Avicenna on the principle of metaphysics, because *being* is obtained from the act of being, but the name of a thing expresses the quiddity or the essence of a being]: Thomas, *De veritate*, q. 1, a. 1). In any case, nothing prevents us from speaking on this point as do our contemporaries and reserving the name of *thing* for the material substance, defined spatially: angels and souls, e.g., will no longer be "things."

success to emphasize its utilitarianism, anthropomorphism, relativity.—Now the critique of knowledge that Aquinas sketched and that one can today push further than he in developing the very principles of his metaphysics is itself above all a critique of the category of the thing, taking the term *thing* in exactly the same sense. For the Holy Doctor not only is the material "thing" the proper and proportionate object of our earthly intellection, but even the primordial idea of "concrete being" (for what Thomas named *ens concretum* is precisely what is called "thing" by the moderns); this primordial idea is found implied and utilized in all the notions we form even of immaterial beings; it is the representative form that the real assumes in order to become an object for us; and if our ideas of spiritual beings are only analogous ideas, it is precisely because we are incapable of directly *envisioning* these beings, and because we know them only by representing [*figurant*] them in the image of those material things we conceive here below.

If the coincidence we underline between two assuredly quite different philosophies seems to us worth noticing, it would be false and childish to exaggerate it to the point of masking the irreducible diversity of their viewpoints. Contemporary Scholastics have perhaps not always guarded enough against this failing which consists in leaning on purely verbal relationships or [478] accidental likenesses in order to insinuate that everything has been said by Aquinas. Probably nothing is more apt to discredit Thomism. Is the coincidence here in question one of those surface analogies, or does it touch essential points of Thomist metaphysics? That is something the reader will have to judge.

One thing is nevertheless beyond doubt, something that already seems very significant. Consider the theses characteristic of Thomist metaphysics—by that I mean those summed up in the axiom: *Forma irrecepta est illimita* [A form that is not received (in matter) is unlimited]: distinction between essence and *esse* [existence], principle of individuation, and the others related to them—and you will realize that in Thomists' eyes *to have understood these theses is to have critiqued the category of the thing* (in the sense in which we have taken this expression). What they constantly reproach their opponents for doing in discussions of metaphysics is allowing themselves to be de-ceived by language (which directly reflects our knowledge of material objects) and speaking of pure forms as though they were concrete beings, and of elements of being (*ens ut quo* [being as that by which (it is)]) as though they were complete beings. They reproach them for what could perhaps be named, following a Kantian formula, the *fallacia formae reificatae* [the fallacy of the reified form]. On a related problem, but nevertheless linked to his fundamental theses, that of the increase of forms, Aquinas writes: "Multis error accidit circa formas ex hoc quod de eis iudicant sicut de substantiis iudicatur: quod quidem ex hoc contingere videtur, quod formae per modum substantiarum signantur in abstracto, ut albedo, vel virtus, aut aliquid huiusmodi; unde aliqui modum loquendi sequentes, sic de eis iudicant ac si essent substantiae" [A common error happens in respect to forms for the reason that people judge about them in the same manner as substances are judged. Indeed this seems to happen for the reason that forms are signified in the abstract through the mode of substances, as whiteness or virtue or something of this kind; whence some following the mode of expression thus judge about them as if they were substances].[3] Whether it is a matter of a subsistent form or an element of being, the error is similar. [479] To multiply pure spirits in the same species is implicitly to place them in space and consequently to affect them with materiality. To represent prime matter as realized without form is to make it a material substance and so to pose again the problem for whose solution prime matter had been imagined. In both cases there is an error made on the very notion in dispute and to which contradictory attributes are assigned, implicitly affirming and explicitly denying that it is a thing. When some modern Scholastics explain this, it is strangely significant to find again under their pen the very expressions now current among the Bergsonians to stigmatize intellectual atomism: juxtaposition, quantitative imaginations, etc.; and these Scholastics are nevertheless the last ones

---

3 *De virtutibus in communi*, a. 11. In the body of the article notice the recourse to the constant principle: "Dualitas in formis unius speciei non potest intelligi nisi per alietatem subiecti. Formae enim unius speciei non diversificantur numero nisi per subiectum" [The duality of forms of one species cannot be understood except through the otherness of the subject. For the forms of one species are not diversified by number except through the subject].

we could accuse of compromising with modern thought.[4] In short, it is a fact of [480] the history of philosophy that can be stated in these

---

4 See the pages in his treatise *De Verbo Incarnato* where Fr. Billot explains, "quomodo inter nihilum et ens *ut quod* mediet ens *ut quo*," [as being *as that by which* (it is) would lie in the middle between nothingness and being *as that which* (it is),] and especially this critique of those who do not go beyond imagination: "si praedicta imaginatio esset vera, sequeretur … nullam dari compositionem in rebus, aut certe omnem compositionem esse instar cuiusdam iuxtapositionis," [if the predicated image would have been true, it would have followed that … no composition would be given in things, or at least all composition would be the equivalent of a certain juxtaposition,] etc. (*op. cit,* p. 51). This is said about the distinction between the essence and *esse* [existence]; further on Billot deals with the notion of *everything*, in the question of the hypostatic union: "Origo huius opinionis (Scoti) in hoc est quod de totalitate substantiali iudicant secundum *phantasma* totius et partis in rebus quantitativis" [The origin of this opinion (of Scotus) in this matter is that people judge of the substantial totality according to the quantitative *image* of the whole and part in things] (ibid., p. 69). See in Billot's *De sacramentis* (Third edition, book I, p. 413) the critique of the Suarezian theogy of quantity and place; again elsewhere, treating predestination (*De Deo uno et trino*, I, p. 285, see p. 288), he perceives the root of an erroneous conception of predestination in what we could call an atomist notion of God's knowledge: "quasi scilet singuli homines solitarie caderent sub Dei providentia, id est, velut praecisi et abstracti ab integro ordine rerum in quo inveniuntur. Sed non habet amplius locum si … non fingamus praedestinationes disgregatas … " [as if each of the humans would have fallen solitarily under the providence of God, that is, as cut off and detached from the whole order of things in which they are found. But this would not have a place any more if … we did not conceive of the predestinations as segregated.] One can venture without rashness that it is not assiduous frequentation of Bergson's works that has suggested these ideas to the great metaphysician of the Gregorian University. One of the great scandals of Thomist metaphysics in its opponents' eyes is the attribution of an "entity" proper to "relations." This is all the more shocking as more nominalist and Cartesian prejudices are brought into metaphysics; on the contrary, insofar as one forms of reality a more spiritual and less spatial conception, one also experiences less repugnance to admitting that the "order," for example, can be a reality in its own way, not "identical" to ordered *things* (see Sertillanges, *Saint Thomas d'Aquin*, book 1, p., 117). As a Scholastic type of an atomist conception of reality, see Palmieri, *Institutiones philosophicae* (Rome 1874), thesis XVII, especially p. 406: "Omnis enim res est aliquid absolutum" [For everything is something absolute].

two sentences: the entire Thomist[5] system consists in the concept of form, and the whole mistake for which Thomists reproach their opponents is to represent *forms* as *things*.

✳

There is no need for long developments to recall to readers of the *Revue néo-scolastique* what specifically Thomist theses are grouped around the principle: *Forma irrecepta est illimita* [A form that is not received (in matter) is unlimited]. Aristotelianism is characterized by the act–potency distinction; Thomism separates itself from the other peripatetic systems by the sharpness with which it distinguishes two degrees of potentiality. God alone is absolutely actual and absolutely simple: God is separated *Esse* [Existence]. In material things there is a double composition: matter, potential element, and form, actual element, compose the essence, which is itself potential vis-à-vis the act of existing. Pure spirits are composed only of essence and existence: they are "substantial forms," directly capable of the act of existing.

Thanks to these sharp distinctions Thomism is freed from the bothersome confusion, not entirely dissipated in Aristotle, between the *form* and the *essence* of bodies (the physical form, such as the soul, and the "metaphysical form," such as humanity). But these distinctions presuppose the principle already mentioned, i.e., that [481] every form not received in a subject is infinite in its line,[6] and consequently alone in its species.

---

5 My intention here is to speak of what gives the Thomist system its original character among Scholastic systems, not of what it has in common with them.—If one uses the term *system* about Thomist metaphysics, it is to conform to what appears to be received usage and not at all to give it the same rank as the other Scholastic metaphysics, or to recognize for it only the merit of a higher probability. This is a position as strange as the one of those who are said to "adopt" a system when they see, according to Brunetière's saying, only a theory whose pieces alone are good.

6 "Esse earum (substantiarum intellectualium) non est absolutum, sed receptum, et ideo limitatum, et finitum ad capacitatem naturae recipientis: sed natura vel quidditatis earum est absoluta, non recepta in aliqua materia. Et ideo dicitur in libro *De causis* quod intellegentiae sunt finitae superius et infinitae inferius: sunt enim finitae quantum ad esse suum quod a superiori recipiunt; non tamen finiuntur inferius, quia earum formae non limitantur ad capacitatem alicuius materiae recipientis eas; et in talibus substantiis non

This is the celebrated doctrine of the "principle of individuation." Aquinas is accustomed to formulate it concretely, saying, for example: "There cannot be two angels in the same species,"[7] or again: "If separated whiteness existed, there could only be one [white thing]." In abstract terms we could say: number presupposes space, or again: "Numeric multiplicity implies representation in material terms ... . Beyond beings circumscribed in space all diversity is specific, all reality strictly individual, and, properly speaking, incommunicable."[8]

---

invenitur multitudo individuorum in una specie, ut dictum est ... " [Their (intellectual substances) being is not absolute, but received, and therefore it is restricted and limited to the capacity of the recipient nature; but their nature or quiddity is absolute and not received in some matter. And hence it is said in the *Book of Causes* that intelligences are limited from above and unlimited from below. For they are limited insofar as their being is concerned, which they receive from a higher reality; however, they are not limited from below, because their forms are not restricted to the capacity of some matter receiving them. And in such substances we do not find a multitude of individuals in one species, as has been said ...] (*De ente et essentia*, ch. 5). The unicity of a separated substance is like its extension; its "infinity" like its comprehension.

7 The French text says: "Il ne peut y avoir que deux anges de même espèce": There can only be two angels of the same species." We consider the presence of the word "que" to be a typo and the "ne" to be a negation, not a restriction. Translators' note.

8 These are Moisant's expressions in a subtle article in the *Revue de philosophie* (volume II, p. 463), where he relates to Bergson's ideas on number and space the Thomist doctrine on individuation. In Aquinas, see particularly *De spiritualibus creaturis*, a. 8: "Si autem angelus est forma simplex abstracta a materia, impossibile est etiam fingere quod sint plures angeli unius speciei ... si enim intelligitur albedo absque omni subiecto subsistens, non erit possibile ponere plures albedines ... et similiter si esset humanitas abstracta, esset una tantum" [But if the angel is a simple form detached from matter, it is also impossible to conceive that there would be many angels of the same species ... for if whiteness is understood as subsisting apart from every subject, it will not be possible to posit many whitenesses ... and similarly if humanity were detached, there would be only one]. The principle is from Aristotle: ὅσα ἀριθμῷ πολλά, ὕλην ἔχει [all things that are many in number have matter] (*Metaphysics* Λ. 8., 1074, a. 33); Plato had already glimpsed this principle (*Republic*, X, 597 cd); Kant also recognized it when he said that the Leibnizian principle of the identity of indiscernibles would hold for the intelligible world but not for the spatial world (*Critique of Pure Reason*, Appendix on the amphiboly of the reflexive concept, n. 1). Among

From that we conclude that in spiritual beings, nature [482] and subject (*suppositum*), essence and hypostasis, are identical, but that they are (inadequately) distinct in embodied beings. *Socrates non est sua natura* [Socrates is not his nature].

The essence–existence distinction,[9] which extends further than bodies and applies even to created spirits, is itself also connected to the principle of unlimited form. The two meanings that the word "reality" [*réalité*] has in French, and sometimes also the word "being" [*être*], can help us understand, I think, this famous distinction. Sometimes reality is taken in the formal sense, as when opposing reality to nothing [*néant*], to non-existence; we then speak of the reality *of* a thing: this is existence, *esse*. Sometimes reality is understood in the material sense: then *the realities*[10] designate real things as op-

modern philosophers who have decidedly taken the opposite stance one can cite Renouvier who on this point expressly appeals to Scotus (*La nouvelle monadologie*, p. 39). I have no intention of taking up again here the arguments one finds indicated or developed in the Thomist Scholastic manuals; the better procedure in this matter consists perhaps in trying to *suggest* by a concrete example this notion of formal unity realized in a substantial being: e.g., an art work. Is it not clear that, while the material exemplars of the Venus de Milo can be multiplied, *the* Venus de Milo itself cannot be multiplied? There are as many humanities repeated as there are existing humans, because matter is intrinsic to humanity, is of the essence of humans considered in their proper being. But if the proper being pertaining to the Venus de Milo—when one speaks of it in art history, e.g.—is to be an abstract type, it is clear that it is not multipliable at all, and if the types in art history were to become subsistent beings, they would not for all that be more multipliable. So if there are subsistent intelligibles (which *ex hypothesi* is what angels are) one could not, as Aquinas says, even pretend they are multiplied in the same species.

9 "Esse abstractum est unum tantum, ut albedo, se esset abstracta, esset una tantum" [Detached existence is only one, as whiteness if it were itself detached would be only one](I C.G. 42, 13). One can thus say that the real distinction (of essence and *esse* [existence]) is a particular case of the principle of individuation.

10　It is in this sense that Molière says of a prude in *The Misenthrope*:
　　"Elle fait des tableaux couvrir les nudités
　　Mais elle a de l'amour pour *les réalités*"
　　[She has the nudities in paintings covered
　　But she has love for *realities*].

posed to false or feigned things, etc.; so we understand by this word not only what makes it the case that things are, but what makes it the case that they are these or those things; we speak of the realities *which* the things *are*, the *existing essences*. *Realities* are real because they possess *reality*. Likewise we can say *beings*, in the material and concrete sense, to designate things, essences; and sometimes, but more rarely, we say *the being* [*l'être*] of a thing to signify its [483] existence. *Esse* [existence] designates not precisely what is most actual but actuality itself, *formalissime* [most formally]; essence is the restriction, the limitation, the finitude essential to everything determined in a certain manner of being; it is the very *manner of being* (aughtness, so-ness, ness-ness, as an English Hegelian puts it[11]). We see that the two elements are intimately blended and united, like matter and form, and not juxtaposed like two material substances; nevertheless the principle of unlimited form makes it clear that they are not identical, but that there is between them a distinction that is not the work of our minds.

These are the main outlines of Thomist metaphysics, if the word "metaphysics" is taken in the sense of the Ancients who designated thereby "the science of the most general conditions of being."

❊

But these principles cast an abundant light on metaphysics in the modern sense of the "science of the most general conditions of knowledge."

To the three elements of being that we have mentioned: *esse* [existence], form, nature composed of matter and form, there correspond three types of intellectual knowledge, all three studied in detail by Thomas. God knows beings by their existence, *per viam sui esse* [by way of their existence];[12] angels know them by their form, *per viam*

The essence–*esse* [existence] distinction has been marvelously explained by Billot in the pages of *De Verbo incarnato* (cited above, p. 479, n. 1).

11   Hutchinson, Stirling, *The Secret of Hegel*, p. 375.

12   When I say that God knows beings *per viam* sui *esse* [by way of *their* being] and angels know *per viam* suae *formae* [by way of *their* form], I mean directly that God knows beings by their own *esse* [existence] while angels know things by the forms these things have. But it would be equally true

suae formae [by way of their form]; we humans know them by their material essences, or in some materialized way, *per viam quidditatis ex materia et forma compositae* [by way of the quiddity from the matter and form of the composite]. Knowledge of things by their existence, [484] by the actuality in the most formal sense, is creative, purely *a priori*, simply exhaustive; angelic knowledge is intuitive, but no longer exhaustive; human conceptual knowledge, derived from the impressions things make on us, is *a posteriori*, abstractive, and always perfectible. The first can perhaps be called an *embrace* or an *intellectual grasp*, the second an *intuition*, the third a *representation*.[13]

As the whole perfection of divine knowledge comes from God's knowing things by their *esse* [existence] and so from exhausting what they *are*, so also all the imperfection of human representation comes from approaching being by this potential aspect that the essence composed of matter and form is. God knows matter, knows it insofar as it is. Pure spirit knows it insofar as it is informed. We who know it neither by its being nor by its form nevertheless cannot represent it apart from this potential element; thus, the general quality of *materiality* is joined to the notion of being in order to characterize the proportionate object of our concepts. Now this quality, in Thomist metaphysics, is the inadequation of the hypostasis to its essence, the individuality that restrains its nature. To express in Thomist terms the imperfection proper to human knowledge one will thus say it consists in *translating the matter–form distinction into a distinction between nature and subject*.

---

to say that God know things by God's own *esse* [existence], and the angel knows them by its own form, and even these are two correlative aspects of the same doctrine.

13   If I reserve the term representation to the human idea, this is not to deny that all the representative perfection of our concepts can be found in the higher intellections (just as when I call the angelic idea *intuition* this is not to deny that divine ideas are intuitive), but because I want to underline this capital principle: the essential difference that makes divine knowledge more perfect than ours—and more perfect even as representation—is not taken from its representational nature, but from elsewhere, namely, from its active and creative nature. *Nomen commune remanet infimo ordini quasi proprium* [The common name remains as it were proper to the lowest order], as Thomas says (I, q. 108, a. 5, ad 1).

This is the first approximation we give when we say that our conceptions do not directly attain *the* individual, [485] thus bringing out their *abstract* nature.—We go deeper when we see with Thomas that this abstract idea is nevertheless affected by a certain *concreteness* insofar as it always encloses an internal reference to *some* individual, to *one* subject *in general.*—Finally, we can discern in the very nature of the knowing subject the reason for these properties of the human idea, and bring its abstract character back to the *utilitarian* character that knowledge necessarily has in a progressive [*progressif*] being. Let us follow these three stages.

It is well known that in Aquinas's noetic our concepts represent abstract essences, not individuals. We do not have intuitions of material singulars. This way of thinking was demanded by the principle of individuation. For *signate* [*signée*] *matter* is impermeable to our intelligence. In contrast, a thisness [*haeccéité*], being of a formal order, could be represented intellectually: so one should not be surprised to see Scholastics like Scotus and Suarez who reject individuation through matter admit that our concepts directly represent individuals. But it is the Thomist notion of the concept which is confirmed by experience. This is generally recognized today: the representation we form even of particular objects[14] appears to us as a complex of notes that could just as well be realized in another subject. And language also adds its testimony to the psychological analysis.[15] In short, "our intelligence renders abstract everything it touches."

---

14   Aquinas never denied that we have some intellectual representations of particulars and it serves no purpose to object against his position that we can make them figure in our syllogisms. All he wants to maintain is that this representation presupposes a reflection on the act of knowledge and the phantasm, on the "functional unity" of the subject. *De Anima*, a. 20, ad 1 in contr.; *De Veritate*, q. 10, a. 5.

15   Nouns called "substantives" designate of themselves a quiddity, a multipliable and thus abstract essence.—Pronouns, as contemporary linguists have very well noted, are not, as was formerly said, simple substitutes for substantives (*pro nomine* [for the name]); they designate, like adverbs of place, the sensible immediation. In a judgment where a noun is affirmed of a pronoun, we clearly ascertain the natural movement of the mind which, in order to become fully conscious of its thought, first disjoins its two terms and then synthesizes them: *This is a human being.* This is what Mercier renders in his felicitous formula: "*The intelligible quiddity I conceive is identi-*

[486] Thomas went further. He saw that by exhibiting an abstract nature our concepts nevertheless present that nature with an internal reference to a subject, or better, to *some* subject. He does not say that the specific nature, object of our idea, is directly known to us as belonging to this definite, determined subject: this would contradict the preceding proposition. He believes that the aforesaid nature connotes an undetermined subject which is not identical to that nature (since the nature is itself clearly determined) but which possesses and participates in that nature without exhausting it. In this internal distention of our idea, in this intrinsic reference, in this need that labors with something that is not itself, I see the characteristic note of the "category of the thing." This belonging to a vague subject, this absence from itself outside itself, is the root of its abstraction. And this is what we cannot suppress. Whether by a reflection on our act and on our phantasm we connect the abstract idea to a sensible immediation (see above note 14, p. 158), to a given sensed in space, or whether, in philosophical contemplation, we deny by a reflex judgment of reason[16] this distinction between *nature* and *subject* imposed by the corporeal conditions of our intellection, we will never succeed in blending into an intellectual intuition our apprehension of the nature and of the subject. That is why we have a quasi-natural tendency to speak mistakenly even of accidental qualities, making them into *things* (see above note 3, p. 151); that is why we have so much difficulty comprehending the uniqueness and the "infinity" [487] of separated substances in their species; and that is why our words and conceptions are improper for expressing God's attributes correctly.[17]

---

cal—at least materially—with the concrete reality I am conscious of perceiving" (Mgr. D. Mercier, *Critériologie générale*, n. 143).

16 P. Rousselot, *Intellectualisme*, pp. 83-94; Eng trans. *Intelligence*, pp. 73-81.

17 The capital text on this matter is found in chapter 30 of book I of the *Summa contra Gentiles*: "Intellectus noster, ex sensibilibus cognoscendi initium sumens, illum modum non transcendit, quem in rebus sensibilibus invenit, in quibus aliud est forma et habens formam propter formae et materiae compositionem ... . Unde intellectus noster quicquid significat ut subsistens, significat in concretione; quod vero ut simplex significat, non ut quod est, sed ut quo est: et sic in omni nomine a nobis dicto, quantum ad modum significandi, imperfectio invenitur, quae Deo non competit ... "

Aided by the principles Aquinas has given on intuitive knowledge (angelic and divine) we can push the critique of the conceptual mode of thinking still further than he did and see why our general schema of being, our category of *thing*, is affected by this internal tension, this distention between nature and subject. For pure spirits this distention disappears: they see directly, in their idea of generic or specific nature, the concrete subjects which realize and fulfill this nature.[18] Why? Because they approach being by its form, by its quasi-exemplary idea,[19] by that in which participation renders formally *such* all objects that are *such*. And why do they approach being through its form? Because they are themselves pure forms and are consequently sympathetic with, akin to, harmonized with what is formal in being, with what gives it its specific actuation.—The human soul, in contrast, which is the form in a subject, is sympathetic, in its being, with form insofar as this form is participated in by some subject,[20] i.e., sympathetic with the generic or specific quiddity [488] which

---

[Our intellect, taking the origin of its understanding from the senses, does not transcend that mode which occurs in sensible things, in which the form and the possessor of the form are different on account of the composition of form and matter ... Whence whatever our intellect signifies as subsisting, it signifies in concretion; because indeed it signifies as simple, not as that which it is, but as that by which it is. And so in every name said by us, in regard to the mode of signification, there is found an imperfection, which is not fit for God.] We can, in the entire complex our representation is, aim by reflection at one of the two poles, either nature or supposit, but we can never purify our idea of the duality of nature and supposit. The same doctrine is taken up again in the *Summa theol.* I, q. 13, a. 1, ad 2.

18   *De Veritate*, q. 8, a. 14: "Quilibet enim Angelus per eandem formam multa intelligit, ad minus omnia singularia unius speciei per unam speciei formam" [For any Angel understands many things through the same form, at least all singulars of one species through one form of the species].

19   *De Anima*, a. 20, etc.

20   "Modus cognitionis sequitur modum naturae rei cognoscentis. Anima autem nostra, quamdiu in hac vita vivimus, habet esse in materia corporali; unde naturaliter non cognoscit aliqua, nisi quae habent formam in materia, vel quae per huiusmodi cognosci possunt" [The mode of knowledge follows the mode of the nature of the knowing thing. But our soul, as long as we are living in this life, has its being in corporeal matter; hence naturally it cannot know anything other than what has a form in matter, or what can be known through such a form] (*Summa theologiae* I, q. 12, a. 11).

includes form and matter.[21] Now to say that the human soul is a form in a subject is to say that a human being is a hypostasis that does not equal its essence, a person who does not intelligibly possess his or her nature; and if that is what we are, to actuate and realize ourselves, to pass from potency to act is for us to tend toward this conquest, this adequation. So, on the one hand, the meaning of the characteristic operation of humanity, which is our intellection, ought to be taken from the innate desire the human subject has to equal itself, to gain its nature; on the other hand, the specific note of this intellection is the distension we have spoken of between the nature conceived and the (external) subject connoted. From the moment when our internal distension would cease, the representational distension, the distension of our concepts would also cease. We would *envisage* our essence, our substantial selves;[22] we would live our souls, our entire souls,[23] and in the same moment we would know the external being by sympathetic intuition. All material *apathy* would vanish in spiritual *sympathy*; having no remainder in ourselves to reduce, our souls would also find no further obstacle to penetrating objects. In short, the profound root of conceptual distension, of abstraction proper to the category of thing, is the incompleteness of our spirituality; if we cannot bring our object to full clarity, it is because we have not brought ourselves to full clarity.[24]

In sum, insofar as the soul has not arrived at self-reflection, at peacefully and entirely looking at itself in being, which it cannot do insofar as it is embodied, its effort to reduce the sensible given to terms of the spirit [489] can be described in the following way: the soul's work is in two parts; one part assimilates, clarifies, humanizes,

---

21   Not *this* matter but of matter *in general,* according to Aquinas's well known doctrine (*De ente et essentia,* c. 2; *Summa theologiae* I, q. 75, a. 4; In 7 Metaphysics, l. 9).

22   Notice how Rousselot takes vision (intuition) as a paradigm, and to get there uses feeling or love, not actual vision. Note of the editors.

23   "To live is to feel one's soul, one's whole soul," wrote a novelist recently, taking up and transforming a saying of Joubert.

24   I have tried to present this point in two articles in the *Revue de Philosophie,* 1 March 1910 and 1 June 1910: "Spiritual Love and Apperceptive Synthesis" and "Being and Spirit." [See chapters 3 and 4 of this volume, pp. 119-148.]

and puts the sensible given at its disposition: this is the quiddity; the other part provisionally renounces attaining and exploiting it: this is the subject, the hypostasis.

But at the same time as the soul disposes these two terms, clarifying the one and leaving the other in the dark, it affirms their union, their real identity in being: by saying *thing*, it says *some* thing, *a* thing; by saying *this*, it says this *being*, this *thing*. To suppose this real synthesis of subject and nature is to affirm that being finds itself in individuality itself; it is to declare that a new glance upon the "remainder" will make being appear again, that the "remainder" can always be translated into the soul's terms, to yield determinations ever more particular, to reveal a little more of its own originality. The individual real being will never be exhausted and yet the soul by the very use it makes of its concept of being affirms its sympathy, its connaturality with total being as powerfully as though it hoped to exhaust the real in this way. Full confidence that reason is made to assimilate things: such is the strength of conceptual knowledge. Inextinguishable persistence of a remainder: such is the essential defect of the concept.

❈

From the critique of the category of *thing* that I have above tried to sum up, two consequences ensue in relation to the problem of metaphysical knowledge; they can be formulated thus: *there is on earth neither intuition nor adequate view of being, but there is a science of being.*

To the questions, "Can one ask and can one know what being is?" there are those who respond, "Certainly, and I am going to give you such an adequate explanation." There are others who will say, "Being cannot be explained, but I am going to make you experience it." The first presuppose the coincidence [490] of the conceptual viewpoint and the total viewpoint; the second, who have recognized the powerlessness of concepts, believe they can suggest a way of becoming free from the concepts' limitations and of raising themselves up to a supra-rational mode of knowing. The first consequence to draw from the Thomist principles set forth above is the vanity of these two philosophical methods. The matter is clear and we can be brief.

If the first condition for having intuition of being is having intuition of self, and if the first condition for self-intuition is being freed from corporeal ties, then the conviction that we could envisage the absolute here below is the illusion of an ultra-refined subject who mistakes the acute consciousness of a sensation for the coincidence with being. If the abstract idea of being is here below the proper effect of our intellection and as it were our soul's own word, then all effort to get rid of *all* abstraction risks making us fall from the relative perfection that the concept is in order to make us return toward purely sensible knowledge, toward instinct. There are no doubt aesthetic perceptions in which the sensible part, harmonized with intellection, vibrates in unison with the reasonable soul—and nothing more deliciously imitates the dreamed-of intuition than these kinds of knowledge. But are they the intuition itself? "We call intuition that kind of *intellectual sympathy* by which we are transported to the interior of an object in order to coincide with what is unique and consequently inexpressible in it."[25] Aesthetic perception does not truly transport us to the *interior* of the real since it is received by the senses, since it is by the sensible *suchness* [*talité*] that we are harmonized with the intelligible *quality*. "For our consciousness to coincide with something in its principle," it is said, "it would have to twist and turn [491] back on itself so that the faculty of *seeing* would become one with the act of *willing*."[26] This is very true, but this consciousness of a perceptive sympathy which would reveal to the spirit its kinship with the object, once more presupposes that the spiritual soul possesses itself as soul, that it is conscious of its substantial self and not only of its actual self. If metaphysics is truly "the science that claims to do without symbols" and the "means of possessing a reality absolutely instead of knowing it relatively,"[27] then metaphysics is not for this earth. And to want to extract it with full force even from the

---

25 Bergson, *Introduction à la métaphysique*, in *Revue de métaphysique et de morale*, 1903, p. 3.

26 Bergson, *L'évolution créatrice*, p. 258.

27 Bergson, *Introduction à la métaphysique*, p. 4.—One is correct in thinking that I do not claim in this whole paragraph to set out from principles supplied by the author I am criticizing. But it seems worthwhile to me to relate the Bergsonian notion of intuition to the true notion of intellectual intuition. Few authors touch on some of the most precious truths of the

subtlest of aestheticism is to risk ending up in what one critic has not judged too severe to call a *zoomorphism*.

At the opposite extreme, others think to arrive at a clear view of being by *analysis* of its lower elements and materials: intelligence is reduced to cerebral life, cerebral life to movement, etc.; whoever would understand matter would understand everything. That an explanation like this is no explanation of being, I trust, presents no difficulty for the reader. Even supposing completion of such analysis (which implies contradiction), philosophy would not advance one step. A being's multiplicity does not account for its unity; the synthesized does not explain the synthesis. "Per ligna et lapides non cognoscitur domus, sicut cognoscitur per formam suam, quae est in artifice" [The house is not known by pieces of wood and stones, as it is known by its form which is in the artificer].[28] The opposite error has been often and brilliantly fought by philosophers of the last century. Before Ravaisson's winged arrows pierced it through, Comte had already made [492] it feel the weight of his heavy bludgeon.[29] To grasp what being is we must not look at it from the side of its diffluence, of its breakdown. This is to make an effort to descend lower than the concept.

---

spiritual world more closely than Bergson does; and yet it seems so improbable that he will ever be able to enter there!

28   *De Veritate*, q. 2, a. 4, ad. 7.

29   There are two strong and curious pages that Comte has devoted in the *Discours sur l'ensemble du positivisme* to "the scientific aberration to which public instinct without injustice applies the qualification of *materialism* because it indeed tends always to degrade the noblest speculations by assimilating them to the grossest." He cites as examples of this materialism the tendency to reduce geometry or mechanics to calculation, physics to mathematics, chemistry to physics, biology to chemistry, social science to biology, and adds: "Everywhere it is the same radical vice, abuse of deductive logic, and the same necessary result, the imminent disorganization of higher studies under the blind domination of the lower. All scientists properly so-called today are therefore more or less materialists according to the simplicity and generality more or less pronounced of the corresponding phenomena" (*op. cit.*, pp. 49-50). See the classical pages of Ravaisson, *La philosophie en France au XIXe siècle* (4th ed.), p. 248 ff.; if one is making a collection of "authorities" on this subject, see also Ritschl, *Rechtfertigung und Versöhnung*, III (3rd ed.), p. 199.

But panlogism, i.e., the doctrine of those who think there is a conceptual and discursive science adequate to being, that there are reasonings that render being, all the way to its ultimate foundations, clear to intelligence, rests on no less fragile bases if it is true that a never reducible *remainder* is of the very essence of the concept. Panlogism falls into an error like that of materialism because the viewpoint whence it thinks to perceive absolute truth is not the viewpoint of supreme actuality. Hegel, for example, very well understood "that a speculative determination could not be exactly expressed under the form of the proposition"; but if he thought to arrive by philosophical reflection at this "thought" which is, he says, "the highest … the sole form under which eternal and absolute being can be grasped," and if, on the other hand, he denied the infinite, personally subsistent absolute, pure of all opposition of contraries, he has fundamentally undermined his prodigious intellectualism. Whoever deems that the concept is the final and supreme form [493] of intellection should stop saying that intelligence is the faculty capable of embracing the whole: feeling [*sentiment*] would rather be what embraces the whole, the feeling that Hegel called "the form most unsuitable to spiritual content."[30] For us French, the best known form of absolute rational-

---

30 Hegel, *Logic*, Vera trans., vol. 1 (2d ed.), pp. 216, 408. The thought arose, as I was writing the lines above, of the interesting volume of E. Belfort Bax, *The Roots of Reality* (London, 1907). Bax holds much against the idealism of the English Hegelians; agreeing with them on the impossibility of the personal God such as Christianity holds, he very logically concludes that it is an intolerable panlogism to speak of a *wound-up absolute* [in English in the text. Translators' note], of *ens realissimum* [the most real being], of a *durchsichtige Ruhe* [transparent rest]: all is potentiality, because everything is in progress. All reality is a synthesis of the logical and the alogical, of *what* [in English in the text. Translators' note] and *that* [in English in the text. Translators' note]; the alogical is "uncategorizable"; it can be *indicated* but not *expressed* conceptually. It follows from this that an element of being (*thisness, alogical immediacy* [in English in the text. Translators' note]) always escapes speculative thought, and that philosophy has no other ideal than an interpretation of the world in terms of reflexive thought; nevertheless, if all humans constituted the cells of one same social consciousness, this consciousness would apperceive the real intuitively. Bax's analysis is correct to the degree that he understands by *logic* the *conceivable*, the *rational*, but his analysis is incomplete. Since he lacks the true notion of the personal Absolute, of the "pure and eternally subsistent intellectual flash [*éclair*]" (see

ism is what we usually call today the intellectualism of 1850, and of which Taine's philosophy remains the most accomplished example. Everything is deduced from "the eternal axiom" and "there are only facts and laws." This last formula—I no longer recall whether Taine himself said it—sums up the system marvelously, and brings [494] out very well the violent opposition of panlogism to the leanings of the present generation: facts and laws were the absolute for panlogism, the real reality; for those who came afterward facts and laws are all that is the most relative and the most elaborated, not to say the most fake. For Aquinas, the "facts" are the partial aspects of this last corner of the universe that is the world composed of matter and form, and the "laws" as such, being *utterable* [*énonciables*], are relative to the lowly intelligence of the rational animal.

Among the different forms of rationalism that Thomas has refuted, does the reader recall those curious Arabic theories according to which human beings could arrive, already in this life, at knowledge of "separated substances," of spirits, whether "by study of the speculative sciences" or in general by means of the intelligible species that corporeal objects awake in us? We certainly have to guard against the antiquarian mania that consists in tracing all of the alive errors today back to the weird and dead imaginations of the past; if we reread these chapters, however, we will perhaps find some profit in

---

Garrigou-Lagrange, *Le sens commun et la philosophie de l'être*, p. 142), he also lacks the correlative notion of *esse* [existence], the divine aspect of things by which the *that* [in English in the text. Translators' note] itself, the *hoc aliquid* [this something], the subject, appears in full clarity to divine intellection; under the distinction between the *that* [in English in the text. Translators' note] and the *what* [in English in the text. Translators' note], between nature and subject, we must see the distinction between matter and form, joined with the distinction between essence and *esse* [existence].—It would indeed be desirable to be given a critique of Hegelian metaphysics done in light of Thomist distinctions: this metaphysics, so inconsistent when one seeks in it a doctrine of God, shows a marvelous fecundity when we study it for the nature of material being, for the category of the thing, for human consciousness.—As for the *ens realissimum* [most real being], it is important not to forget that if we know that the Absolute subsists with no opposition of contrariety, we do not believe that it subsists without the opposition of personal relations, and we could say *transeat* [let it be put aside] to anyone who would think to prove that the hypothesis of a *unipersonal* God implies a contradiction.

them; we will see that Thomas refutes Alexander, Ibn-Rosch, and Ibn-Bâdja by appealing to the principles we have mentioned: the essential relation of our concepts to quiddities composed of matter and form, the essential link of the abstract principles that human speculation contemplates here below with the objects of the sensible world, the incapacity of all these principles, even if they composed a finished whole, to permit us the most furtive glance at the essence of subsistent intelligibles[31] (the essence of our human soul is no exception).

[495] The condition for grasping or contemplating corporeal being itself is to grasp or contemplate spirit. But conceptual thought is radically unfit for grasping and contemplating spirit, so it is radically incapable of grasping and contemplating being, and can only represent being. Philosophy can never "provide the being of which it studies the notion, never contain the life of which it analyses the exigencies … never realize the very thing of which it must say that it [philosophy, conceptual thought] conceives it necessarily as real."[32]

---

31 Against Avempace (Ibn Bâdja): "Quidditas … generis vel speciei horum sensibilium, cuius cognitionem intellectivam per phantasmata accipimus, comprehendit in se materiam et formam. Est igitur omnino dissimilis quidditati substantiae separatae, quae est simplex et immaterialis, etc." [The quiddity … of a genus or species of these sensible things, whose intellective cognition we receive through phantasms, includes matter and form within itself. Therefore it is altogether dissimilar to the quiddity of a separated substance, which is simple and immaterial, etc.], III C.G. 41.—Against Alexander, ib., c. 42.—Against Averroes, c. 43, arg. 4 and arg. 6: "Sed nec omnia intellecta speculativa simul accepta adaequant illam perfectionem, intellectus agentis, secundum quod intelligit substantias separatas, cum omnia haec non sint intelligibilia nisi in quantum sunt facta intellecta, illa vero sunt intelligibilia secundum suam naturam" [Yet not even all the objects of speculative understanding taken together are sufficient for that perfection of the agent intellect according to which it understands separated substances. Since all of these objects would not be intelligible unless inasmuch as they have been made objects of understanding, whereas those (intelligible substances) are indeed intelligible according to their own nature.]

32 M. Blondel, *Lettre sur les exigences de la pensée contemporaine, Annales de philosophie chrétienne*, vol. 34, p. 145.

❋

There is no intuition of being here below; is there a science of being? Does the critique of the category of the *thing* not come down to suppressing metaphysics as knowledge [*science*]? We could have two reasons to think so. First, it may seem that if the ideas we form of spiritual beings are constructed on the pattern of material quiddities these ideas include a contradiction. Second, one can think that the assertion, "it is," which signifies logical exigency—the heart of judgment and reasoning, referring essentially to the *ens* [being] of the conceptual representation—has only one legitimate function: it shows the inclusion of abstract ideas or the *nexus* among things of sense experience. The assertion is thus powerless to certify for us a necessary connection between factual data and transcendental realities, to allow us to affirm the soul and God.

Thomist metaphysics, extended in the sense we have said, dispels the artifice of these objections, presented under this form or under any more clever form. [496] Thomist metaphysics lets us see, first, by the very analysis of our idea of being, that the category of thing, far from prohibiting the representation of the soul and of God, on the contrary, implicitly presupposes its affirmation. Thomist metaphysics thereby reveals the sense of spontaneous movement by which intelligence concludes the world of spirits from the world of bodies and this shows that metaphysics is just as natural and just as justified as life.

We have seen that it is essential for human intelligence that conception of a quiddity includes within it the thought of its belonging to some *hoc aliquid* [this something], to some subject. At the same time that intelligence disjoins nature and supposit, it synthesizes them. The two terms are not *seen* directly, the one in the other, by an intuition, but they are *judged* united in being; a representation and an affirmation are thus two moments, essential and inseparable, of conception. This is true of even the most general conception, that of *being* or of *thing*: we conceive everything as *a* being, disjoining and rejoining nature and subject, and as the idea of being is included in every conception, one can say that every conception virtually contains the judgment: *This is a being.* But to affirm this unity of the *hoc* [this] and of *ens* [being], a unity that is not for us an object of intuition, is to presuppose a viewpoint wherein nature and supposit coincide, wherein one is seen in the other, without remainder and in full clarity.[33] This is, therefore, to affirm perceptive intelligence, the soul contemplating itself [*s'envisageant*] face to face, pure spirit.—In other words: the whole explanation of knowing activity comes down to the soul's wanting to express the object in function of the soul itself, and all the imperfection of conceptual abstraction comes from the fact that, our [497] body being us, we can neither find ourselves, gaze at ourselves completely in the object, nor (which amounts to the same thing) express the entirety of the object in function of ourselves. Material individuals that we are, we cannot bring an object to light in its total reality, as to its very individuality, but only as to its quiddity. Yet by the very fact that the conception of this quiddity includes the idea of being and the judgment *this is a being*, it happens that at the same time we run up against the opaque residue of the supposit, we nevertheless proclaim that the residue can also be expressed in terms of the soul, that the residue is also an object for the soul, for that is what *being (ens)* means. So in the least conceivable quiddity, in the least representation that the soul forms by means of the category of thing, the supposition is implied, or one could say the presumption, that the soul can *get through* the object, *have it over and done with, bring it to light*, and, consequently, bring itself to light. To think the idea of being (where *this* and *being* are separated and reunited) means: *if I were to see the object intuitively, I would see these two elements one inside the other.*[34] To form a representative conception is to

---

33 To say that a bodily essence can be an object of intuition is not to say that it can be an object of intuition in its singularity, all by itself. Saying this does not prejudge the question whether it is not for these essences a condition of being and of intelligibility, not only that a creative knowledge sustains them but also perhaps that there are human souls to which these sensibilities are ordered.

34 To understand the genesis of the idea of being I could thus express myself as follows. The movement of the spirit would go on to exhaust, in one act if it could, the entire given, the whole of being confusedly presented to it in the first apprehension. But it cannot succeed: I have not yet elucidated completely the intelligible content of our first sensation. Thus the spirit, driven by the necessity to live, presupposes, so to speak, that the problem is solved, and forms the idea of being; in this idea the given, while still irreducible, is presumed clarified and is proclaimed object for the soul, an object

suppose, to imagine [*rêver*] perceptive intelligence. To conceive being is to imagine [*rêver*] the spirit.

We can go farther. Along with the synthesis of nature and subject, the simplest human conception includes a synthesis of essence and existence. This is clear with [498] regard to the natural and primitive act by which the spirit all at once conceives being and affirms its existence, without distinguishing conception and affirmation; in this case, with the judgment: *This is some being* [*C'est de l'être*], the concept also eminently contains the judgment: *Being exists.*—This is also true of simple representations of the possible: these representations (like, moreover, negative judgments) implicitly include, under the judgment: *This would be a being,* (or under the judgment: *This being does not exist*), the judgment: *Being exists*).[35] Now we can reason

---

lined with a soul, so to speak, or enriched with a soul [*étoffé d'âme*], in order to be susceptible to being acted upon. We could speak in almost the same way of the formation of universals: memory (= consciousness of the identity of the reaction) represents a quiddity as *already seen* but *not yet exhausted,* and we consider this quiddity as *provisionally sorted out* for the sake of practical action.—But these are ways of speaking whereby we transform a single and spontaneous movement into distinct elements and reflected acts.

35 The affirmation of existence, of reality, is not added onto the representation of the possible (see the remarkable treatise of J. Maréchal: *A propos du sentiment de présence*, an extract from the *Revue des questions scientifiques*, Louvain, 1909); it is the possible, on the contrary, that complicates the affirmation of the real. When I conceive an object as inexistent or purely possible, a proposition as erroneous or as doubtful, in the representation of this object or of this proposition is included the representation of a thinker, of a self or rather of a *one* who is thinking, with which I do not agree to identify myself. "This is not" is equivalent to: "One would be wrong to believe that this is." But this affirmation, like all others, presupposes the affirmation of the existence of the whole, for it could be explained in this way: "Someone who would see the whole of being would not see this there."—In the affirmative judgment we again meet up with this *one* who is thinking to which the self is opposed but, in the latter case, the self agrees to identify itself with it. The fact of this opposition of a *one* who is thinking to the *self* that glimpses itself is characteristic of spirits in which the subject does not coincide with its nature: doubt, opinion, judgment, representation of an object while prescinding from its affirmation as real, are proper to the reasonable animal and foreign to the intuitive spirit in its natural state (See St. Thomas, I q. 58 a. 1, a. 5; Kant, *Critique of Judgment*, § 76; Bergson also says, in *L'Évolution créatrice*, pp. 306 and 312: "... an intelligence that

about the synthesis of essence and existence, which the judgment *being exists* expresses, as we reason about the synthesis of nature and subject, which the judgment *this is a being* expresses. To affirm the synthesis of essence and existence, whose intuition we do not have, is to affirm implicitly that there is a point of view from which one is seen in the other (or indeed to make bodies an absolute of existence). To say: *This is*, is to say: *Someone who would see all of being would see this there.* Forming this synthesis is equivalent then to presupposing, [499] to presuming, to imagining [*rêver*] the absolute creative Truth.—Every act of intellection presupposes not only that reality is intelligible, that reality can be brought to light, but also that reality is somewhere understood, somewhere completely brought to light: therefore it presupposes God.[36]

Now if this is the case here, it is not too difficult to show how our ideas of spiritual beings do not contain a contradiction. If the category of thing, the natural schema of our objects, unified the spirit in the direct apprehension of the material singular, of a supposit determined in a nature, then the category would be closed, so to speak, and we would no longer have a means of going out from it. But the disjunction of the two terms and their synthesis is essential to our spirit: it disjoins them and in this way goes beyond the material reality (always singular); at the same time it synthesizes them, that is to say imagines [*rêve*] that it unifies them; it can therefore picture the spirit by the negation itself of the distension between supposit and nature. If my idea of the soul is simply my idea of my consciousness purified of the aforementioned distension, my idea of the soul is no

---

was only intelligence, that had neither regret nor desire ... could not even conceive an absence or a void ... negation is not the work of pure mind, I should say a mind (detached from everything changeable (*mobile*)) placed before objects and concerned with them alone. ... It is of a ... social nature") [see Henri Bergson, *Creative Evolution*, trans. Arthur Mitchell (New York: The Modern Library, 1944), pp. 307, 313-314].

36   The scholastics have no difficulty admitting this, since, on the one hand, they hold that the object of the first intellectual apprehension is "being in the concrete, something that is, τὸ ὄν" (Garrigou-Lagrange, *Le sens commun*, p. 18) and that, on the other hand, it is true to their principles to say that this being, not being its *esse* [existence], not being an absolute existence, but "something that is," postulates by its very notion a creative knowledge that supports it.

more contradictory than my idea of thing, since it is required by it. Likewise, my idea of God is possible, as that of the object that would fully unify me, and in the apprehension of which I would synthesize at once the whole real world. To picture God and the soul is to gain awareness of the conditions of thought; when the human forms these two ideas according to the concept of thing, the role of the intelligence, one could say, "consists simply in unraveling the content of which the concept has been [500] filled."[37]—The justification of the category of being does not occur, moreover, without the justification of the movement of the spirit expressing the *nexus*, the logical exigency of beings, since we have seen that this *nexus*, that this exigency is intrinsic to the aforesaid category.

Very well, someone will perhaps say, you show the subjective necessity of affirming God and the soul. You show that, if it is necessary to live the human life (in which the intelligence is the essential part, and in which the category of *thing* is the characteristic instrument), it is also necessary to affirm the soul and God. But you who reason in this way about the *idea* of being,—considered both as notion and as action,—do you abandon the ancient proofs, which started from *being itself*, and which, through efficient, final, and exemplary causality came directly to the conclusion of the real existence of the soul and God?—We do not abandon them in the slightest. On the contrary, the analysis of the movement of the spirit who proves comes to cover over and sanction anew the ancient proofs, and makes us more keenly aware of their legitimacy. It explains, indeed, what remains obscure in what they presuppose in common, which is this twofold judgment: *Being exists*, and *the existent is being* (= reality is intelligible).

The modern scholastics very clearly understood that, for the science of being as set forth by St. Thomas to be justified to the eyes of the spirit, it suffices that the value of our idea of being would be admitted. For, if this idea, in which essence and existence are synthesized, contains an existential affirmation, it also contains the implicit assertion that our intelligence is capable of becoming aware of what

---

37 This felicitous metaphor was used by A. Valensin in regard to *the theory of experience according to Kant* (*Revue de philosophie*, July, 1908).

is existent.[38] It gives therefore at the same time the starting point [501] and the instrument of metaphysics. The whole of metaphysics responds, we could say, to this question: what should one affirm, or what should exist, *since being exists?*" God and the soul are affirmed as necessary conditions of this proposition; the demonstrations that we give about them fill, so to speak, the gap that separates the two terms that this proposition synthesizes; this can be seen, for example, in the proof of God that is drawn from the degrees of perfection, thanks to the distinction of essence and existence (the *Quarta via* [Fourth way] of the *Summa*); this is true also of the other demonstrations.

But this synthetic proposition itself, by what right does the mind affirm it? One should not even consider reducing it to an analytic proposition: we will never deduce the existence from our representation of being. It seems then that at the very origin of the intellectual life, there is, by the fact of this synthesis, something like a postulate, a presumption; a legitimate postulate perhaps, a highly justified presumption perhaps, but still we would want to know the legitimacy and the rightness of it. Why is it necessary that the gap which separates essence and existence be closed? Why is it necessary to affirm that being exists, and to admit everything which is a necessary condition of this proposition?

Several contemporary scholastics are extremely reluctant to allow this critical question. To admit it, even for an instant, they think,

---

38 The mental life does not begin with an explicit judgment, which is always an act of reflection. It begins with an immediation, with an apprehension of moving being, which we can still find in ourselves under the heap of acquired conceptions. Power and act, writes Zigliara, are two notions "quae immediate in mente pullulant ex tradita entis notione ... De facili infertur, potentiam et actum ... in mutua quadam oppositione consistere" [which directly in our mind sprout from the passed down notion of being ... is easily inferred, potency and act ... standing together in a certain mutual opposition] (*Summa philosophica*, v. I, pp. 342, 354). These expressions, and others which the Scholastics have used in order to make us understand the reflective and philosophical notions of power and act, can serve to suggest what is, in direct and primitive apprehension, the *fluctuating* [*la palpitation*] between power and act, between essence and existence which essentially characterizes this. This apprehension eminently contains both the judgment: "The existent is being" (See Garrigou-Lagrange, *Le sens commun*, pp. 219-220), and the synthetic judgment: "Being exists," which is just as essential as the first.

is to have already completely given up, to have completely given in to skepticism. Therefore they bind themselves to the mast and plug their ears, so much do they fear to hear the siren. [502] They only have a first and last response: "It is obvious." But this answer leaves the question intact, and these terrors, moreover, show that they have not understood the question well. One cannot deny the legitimacy of the assent rendered to the evidence, nor deny either the legitimacy of the problem that the evidence poses. If evidence poses a problem, the true agnostics are those who avoid it,[39] who forever entrench themselves in the evidence, and refuse to examine it in the integral dynamism of the knowing subject. Now, evidence poses a problem by the act of judgment mentioned above, which is synthetic, and which, being immanent in our category of being, necessarily transfers its initial obscurity to the heart of the analytic deductions themselves, to the heart of the substitutions of equivalence that appear at first in the most resplendent clarity.[40]

---

39   See the article of the *Revue de métaphysique et de morale* (1896, pp. 551-567), where long ago, in regard to Descartes, Blondel spoke of this "kind of agnosticism immanent in the method of evidence and in the absolute justification of the understanding ... (From the principles of Cartesianism it ensues that) in our most immediate intuitions, among our most clear ideas, the middle term that would render them analytic and intelligible is inevitably missing" (pp. 557-558). To speak of it in passing, Blondel is one of those people who have best shown that knowledge is neither exclusively, nor especially, representative; I do not know, however, if this penetrating philosopher has thoroughly mastered the Thomist idea of intellection; indeed, in one of the articles he signed Testis in the *Annales de philosophie chrétienne* (December, 1909, p. 274), he seems either not to see that in the creative and beneficent intellection of God knowledge and love are identical, or not to grant that it is the intelligence which makes us penetrate, in Heaven, the very interior of God. But if our perfection truly comes to us from an Other than ourselves, is not the act which should finally perfect us the one that renders this other more profoundly immanent for us? Since God is our Beatitude, and we are not his, our perfection consists even more in receiving Him than in giving ourselves.

40   What then? one will say. A = A, is there here anything obscure? Certainly not regarding what is perceived, considered precisely as such, but there is something obscure regarding perception itself; it is important to ask what this identification is, which presupposes the disjunction of the *same* and abstraction. Yet perception is internal to what is perceived, unless one

The solution to this problem does not consist in demonstrating that being exists: we have already said that this is impossible. [503] It consists in showing why and how *we affirm* that being exists. This explanation, or exposition, can assuredly be made only in terms of a certain metaphysics. But if it is made in terms of the metaphysics that emerges from the "philosophy of being," and that satisfied dogmatic reason before any critical question would have arisen, the problem will be resolved. We will not have, no doubt, analytically deduced the principles themselves (which implies a contradiction), but we will have caused the explanation of what is obscure in them to emerge from the principles themselves, namely from their affirmation, and thus the spirit will have peace.

Where then does this surplus of confidence come from, which the soul seems to grant to its idea in primitive affirmation? Where does this sort of presumption come from, which causes it to say in all intrepidity, at its first contact with the sensible given: *being exists, the world is intelligible, reality can be brought to light* (interdependent affirmations, as we have seen)? This is indeed obvious to the soul, but how can it be obvious, since afterwards this turns out to resist all of the ordinary means the soul has of reducing a synthesis to what is obvious? Why does the soul not restrict itself to the proposal of a problem or of a task, but from the first presuppose, so to speak, that the problem is resolved? Why does it boldly risk declaring the synthesis of essence and existence, whose consequences will only have to be later unfolded? The Thomist metaphysics shows that one must answer: because for the soul this is precisely equivalent to accepting its human nature, desiring its own good, consenting to being what it is. The human is essentially a spirit whose hypostasis does not equal its nature, a spirit incompletely spiritualized; it does not perceive itself yet as a whole spirit, wholly of God and for God; it must attain this through progress and exercise; it must "gain its soul" by its usage of the sensible world, which is for it altogether both a restriction and a means. For, the sensible world [504] represents the difference between the human person and nature; the essence of the natural being consists, in the final analysis, in its aptitude to serve as a means

---

wants to ascribe an absolute existence to an abstraction, to an axiom, which is precisely the error of panlogism mentioned above.

for humans to conquer themselves and to rise up to God. To affirm
then the consistency, the reality, the solidity of these essences, is to
affirm for the soul the possibility of realizing itself, of gaining itself,
and of gaining God in its own way, which, for it, is all the same. We
can, moreover, in the fluctuating duality that characterizes the first
apprehension, find the distinct trace of two loves which drive the
soul: insofar as it translates the sensible given into a quiddity, into an
essence, the soul desires itself, it wants to realize itself as humanity;
insofar as it affirms that being exists, it wants to realize itself as being,
it desires God. But these two loves are not external to one another;
the love of God, as Aquinas explains it, is internal to the love of self;
it is as it were its soul.[41] It is also the first source of our intellectual
light; if the soul is sympathetic to being as such, it is in the end because it is capable of God.[42]

---

41   *Contra Gentiles*, VIII, 24; see I-II q. 109 a. 8.

42   I have attempted to explain elsewhere (*L'intellectualisme de saint Thomas*, p. 40, n. 2 and p. 65) [see *Intelligence*, p. 41, n. 63 and pp. 58-59], that,
if the soul is πάντα πως [in some way all things], it is because it is θεός
πως [in some way God], and not conversely. "I do not admit," Fr. Gardeil
writes, "that intelligence in itself defines itself from the outset as the faculty
of the divine, as Rousselot attributes to Saint Thomas" (*Le donné révélé*, p.
188). I confess to not seeing myself in this *from the outset,* having never ven-
tured this outrageous statement, that the notion of "faculty of the divine"
would be first, *via inventionis* [the way of discovery], that one would have of
the intelligence, and this is what suggests the phrase *from the outset*; I have
said that it is the most profound state that one could reach, and one can say
that it is first in this sense, but *from the outset* does not signify this. If one
judges that it is more profound to say that intelligence in itself is the "faculty of being, of being that is distributable *by analogy* into the two orders
of reality, the divine and the contingent" (Ibid.), does one not succumb to
the mirage of a *common notion anterior* to the created realm and to God,
a notion which is the very negation itself of the doctrine of Saint Thomas
on analogy, the one we want above all to preserve? Does not one also succumb to this, when one says that it is not "the intelligence that makes use
of the senses," but "the intelligence pure and simple," which is the "proper
faculty of *the* conceptual reality of being"? (Gardeil, l.c.). In the school of
Fr. Gardeil, one marvelously explains how the intelligence makes use of
the idea of being, how, once this idea is given, the soul endeavors to render
everything intelligible in terms of this idea of being. The explanations that
either Fr. Gardeil in the first book of the *Donné*, or Fr. Garrigou-Lagrange
in his various works, give on this subject are very rich in meaning and very

[505] It is thus not in accordance with the truth, nor with the principles of Aquinas, to believe that one could balance and justify the whole mental synthesis by only appealing to the representative elements of consciousness; nor to speak of the conceptual apprehension of being as if it did not contain, in its very core, any darkness, as if it was what is so well named "an immediate and saturating apprehension of concrete reality."[43] Yet we should not say either that this meaning of the idea of being, that this awakening of the soul that consents to its nature, would be properly speaking free. Although it may be an act of spiritual spontaneity, it is not the result of a choice, and it is no more a free act than the appetite for happiness is. Why is it not the result of a choice? Because it is precisely the *first* awakening of the soul, because it is the *first* move to the act of this appetite for the divine which is intellection, and because, as Thomas explains, the first movement of the appetite of a creature is always [506] given to

---

worthy of consideration; but after we have established the evidence of being and the fact of its affirmation, it remains for us to explain it: it remains for us to explain the category of being itself, and how it consists in rendering everything intelligible in terms of the soul. Not seeing or not accepting this task, not consenting to critiquing conceptual being, to engaging in as it were the "deduction of the category of thing," is to stop philosophy too soon, and to mutilate it.—And if, elsewhere, Fr. Gardeil, bringing together two conceptions of the world, the dynamic and ontological, the Augustinian and Thomist, judges them irreducible, and, for his part, by preferring one, concedes, however, that it does not explain what the opposite conception explains (*Le Donné révélé*, p. 283), the reason for this is that he refuses to ask himself, with respect to Thomist principles, the questions that allow us, if we penetrate these principles more deeply, to make the philosophy of the Good to coincide with the "philosophy of being."—It seems to me also that, if Fr. Gardeil stated the truth about the reciprocal irreducibility and the relative legitimacy of the two "systems," the properly philosophical work would consist in discovering what characteristic of the human spirit so radically prevents it from arriving at a comprehensive metaphysics, which reconciles the points of view of the being and the good. There you have it in order to delight the critical minds (*les criticistes*),—unless of course the Thomist system is more comprehensive than the eminent Dominican thinks.

43 Blondel, *Le point de départ de la recherche philosophique* (*Annales de philosophie chrétienne*, June, 1906, p. 248).

it by God.[44] We see what an essential difference separates our doctrine from that of moral dogmatism, according to which, "in order to know being and to believe in it, one must cooperate in giving being to oneself in one's freely willed life."[45] In moral dogmatism, we do

44   *De Malo* q. 6, q. 16 a. 4; I q. 63 a. 5; *Summa theologiae* Ia-IIae q. 9 a. 4, q.17 a. 5 ad 3.

45   In order to separate our cause from that of moral dogmatism, it is not necessary to identify moral dogmatism with an absurd theory, obviously destructive of the notion of truth and of God Himself, with which the Scholastic polemic has sometimes confused it. This theory would consist in saying that our liberty alone engenders our certainty, without any reciprocal priority of the light on the will. The partisans of moral dogmatism understand well, on the contrary, if I am not mistaken, that if the good will introduces the light, the light, in the same act, enlightens the good will.—But in the first awakening of reason, we would not be able to speak of the reciprocal priority between intelligence and free will: Thomas shows this in the passages cited earlier, and moreover this is rather clear on its own. This is why, since it is necessary to give an explanation of this kind of *presumption* which is at issue in the text, the recourse to divine attraction is necessary. I cannot discuss here the interesting theological question of whether this divine attraction can be called a grace; what is certain, is that it is not, on its own, identical to the conversion of the heart, since the Catholic Church believes that a human who has never been in the grace of God can have a firm and true certainty of His existence. I can say, however, that there remains a true disequilibrium *ex parte subiecti* [on the side of the subject] in the certainty of this human, since the soul implicitly affirms, in its primitive intellection, its possibility of attaining its final end, the supreme truth, and that, in the actual order, it cannot achieve this by remaining such as it is.—Augustine has a beautiful passage where he distinguishes this first divine attraction, this awakening of reason which he calls "the creation of the internal eye," from the meritorious illumination of the Catholic faith. This is about the verse: "illuminat omnem hominem venientem in hunc mundum" [(the Light that) enlightens every human coming into this world]. "Aut si rationem ipsam," he writes, "qua humana anima rationalis appellatur, quae ratio adhuc velut quieta et quasi sopita, tamen insita et quodam modo inseminata in parvulis latet, illuminationem voluit appellare, tanquam interioris oculi creationem, non resistendum est, tunc eam fieri, cum anima creatur, et non absurde hoc intelligi, cum homo venit in mundum. Verumtamen etiam ipse, quamvis iam creatus oculus, necesse est in tenebris maneat, si non credat in eum qui dixit, *Ego lux in saeculum veni*, etc." [Or if (the clause concerns) reason itself, by which the human soul is called rational (whose reason even as still quiet and as it were asleep, is yet hidden as innate and in some way implanted in infants), and it in-

not see how, before the conversion of the heart to God, the speculative proofs of His existence would be sound; in our doctrine, this appetite for the divine that intelligence is suffices for this.

❈

I do not doubt that the preceding explanation could give rise to objections of more than one kind, either objections that I was unable to anticipate or that I did not want to forestall in order not to [507] be even more lengthy. Still let me make a remark about two kinds of possible opponents. Some of them will say that we have here a critique of knowledge only in the title, because, from one end of the study to the other a certain metaphysics is presupposed. Others will demand that we further reassure them about the case that we make for the ancient Scholastic proofs, and about the criterion of intellectual evidence.

To the first I respond that it is exactly the same thing to presuppose everything and to presuppose nothing.[46] The abstractive and

---

tended to designate illumination, as if it were the creation of an inner eye, then it cannot be denied that it is made at the time when the soul is created; and there is no absurdity in this being understood to occur when the human comes into the world. Nevertheless, although the eye is now created, it is necessary that the human would still remain in darkness, if such a one would not believe in Him who said *I came into the world as Light,* etc.] (*De peccatorum meritis et remissione,* I, 25, 38. Mignc, 44, 130).

46   One scarcely wonders today "if the external world exists," and this is with good reason, for the negative response is not only opposed to common sense, but contradictory in its terms if it is true that our idea of existence is suggested to us precisely by what we call bodies. Bodies are, as Plato said, ἄ νῦν εἶναί φαμεν [those things which we declare now to exist]: if it is from them that we first of all draw the notion of being, we indeed have to say that they "are" in some manner. Yet it by no means follows from this that what was underlying this incorrectly formulated question was nothing other than a false problem. There was a true problem, and one which remains intact, for the entire question is about knowing—no longer from the outset as before, *how* the corporeal world is, or *what* it is—but what we mean by saying: it is.—We can speak about the whole of experience as we do about the "reality of the external world"; all of "life" is *given* to philosophical reflection, and we ask ourselves: *Was soll sein weil das Leben ist?* [What has to be the case because life exists?]. Thus, in order to be sure not to presuppose anything, there is no other way than to presuppose everything.

arbitrary method is that which isolates a partial element from the beginning, for example, the *Cogito* [I think]. It appears to me, I admit, that the metaphysics upon which I rely,—the Thomist form of Aristotelianism,—is, from the dogmatic point of view, a demonstrated metaphysics. The marriage of these two words appears very puerile to certain people; others, on the contrary, are so little concerned with "contradictions of the philosophers," that all the dogmatic metaphysicians have had in terms of truly personal intuitions and correct reasonings seems to them to become comprehensively and harmoniously integrated into this system. If this is the case here, then there is no more apriorism in recognizing that the fact of this demonstration [508] and the fact of this convergence are given to me, than in recognizing that a world of images is given to me. This, moreover, in no way prevents us from granting that a time arrives when we notice that we should not content ourselves with the fact of intellectual evidence, but that we have to become aware of the meaning and the value of this fact. I grant therefore that from this moment the doctrine of the spirit should not only complete, but include and explain the doctrine of being, and that consequently the true agnostics would be those who, *having understood the question*, refuse to answer it, and take refuge in the stronghold of the evidence without wanting to leave it. Yet I consider that Thomism is capable both of obtaining the intellectual evidence and of giving an account of it.

As for the ancient demonstrations of the Scholastic metaphysics, let us repeat once again, everything that we have said above does not come to weaken them in the least, but to strengthen them. This is the case in particular with the proofs of the existence of God, especially of the one that is drawn from the distinction between essence and existence in all finite beings. When we have *seen* the truth of this distinction, all the explanations of the world other than that through the infinite *Esse* [Existence], appear, rigorously speaking, as inconsistent, as infantile as the Indian explanation which has the world held up by an elephant, and the elephant by a turtle. This hypothesis is ridiculous, because it claims to explain *being* as such and the whole of being through a particular, definite, determined *essence*, completely relative to the whole of being. As long as one makes the same mistake, the imagination can be less shocked than by the elephant and the turtle, but the scandal of reason is not less. Atoms, nebulae, changing matter, living cells, spontaneous centers of consciousness, monist conceptions or pluralist conceptions, everything that places a *qualified essence* at the origin of things reveals a similar fragility. I would speak proportionately about proofs of the soul. Yet, once [509] these great discoveries are made, these great intuitions are possessed, is metaphysics completed forever? Far from it indeed. Does metaphysics only grow by the addition of new arguments against materialist conceptions, arguments which the progress of the sciences would supply to it? Farther from it yet. *Metaphysics renews itself from the inside*, assuming a consciousness always more vivacious of its originality, its principles and its certainty. It was renewed in this manner when Thomas rethought Aristotle in the pure light of Catholic truth. Is the metaphysics he has given to us not *the same* as that of the Philosopher? And, nevertheless everything is transformed because everything is deepened. Would we see a less brilliant renewal, the day when some masters of the traditional thought would thoroughly understand that the science of the soul is internal to the science of things, and would give us finally, according to the very felicitous phrase of Piat in regard to Leibniz, "an internalized Scholastics?" *Dig within*, said Marcus Aurelius; *there lies the well-spring of good; ever dig, and it will ever flow.*[47]

---

47 Ἔνδον βλέπε. ἔνδον ἡ πηγή τοῦ ἀγαθοῦ, καὶ ἀεὶ ἀναβλύειν δυναμένη, ἐὰν ἀσὶ σκάπτῃς (Marcus Aurelius, *Meditations*, VII, 59 [translation of Maxwell Staniforth, London: Penguin Books, 1964, p. 115. Translators' note].

[1] REMARKS ON THE HISTORY OF THE
NOTION OF NATURAL FAITH

As I indicated in a previous issue of *Recherches de Sciences Religieuses* (1910, no. 3, p. 245, note), what most fundamentally distinguishes the modern theories of the act of faith in Catholic theology from ancient theories is the fact that modern theologians commonly admit the existence, as *at least possible*, either: (1) *concurrently* with infused supernatural faith, of a faith acquired through the lights of natural reason alone, and still objectively certain, or: (2) *prior to* the act of faith, of a conviction on the basis of revelation similarly acquired through reason alone. These are two slightly different forms of the same dualist conception of faith which could be called without injustice the *modern* conception or even, as I shall show, the *Scotist* conception; this modern conception is opposed to the ancient theory of Augustine and Aquinas, which essentially requires grace for the legitimate certainty of the assent of faith. At the end of the above mentioned footnote, I announced a study on the origins of this dualist theory. I have learned since then that an exhaustive work was in preparation on the theology of the act of faith in the Middle Ages. Ligeard has published here (*Recherches* 1911, no. 4) one page of this work in his "Rationalisme de Pierre Abelard." It did not occur to me to mention the famous text he refers to and quotes, but his conclusion on the general course of the doctrines was exactly the same as the one I previously came to.[1] Some remarks [2] I propose here will no doubt only raise a weak interest when his complete work is pub-

---

1 H. Ligeard, *loc. cit.,* p. 396: "He thus imagines distinguishing two moments in the production of the act of faith, which each have their specific character. At the beginning there would be a strictly rational demonstration, which is the exclusive work of intelligence: grace emerging afterward would transform this first act and would thus generate supernatural faith, free and meritorious." Ligeard further speaks of "other attempts" and only mentions Hermes, as if we only had isolated endeavors. Why hide the fact that several modern theologians, who, moreover, perfectly know the fifth canon *De Fide* (Denzinger-Bannwart, 1814) and which the Fathers of the Council did not target, persist in their desire "to graft a free act on a necessitating demonstration of revealed faith"?

lished. Yet there is a very irritating and tenacious misunderstanding permeating this whole question and those who deem that faith is only reasonable when it is supernatural are very persistently and with the best intent accused of compromising or denying the rationality of faith. Thus I do not hesitate to offer to my theologian and courageous reader this little attractive mix of reflection and texts.

I

Everybody acknowledges that the ancient Fathers[2] did not raise the question of natural faith, at least not in the precise terms in which we formulate it. There are several reasons for this. The main one is that, although they very well knew that reason can find some truths through its own forces, whereas other truths are only known through Christian revelation, they did not take the same care nor the same interest as the Scholastics to mark the limits of these two fields. In order to prove that faith or purely rational credibility are Patristic notions one would refer in vain to those texts where the writers of the first [3] centuries announce that they are going to prove the perfect rationality of Christian faith. These texts, which are very numerous, do not touch on the question even with one line. Indeed even in the same passage where an ancient theologian may declare his intention to prove the rationality of faith, it comes as no surprise that he goes on to attribute to divine inspiration the knowledge not only of Christian dogmas, but even of moral and philosophical truths, or that he attempts to demonstrate not only the credibility, but also the mysteries. This indecision regarding the distinction of the two domains is characteristic of ancient theology. Those recognize it wholeheartedly who are proponents of the purely rational credibility and who are the most eager to find some trace of it in Antiquity.[3] But even independently of that imprecision, the fact that a writer vigorously affirms

---

2 I do not say anything here on the New Testament about which I formulated some time ago some reflections that naturally come to mind (*Recherches*, no. 5, p. 469-73). In order to provide some guidance in the neo-testamentary conception, let me at least mention a suggestive article by Lacey on the two elements of faith according to John ("The Two Witnesses," in *Journal of Theological Studies*, October 1909, p. 55-60).

3 See Fr. Gardeil in *Dictionnaire de théologie catholique*, art. "Crédibilité," col. 2240.

the rational validity of Christian faith in no way allows us to say that he does not believe that grace is necessary for the *perception* of these proofs, however valid they are. If sometimes the Fathers only speak of the proofs of our belief and thus seem to be completely engrossed in the object; if sometimes they only speak of grace and seem to see only the subject, they also often distinguish with a perfect clarity, in the unity of an act both divine and human, the two elements that are constitutive of Catholic faith: human experience, "hearing," provides the material of the proof, and illuminating grace gives the understanding, perception causing synthesis to take place. Augustine, for example, says with much precision and elegance:

> Et si ab hominibus audiunt, tamen quod intelligunt, intus datur, intus coruscat, intus revelatur. Quid faciunt homines forinsecus annuntiantes? Quid facio ego modo cum loquor? Strepitum verborum ingero auribus vestris. Nisi ergo revelet ille qui intus est, quid dico, aut quid loquor? Exterior cultor arboris, interior est Creator. [And though they do listen to humans, yet what they understand is given within, shines within, is revealed within. What do humans do who announce from without? What am I doing now when I speak? I am pouring a clatter of words into your ears. Unless, therefore, the one who is within reveals it, what do I say or what do I talk about? Outside is the planter of the tree, inside is its Creator.] (In Joannem tr. 26, no. 7. P.L. 35. 1609-1610.[4])

[4] It would be easy to mention one hundred texts of the same kind by the Fathers[5] and in the literature of the Augustinian centu-

------

4 Let me point out that, in this passage and in other similar ones, natural *reason* is not mentioned. However, in the rhetorical manner Augustine attributes to senses what belongs to the natural human being ("Strepitum *verborum ingero* auribus *vestris*" [I am pouring *a clatter of words* into *your* ears]). But his intention is quite clear: he does not deny that human beings without grace could find a meaning in the preaching they hear. He does not say that human beings only perceive the noise in words like an animal without reason does. What he says is that human beings without grace cannot perceive the preaching in this touching and intimate manner that leads one to believe, to give one's assent.

5 J. Marin in the *Apologétique traditonnelle* and Fr. Gardeil in the article *Crédibilité* mentioned above have given us two useful collections of texts referring to this matter. A chapter from John Damascene was referred to in the Halesian *Summa* and quite often since then, as giving a Patristic founda-

ries of the Middle Ages.[6] I only quoted the text above as a sample. It quite nicely makes understandable the *organic* conception of the act of faith, which is so different from the *dualist* theory: supernatural light that vivifies intelligence immediately enlightens the speech that has been heard without the necessity, without even the conceived possibility of the purely natural assent to divine truth. *The light of grace constitutes intelligence which is the proper potentiality of the act of believing.*

[5] II

Let us now move to the first half of the 13th century and investigate three theological works of great interest: the *Summa* of William of Auxerre; the *De Fide* of William of Auvergne; and the *Summa* of Alexander of Hales. I will refer to well-known texts, while trying to underline the main thought. I shall on purpose leave aside many of the notable or odd features in the theories of faith proposed by these three writers and I shall only concern myself with bringing

---

tion to the notion of natural faith. But the author only distinguishes there faith from hope or trust. Here is the text (*De Fide orthodoxa*, IV. 10. P.G. 94, 1125): Ἡ μέντοι πίστις διπλῆ ἐστιν. ἔστι γὰρ πίστις ἐξ ἀχοής. ἀχούντες γὰρ τῶν θείων πραφῶν, πιστεύομεν τῇ διδασκαλίᾳ τοῦ ἁγιου πνεύματος. αὕτη δὲ τελειοῦτοι πᾶσι τοῖς (ἔργοις ...) ἔστι δὲ πάλιν πίστις ἐλπιζομένων ὑπόστασις, πραγμάτων ἔλεγχος οὐ βλεπομένων, ἤ ἀδίσταχτος καὶ ἀδιάχριτος ἐλπὶς τῶν τε ὑπὸ θεοῦ ἐπηγγελμένων, καὶ τῆς τῶν αἰτήσεων ἡμῖν ἐπιτιχίας. ἡ δὲ δευτέρα, τῶν χαρισμάτων τοῦ πνεύματος. The beginning seems clear enough in order to dissipate all the doubts the last words could raise.

6 Here is a passage from Hermann, a converted Jew from Cologne (12th century), which strikingly recalls one by Augustine: "Ego autem saluberrima eorum monita tanquam surdus non audiebam, quando aures, quas in suo Evangelio Dominus requirebat, dicens: qui habet aures audiendi, audiat, aures videlicet cordis, aures intellectuales non habebam. Et quod spirituali auditu carebam, ea, quae corporali solum aure perceperam, contemnebam" [Yet, as though deaf, I did not hear their most salutary admonitions, because I did not have the ears which the Lord required in his Gospel saying 'Whoever has ears for hearing would hear,' the ears, namely of the heart, intellectual ears. And because I was lacking in spiritual hearing, I despised those things which I had perceived with the corporeal ear alone (*Opusc. de sua conversione*. P.L. 170 822 D. See 812 D, 814B).

to the fore the object that occupies me: namely, the new conception of a *double end* which these authors deem necessary in order to preserve the two traditional elements (external given and internal grace), whereas before these two elements were unified by one and the same act of faith. Although awkward and naïve in its beginnings, the theory of the double faith fully manifests itself. Yet at its foundation, in its essential postulates, it is such then as it will be later and has remained until now.

"Accidentalis cognitio Dei triplex est" [Accidental cognition of God is threefold], William of Auxerre says. "Quoniam quaedam est quae acquiritur per naturales rationes qualem habuerunt philosophi. Est alia quae innititur testimoniis scipturarum vel miraculorum et haec est fides informis. Tertia est gratuita, quae est per illuminationem quando lux vera illuminat animam ad videndum se et alia spiritualia, et talis cognitio est fides gratuita. Quae dicit in corde hominis: iam non propter rationem naturalem credo, sed propter illud quod video."[7] "Quoniam tali cognitione adveniente assentit anima primae veritati propter se et super omnia, tali cognitione pereunt omnes aliae cognitiones accidentales, et quantum ad actum et quantum ad habitum, licet quidam dicant quod non pereant quantum ad habitum, sed tantum quantum ad actum, sed hoc est falsum… et ita cum fides adest iam non est (h)abilis homo ad credendum per rationes quas prius habebat. Sed illae rationes non in eo generant fidem, sed gratuitam fidem confirmant et augmentant, sicut beneficia temporalia non faciunt in homine caritatem, sed confirmant et augmentant eam quantum ad suum motum…" [Seeing that a certain one is that which is acquired through natural reasons such as philosophers had. Another is that which rests on testimonies of Scriptures

---

7 Compare in one of the arguments *sed contra* [on the contrary] which precede this solution: "Hoc fuit signatum per Samaritanam cui dixerunt Samaritani: *iam non propter* te credimus, sed quia ipsi vidimus et audivimus, *Samaritana significat rationem naturalem, Samaritani venientes ad fidem noviter. Quoniam venientes ad fidem noviter dicunt rationi naturali*: iam non propter te credimus, sed quia ipsi vidimus per fidem" [This was signified by the Samaritan woman to whom the Samaritans spoke: 'Now *we believe* not on account of you, *but because we ourselves saw and heard.*' The Samaritan woman signifies natural reason, the Samaritans those recently coming to the faith. Since those recently coming to the faith say to natural reason: 'Now *we believe not on account of you, but because we ourselves see through faith.*']

or miracles and this is unformed faith. The third is gratuitous which occurs through illumination when the true light illuminates the soul enabling it to see itself and other spiritual things, and such cognition is gratuitous faith—which says in the human heart: Now I do not believe on account of natural reason, but on account of that which I see]. [Since with the coming of such cognition the soul assents to the first truth on account of itself and above all things, with the coming of such cognition all other accidental cognitions vanish, both in regard to the act and in regard to the habit. It is allowable, certain people would say, that they would not vanish in regard to the habit but only in regard to the act, but this is false ... and so when faith is not yet present, the human is capable of believing through reasons which it had earlier. But these reasons do not generate faith in the human, but confirm and increase a gratuitous faith, just as temporal benefits do not create charity in a human, but confirm and increase it in regard to its activity] (*Summa aurea*, I. III, tr. 3, q. 4, Paris ed., 1500, fol. CXXXIII, recto).

[6] We can see in this passage that William opposes *unformed faith [foi informe] and gratuitous faith*, whereas in later theology unformed faith is a faith that is produced by grace, but separated from charity. But what must draw our attention is the conviction the author has that the understanding of testimonies and miracles cannot be in a real sense the cause of faith, without faith ceasing to rely absolutely, as it should, on divine truth. Thus, William is consistent when he states elsewhere, depriving true knowledge of faith from any relation to signs, that faith finds in dogmas themselves, in determinate "articles," its reasons for believing in them, in the same way as intelligence in philosophy sees in the principles themselves the reason to affirm the principles.[8] "Relying on miracles" *is opposed* for him to "believing in God."

---

8 *Summa aurea*, same treatise, q. 1, fol. CXXXI verso: "*Dicitur fides argumentum* non apparentium propter articulos fidei qui sunt principia fidei per se nota. Unde fides sive fidelis respuit eorum probationem. Fides enim quia soli veritati innititur in ipsis articulis invenit causam quare credat eis, scilicet Deum; sicut in alia facultate [i.e., in philosophy] intellectus in hoc principio: *Omne totum est maius sua parte,* causam invenit per quam cognoscit illud; quoniam si in theologia non essent principia, non esset ars vel scientia. Habet ergo principia, scilicet articulos, qui tamen solis fi-

What appears the strangest at first glance in the system [7] of William of Auxerre is the opposition, the incompatibility of these two faiths. What is in actuality the newest and the most remarkable is simply once again their duality. The view on miracles or on the understanding of Scripture now *offends* the light of grace, whereas before in Augustine, as later in Aquinas, the light of grace is what *allowed us to see*, what *allowed us to understand* miracles or the word of God.

William of Auvergne distinguishes two faiths: living faith and dead faith (*De Fide*, ch. 1, *ad fin.* Paris: 1674, vol. 1, p. 7, col. 2). He says of the latter: "Nec virtus, nec virtuosa est, sed est opinabilis appre-hensio" [It is neither a power, nor powerful, but it is a conjectural apprehension] (*loc. cit.*, D). And he seems to claim elsewhere (p. 6, col. 2, F) that in order to believe the truth of Christianity, good will and grace are absolutely required. This is thus not what makes him a

---

delibus sunt principia, quibus fidelibus sunt per se nota, non extrinsecus aliqua probatione indigentia. Sicut enim hoc principium: *Omne totum est maius sua parte*, habet aliquantam illuminationem per modum naturae il-luminantis intellectum, ita hoc principium: *Deus est remunerator omnium bonorum*, et alii articuli, habent in se illuminationem per modum gratiae quo Deus illuminat intellectum" [It is said that faith is not an argument of discernibles on account of the articles of faith which are principles of faith known through themselves; whence faith or a matter of faith rejected the proof of these things. For faith that rests on the truth alone of the very articles finds a basis by which one would believe them, namely God; just as in another faculty [i.e., in philosophy] the intellect finds the basis by which it knows something on this principle: '*Every whole is greater than its part*'; hence if there were no principles in theology there would be neither art nor knowledge. Therefore it has principles, namely articles, which, however, are principles for matters of faith alone, by which matters of faith are known through themselves, not from without by some wanted proof. For just as this principle '*Every whole is greater than its part*' has a certain degree of il-lumination through the way of nature illuminating the intellect, so too does this principle '*God is the rewarder of all good people*' and other articles have in themselves an illumination by way of grace in which God illuminates the intellect]. Compare this with the theory of the *discerniculum experimentale* [experiential discernment], which I mentioned previously ("Les Yeux de la foi," *Recherches* 1910, no. 5, p. 460, n. 2). However, it is possible that Wil-liam only means here the actual adherence to this or that "article," once faith in the whole of religion has been obtained. That is why I used a dubi-tative expression.

forerunner of the new school. However, in the opposition William of Auvergne establishes between belief that would come from signs and meritorious faith that comes from God we find again the very same prejudice that held William of Auxerre captive. William of Auvergne does not see how the same act very easily synthesizes the two elements. He claims that the proofs diminish the merit (it is probably his opinion that Aquinas had in view in 2a2ae, q. 2, a.10, ad. 1) and that faith would not be virtuous if the object were not "improbable." Here is how he explains it in two parables where we take delight in the profusion of his style.

> Intellectus humanus... in se ipso infirmus est et non stans per semetipsum... fulcitur autem infirmitas ipsius interdum evidentia veritatis plerumque probationibus aut suasionibus, quandoque signis, et cum debilis fuerit vel levis ratiocinatio, hoc est probatio vel suasio, non innititur ei confidenter, sed quodammodo se retinet, timens ne non satis fortis sit ad sustentandum ipsum. Et propter hoc manifestum est, quia ipse utitur huiusmodi fulturis, seu suppodiaculis, quemadmodum baculo debili et fragili, cui neque sine timore neque totaliter innititur gestans ipsum. Evidentia autem veritatis, et probatio demonstrativa, fortissima fulcimenta ipsius sunt, et tanquam baculi inflexibiles et infrangibiles, nullaque ex parte nutantes. [8] Manifestum igitur est tibi ex his, quia intellectus non quaerit huiusmodi fulcimenta, nisi ex infirmitate et debilitate sua; et quia intellectus philosophans est sicut viator ambulans... adiutorio baculi se transferens... baculus autem cuius adminiculo ita adambulat, et transilit, demonstratio est, sive probatio demonstrativa. Intellectus autem qui virtute propria credit, nec requirit huiusmodi fulturas, nec illis indiget, magis fortis est magisque firmus, quia propria virtute et firmitate nititur, quam qui aliena; quapropter magis firmiter credit quam ille. [The human intellect ... is weak in itself and does not stand by itself ... rather its infirmity is now and then strengthened by the evidence of truth (commonly through proofs or persuasions, occasionally through signs), and when reasoning would have been feeble or slight (this is proof or persuasion), it does not confidently rely upon itself for this but in a certain way restrains itself, dreading that it would not be strong enough to sustain itself. And on account of this it is evident that it makes use of these kinds of buttresses or supports, as a sort of feeble and fragile stick, which is neither without dread nor totally resting upon it for the carrying of itself. Now the evidence of truth, and a demonstrative proof, are

the strongest props for it, and resemble inflexible and unbreakable sticks, and in no way wavering. Therefore from these things it is evident to you that the intellect does not seek props of this kind, unless from its weakness and feebleness, and that the philosophizing intellect is as it were a walking wayfarer ... transporting itself with the aid of a stick ... Now the stick with whose help it thus walks nearby and hastens past is demonstration, or demonstrative proof. Yet the intellect which believes by its own power, neither requiring these kinds of buttresses nor needing them, is stronger and firmer because it leans upon its own power and firmness, than one which is otherwise; on account of which it more firmly believes than the other one does.] (*Loc. cit.* ch. 1, p. 4, col. 2, GH).

Debes etiam scire, quia intellectus requirens ea quae supra diximus, est sicut venditor incredulus, qui emptori non aliter credit, nisi pignus vel cautionem vel securitatem det ipsi, et probatio sive suasio ut pignus est et cautio securitatis, sine qua non credit huiusmodi intellectus... Notum autem est tibi, quia exactio pignoris aut alterius cautionis, non est nisi ex parvitate seu debilitate credulitatis aut ex defectu ipsius: quare manifestum est intellectum exactorem huius-modi pignoris et securitatum, videlicet probationum, suasionum, signorum, esse credulitate infirmum aut incredulum...; manifestum etiam est tibi, quia magnitudo et multitudo pignorum in domo ven-ditoris, etsi securitatem ipsi faciant, signa tamen sunt et testimonia incredulitatis ipsius: sic pignora et securitates probationum ...." [You should also know that the intellect requires those things which we said were above it, and it is as it were an unbelieving wayfarer who does not believe a buyer unless the buyer would give a pledge or a guarantee or a security to him. And proof or persuasion is like a pledge and a guarantee of security without which the intellect does not believe in this way ... Now it is known to you that the demanding of a pledge or another guarantee does not occur unless from the slightness or feebleness of the belief or from a defect in it: wherefore it is evident that the intellect is a demander in this way of a pledge or security, namely proofs, persuasions, or signs, being weak or unbelieving in its belief ...; it is also evident to you that the magnitude and multitude of the pledges in the domicile of a seller, even if they would make a security for him, are nevertheless signs and testimonies of his unbelief; so too are the pledges and securities of the proofs.] (ibid., p. 5, col. 1, AB).

I know full well that the Bishop of Paris speaks afterward of the miracles which prove Christian faith (p. 8, col. 2, G, especially Ch. 3, p. 16, col. 1, BC). I also know fully well that he confusedly feels (like William of Auxerre) that imperfection resides precisely not in the usage of proofs but in the defiance toward God ("quodammmodo se retinet, timens...") [in a certain way restrains itself, dreading ...][9]; and elsewhere he blames faith that relies on proofs by adding: "Si... propter hoc solummodo crederentur" [If ... they were believed on account of this way alone] (p. 7, col. 1, C).

[9] But all that should not lead us to forget a fact that is certain and supported by a clear text. *William of Auvergne pressed the separation between the grace that causes us to believe and the object that is proper to the mind so far as to exclude expressly from faith the motive of divine veracity.* He writes:

> Fides haec est digna deo credulitas, qua ei, scilicet Deo, ut dignum et iustum est creditur, hoc est sine omni pignore et cautione, scilicet gratis et obedienter, *et non propter hoc quia verax est, aut quia verum est quod ipse loquitur*; sic enim crederetur homini cuivis. [This faith is a worthy belief in God, in which one believes in Him, namely in God, since He is believed as He is worthy and just. This occurs without any pledge and guarantee, namely freely and obediently, *and not on account of the fact that it is truthful, nor on account of the fact that it is true because He Himself speaks*; for in this manner it would have been believed by any human] (p. 7, col. 1, A).

To cancel "all proof and all caution" thus eventually means excluding divine veracity from the formal motive of faith. There is no need to remind readers that this idea is no less contrary to the Vatican Council than to the Catechism. I indicated in the past (*Recherches*, 1910, no. 5, p. 455, n. 1) that the proponents of double faith who bring

---

9 The fact that intelligence needs proofs, which are distinct from the truth itself in which intelligence believes, is assuredly an effect of its present weakness. Thus, the less the mind is well-disposed the more the need for a great sign (*Recherches*, 1910, no. 3, p. 258-59). But the need for any sign does not come from a *personal* indisposition, but from the *natural* state of all humanity as it is now. Furthermore, the multitude of proofs available does not decrease by itself "the promptness of the will to believe," nor, thus, the merit of so believing, as Aquinas shows about the explanations of dogmas by theologians (2a 2ae, q. 2, a. 10).

into opposition "scientific faith" and "faith of homage" cannot follow William up to that point, but that this conclusion would be, according to their opponents, the natural result of their thought.[10]

[10] According to Fr. Mandonnet, who has not been contradicted by the scholarly critiques of Quaracchi,[11] the Halesian compilation

---

10 Given the era in which the dualist theory of faith was born, would it be useful to compare these authors' doctrine with the philosophical theories of knowledge that then started to gain in popularity? It would be tempting to do so. The two Williams, one could say, are contemporaries with the introduction of the complete Aristotle in the medieval Latin schools; Augustinian psychology loses ground. The certainty coming from divine illumination starts *to be opposed* to intellectual knowledge drawn from the input of the senses. Does the theory of double faith not flow very naturally from there? Given the absence of clear texts on this subject, this comparison must be deemed more specious than solid and it indeed seems through the case of Abelard that medieval dialectic was capable of drawing from Gregory's famous word, "Fides non habet meritum..." [Faith does not have merit ...], the theory of two faiths independently of any Peripatetic influence. Regardless of the question of origins, it is hard to deny, I think, that the exclusive domination of Aristotelianism in the School had strong influence on the history of *The Treatise on Faith* in our theology. It was assuredly a progress, and due in part to the study of Aristotle, to have the clearer distinction between what reason knows through its natural light and what faith reveals. It would be a deplorable step backward to return on this point to the old confusion. At any rate the Church has spoken. But it remains that Aristotle's ideas, for those who became his disciples, have certainly concealed too much of the traditional doctrine that sees an illumination of God in intelligence. The doctrine of the agent intellect was little developed in this direction. People did not see any more how grace intrinsically perfects intelligence, excavates it, so to speak, deepens it. The two types of knowledge were *juxtaposed*, the gratuitous one and the natural one. For example, with regard to the question I discuss, people ceased to understand how the infused gift of faith, by elevating intelligence, allows it to discern supernaturally the signs of the supernatural world in sensible things. The natural reason people learned to consider as a separate faculty, seemed capable for its part of such a discernment. Thus, how can we distinguish the knowledge through infused faith? By removing all relation it has to signs? This is what William of Auxerre does. Less extreme, if not less logical, Scotus and his followers only see an entirely *entitative* difference between supernatural and natural faith, which is translated only *accidentally* into the life of the soul through effects.

11 See Heitz, *Essai historique sur les rapports entre la philosophie et la foi, de Bérenger de Tours à saint Thomas d'Aquin.* Paris, 1909, pp. 105-6.

would not have been written in its entirety in the first half of the
13th century, but would depend in several of its parts on Albert, Bonaventura, and Aquinas. I would be surprised if questions 64 and 68
of the third part (*De Fide Informi, De Fide Formata*) with which I
deal here were not old. And even if they were not, there would perhaps be reason to no longer attribute to the Irrefragable Doctor the
place of honor in the elaboration of the idea of rational credibility
(Gardeil, *loc cit*, col. 2268). As far as the result of the present study is
concerned, this historical point is irrelevant. For my exclusive goal is
to shed light on the nature and the essential moments of the development of an idea. It is certain that the Halesian *Summa* makes us see
in full clarity the notion of acquired faith in the intermediary phase
between William of Auxerre and Scotus.

Now in the above mentioned question 64, member 2, Alexander
[11] quotes the text by Damascene mentioned above and adds:

> vult ergo distinguere Damascenus quod est fides acquisita ex
> auditu, sive testimonio scripturarum, sive humana ratione; et est
> fides donum gratuitum a Deo ad assentiendum veritati divinae
> nobis annunciatae. [therefore Damascene wants to distinguish
> the faith which is acquired from what is heard, whether from the
> testimony of the Scriptures or from human reason, and the faith
> which is a gratuitous gift of God for assenting to the divine truth
> announced to us.].

At member VIII he puts these two faiths in demons:

> In daemonibus fides dupliciter est: uno modo fides quae est habitus
> acquisitus ex miraculis et praedicationibus, alio modo fides quae est
> habitus gratuitus. [In the demons faith is twofold: on the one hand
> the faith which is a habit acquired from miracles and prophecies;
> on the other hand the faith which is a gratuitous habit].

He adds that the gratuitous faith of demons is obviously unformed,
i.e., separated from charity. In the first passage, just after the words
I quoted, he very clearly distinguishes his "acquired faith" from "unformed faith" which is as supernatural as formed faith. This is a notable difference with William of Auxerre. Ideas become more precise
and the *naturalism* of the theory more acute.[12] For, in William the

---

12   I use the word "naturalism" without pejorative connotations.

name of *unformed faith* still suggested some link with grace through the idea of a privation. Here is how Alexander presents acquired faith, fully natural, neutral, and indifferent:

> Q. 68, *De Fide formata*, m. II (Alexander explains Augustine when he speaks of *sufficient testimony* in the book *De videndo Deo* (Ep. 147, P.L. 33)): "Loquitur de fide quae est ex auditu exteriori, quae est fides acquisita, non de fide quae est ex inspiratione gratiae interioris, quae est fides gratuita" [He speaks about the faith which is heard from the outside, which is an acquired faith, not of the faith which is from the inspiration of internal grace, which is a gratuitous faith]. (*We thus have two faiths! Compare this text with what Aquinas says, quoted in my first article, p. 242, and we shall feel the whole difference between the organic conception and the dualist conception.*[13]) "Illius causa est ratio vel apertum testimonium auctoritatis, istius vero causa est gratia illuminationis divinae ad cognoscendum veritatem, quae est supra naturam, et assentiendum ipsi propter se. [The cause of that is reason or the visible testimony of an authority; however, the cause of this is the grace of divine illumination for the knowing of the truth which is above nature, and for assenting to it on account of itself] (*As if these two causalities were in opposition, were in the same line! And what more anti-Augustinian than the disjunction between illuminating grace and the interpretation of testimony?*) "Notandum tamen quod ratio et fides quae est ex ratione se habent ad fidem gratuitam sicut praeambula dispositio [12] ad formam. Disponit enim animam ad receptionem luminis, quo assentiat primae veritati propter se: sed per modum naturae, non gratiae: et dicitur ipsam introducere sicut tela filum, et tunc ratio cessat humana, quando ei non innititur fides introducta" [It designates, however, that reason and the faith which is from reason relate to gratuitous faith as a preceding disposition to the form. For it disposes the soul for the reception of the light, by which it would assent to the first truth on account of itself: but by way of nature, not grace. And it is said to introduce itself as a thread into a fabric, and then human reason ceases inasmuch as the introduced faith does not rely upon it.].

This *innititur* [relying upon] would call for remarks similar to those I made about William of Auvergne. For the rest, the *faith of hearing* [*foi de l'ouïe*], which is natural, is quite clearly distinguished from

---

13   See also *loc. cit.*, m. II, ad. 3: "Fide suasa creditur ex testimoniis, sed fide infusa creduntur testimonia" [With persuaded faith it is believed from the testimonies, but with infused faith the testimonies are believed].

the faith of grace [*foi-grâce*]! This is what is essential in the "modern" theory. After that the modalities, the minute nuances, should not be overlooked, but they have to be kept in perspective. They should only be considered once the central point has been brought to the fore. For example, Alexander or any other theologian may affirm that a distinct act of acquired faith always temporally precedes the act of infused faith; others, on the contrary, deem that the act of acquired faith, which is actually indistinct from the act of infused faith, is still contained in infused faith in such a way that it could subsist apart.[14] These are modalities which do not change anything essential to the theory, although they reinforce or attenuate its rough character. There is agreement on the basic points.

Now if there is agreement on the basic points, it is because there is agreement on the theological and philosophical assumptions, on the conception of the natural activity toward supernatural objects. In a more general view, there is agreement on the relationship between the material and the formal element, on the theory of act and potency. This will become perfectly clear when we see the dualist theory of faith reach, so to speak, its full self-awareness in the writings of Scotus.[15]

[13] Here is how Scotus explains his position:

---

14   See the article by de Séguier in the *Annales de philosophie chrétienne*, vol. 37, p. 276 (December 1897).

15   Bonaventura's thought is less clear than Scotus's. Bonaventura does not quite clearly distinguish the perception of credibility from the demonstration of the mysteries. When he speaks of acquired faith, he does not go back to the principles. As is well known, he is inferior to Aquinas and Scotus with regard to synthetic and systematic strength of thought. In his *Commentary on the Sentences* he seems inclined to grant certainty only to infused faith. Compare conclusion 3, d. 23, a. 2, q.2 with the reply to the second objection: "Ideo credit sacrae scripturae, quia patres sui crediderunt... est talis credulitas... cuiusdam assuetudinis" [For this reason one believes Sacred Scripture, because the Fathers believed it ... such a belief is ... from a certain custom], and with the fourth reply: "Haeretici quidem si cognoscunt aliquos articulos, hoc est ex quadam persuasione humanae rationis, immo fictionis suae" [Indeed the heretics, if they know some articles, this is from a certain persuasion of human reason, assuredly of its fabrication] *(Quaracchi,* vol. III, p. 491).

Igitur si nulla fides infusa esset in me, crederem firmiter historiis librorum canonis propter auctoritatem Ecclesiae, sicut fide acquisita credo aliis historiis a quibusdam famosis viris scriptis et narratis. Credi igitur fide acquisita Evangelio, quia Ecclesia tenet scriptores veraces, quod ego audiens acquiro mihi habitum credendi dictis illorum... Credo etiam Romanam esse, quam non vidi, ex relatu fide dignorum; sic est revelatis in Scriptura per fidem acquisitam ex auditu firmiter adhaereo credendo Ecclesiae approbandi veritatem auctorum illorum... Praeterea *Rom.* 10... *fides est ex auditu...* argumentum (apostoli) non valet, nisi loqueretur de fide acquisita... potest esse in peccato mortali, et audiendo praedicantem, et videndo miracula fieri, credit ei, et hoc, quia dictat sibi naturaliter ratio, quod Deus non assistit falsitati alicuius... Ex istis sequitur corollarium, quod propter credulitatem articulorum revelatorum ut homo firmiter credat omnibus articulis revelatis, et determinetur ad alteram partem sine oppositi formidine, non oportet[16] ponere fidem infusam; nec necessitas eius potest ex hoc concludi, quia fides acquisita est super opinione... licet sit infra scientiam .... [Therefore if no faith would have been infused in me, I would have firmly believed in the stories of the books of the Canon on account of the authority of the Church, just as from acquired faith I believe in other stories from certain famous men through writings and narrations. I have believed therefore in the Gospel with an acquired

---

16　Of course, Scotus does not deny infused faith and does not doubt its reality. What he denies is that the reason he mentions suffices to demonstrate the existence of such a faith. I only quoted the most remarkable passages, but everything should be read. Let me point out in no. 5 the number of times *firmiter* [firmly] occurs: this corroborates the *sine oppositi formidine* [without dread of the opposite] and does not leave any doubt about Scotus' thought. The certainty he speaks of is fully rational, the will plays no role in it (See *loc.cit.* p. 8: "Ideo sicut nec haesito" [Therefore as I do not hesitate], etc.) However full this rational certainty may be, it does not have for Scotus the same perfection as that given by infused faith. "Licet enim fides acquisita sufficiat ad assensum et certitudinem actus, prout *credere* opponitur *opinari*, tamen non est ita perfecte certus sicut cum fide infusa, nec esset actus ita intensus, nec sufficit in esse primo, quia fides acquisita non perficit animam ita perfecte sicut infusa; oportet igitur ponere utramque fidem" [For it is granted that acquired faith would suffice for the assent and certainty of the act insofar as *believing* is opposed to *supposing*. Nevertheless it is not as perfectly certain as with infused faith, nor would its act have been as intense, nor does it suffice in being first, because acquired faith does not perfect the soul as perfectly as infused faith. Therefore it is necessary to put forth each faith.] (Ibid., no. 18, p. 26).

faith because the Church preserves the true Scriptures, since I, as hearing, acquire the habit for my believing statements of them ... I also believe a Roman woman to exist, whom I have not seen, from the related faith of worthy people. Thus is it that from the things revealed in Scripture through acquired faith from what is heard I firmly adhere to the truth of these authors by believing in the assenting Church ... Furthermore (see Rom. 10) ... faith is from what is heard ... the argument (of the Apostle) is not valid unless it was speaking of acquired faith ... it is possible to be in mortal sin, and by hearing a prophecy and seeing miracles happen, believe in it, and this is so, because reason would naturally prescribe to it, as God does not defend the falsity of something ... From these things this corollary follows, that as the human would firmly believe all revealed articles on account of a belief in the revealed articles, and would be settled on the other hand without dread of the opposite, it is not necessary to put forward infused faith; nor can its necessity be concluded from this – that acquired faith is above opinion ... granted that it would be beneath knowledge.] (3, d. 23, n. 4. Vivès, vol. XV, p. 7-8).

In the XIVth of his *Quaestionis quodlibetales,* the subtle doctor is no less clear:

Potest... viator ex natura sua, audita et intellecta communi doctrina Ecclesiae firma credulitate assentire his quae ipsa docet de fide [14] et moribus, inter quae principale est de Trinitate in Divinis. De ista credulitate acquisita videtur accipi illud ad *Rom.* 10, Fides ex auditu... Comparando fidem infusam et fidem acquisitam ad actu credendi, in hoc conveniunt, quod quando insunt eidem animae, actus unus etidem credendi elicitur secundum inclinationem utriusque. [The wayfarer could ... from his nature, from the heard and understood common doctrine of the Church, assent with firm belief to those things which it teaches about faith and practices, among which the principal one is that of the Trinity in the Divine. This acquired belief seems to be treated in that passage of Rom. 10; *Faith is from what is heard* ... By comparing infused faith and acquired faith to the act of believing (we see that) in this they are united – that when they are present in the same soul, one and the same act of believing is elicited according to the inclination of each.] (*Quodl.,* XIV, no. 5, vol. XXVI, p. 9)...

> Est tamen differentia una quantum ad hoc quod est actum elicere,
> ista scilicet, quod ex fide acquisita, etiam si sola insit, potest elici
> actus credendi, sicut credimus certis articulis testimonio fide digno
> asserentis, ad quos tamen non inclinat aliqua fides infusa... sed ex
> fide solum infusa non potest quis elicere actum credendi, et hoc de
> lege communi ... [... it is, however, a different matter in regard to
> that which is the eliciting act, namely that which is from acquired
> faith; even if it would be present alone, the act of believing could
> be elicited, as we believe from testimony assured articles through
> the worthy faith of the asserter, to which, however, any infused
> faith does not incline ... but from infused faith alone one is not
> able to elicit an act of believing, and this is in accordance with the
> common law.] (Ibid., no. 6, p. 10).[17]

These texts are crystal clear and certainly suffice to show the extent to which Scotus clearly conceived the theory of the act of faith;
this act involves as a necessary part of its mechanism an acquired
and natural faith that could subsist alone, i.e., without grace, and
still keep a true certainty. But there is more. The theory of the faith
that is purely acquired or natural and still certain is only a particular
case of the Scotist doctrine regarding the relationships of nature and
supernature. He grants to human will the power of actually loving
God above all things, independently of grace. He only sees in the
supernatural act of force or temperance an act raised through the
influence of charity, but substantially identical in its determinations

---

17 Thus, from a *natural and necessary condition*, from an *element* of the act
of faith, one makes a complete act that can subsist separately. See also in an
argument expounded in no. 4 of collatio X (vol. V, p. 185): "Puer baptiza-
tus, licet habeat fidem infusam, non tamen propter hoc potest actum credendi elicere, sed solum quando acquisierit sibi fidem acquisitam credendo
praedicanti et dicenti articulos" [For the baptized boy it is permitted that
he would have an infused faith, not, however, on account of this act can
he elicit the act of believing, but only when he will have acquired for himself an acquired faith by believing the articles that are preached and told].
Compare this new formulation, as above the one by Alexander of Hales,
with the key text by Aquinas (in 4 Sent. d. 4), from which my whole essay
arose. Scotus says: *fides acquisita* [acquired faith] and speaks of an organism
that can be self-sufficient where Aquinas says: *determinatio credibilium* [a
determination of credible things] and speaks of an element constitutive of
the assent of faith alone.

to the natural act of these virtues.[18] He thus grants [15] to reason
the power of stating the fact of revelation and giving one's firm and
legitimate assent to it without the illumination of the Holy Spirit.

All these theological opinions are in fact in harmony with the Scotist ideas on matter and form, potency and act. Aquinas believes that
there is only one substantial form in the body, because the form from
which the supreme actuality comes is prior to the others and more
intimately united to matter.[19] Whoever does not agree with him and
does not grant this is logically led to conceive that all actual beings

---

18   On the natural love of God, see Scotus, 3 d. 27, no. 13 (Vol. XV, p.
367). This passage only treats the *homo purus* [the pure human] (See no. 15
and 21, p. 368 and 374). But elsewhere Scotus seems to assume that one
has to speak similarly of the *lapsus* [the lapsed human] (2 d. 28, vol. XIII, p.
262). See also 1 d. 17, Q. 3, n. 33 (Vol. X, p. 96). See especially the Quod-
libetal Question XVII (Vol. XXVI) where the principle of the substantial
univocity of acts is clearly stated. Scotus says about the act of supernatural
faith: "Aeque perfectus esset, quantum ad quodlibet intrinsecum sibi, si aeque intense eliceretur praecise secundum fidem acquisitam" [It would have
been equally perfect in regard to anything intrinsic to it, if it would have
been elicited equally intensely and precisely according to acquired faith] (p.
220). See lastly on moral acts: "Actus qui est complete circumstantionatus
secundem virtutem moralem, est potentiale respectu virtutis, quam dicit,
meritorium" [The act which is completely circumstantial according to moral virtue is potentially in respect to virtue, as one says, meritorious] (p. 212)
(Let us note, however, that a certain degree of intensity is granted to infused
virtue 3 d. 23, no. 18 and d. 27, no. 19, vol. XV, p. 26 and 373). Among
the nominalists, see Durand, 3 d. 29, Q. 2, no. 24: "Caritas elevat naturam
ad amandum Deum meritorie... non autem oportet quod plus vel aliter
elevet" [Charity elevates nature in order to love God meritoriously ... but it
is not necessary that it would elevate it more or otherwise] and among the
Moderns, Molina, *Concordia*, Q. 14 a. 13. I am surprised that Fr. Gardeil
overlooks the subtle Doctor in an otherwise extremely instructive passage of
the *Revue pratique d'apologétique* (Nov. 15, 1908, p. 274) and relates these
doctrines only to the theologians who fought Baius and Jansenius.

19   Aquinas, *Quaest. disp. de Anima*, a. 9: "Oportet quod forma dans esse
materiae, ante omnia intelligatur advenire materiae, et immediatius ceteris
ibi inesse. Est autem hoc proprium formae substantialis, quod det materiae
esse simpliciter" [It is necessary that the form giving existence to matter,
must be understood to come to matter prior to all other things, and to
be present there more immediately than other things. Yet it is proper to a
substantial form that it would give existence to matter in a simple manner]
(Vivès, vol. XIV, p. 101).

potentially pre-contain *beings already made*, which will be able to escape, so to speak, into actuality in order to subsist apart later once the first being dissolves. Such is acquired faith in infused faith according to the Scotist schema. The logical coherence in Scotus is hardly less admirable than in Aquinas; neither in Scotus nor in Aquinas can metaphysics be separated from Theology.

[16] III

One of the great merits of Aquinas is to have sharply distinguished in the knowledge of faith what is seen from what is believed. One *believes* the mystery (for example, of the Trinity) and one *sees* that one has to believe it. The more considerable the place this master receives in the history of the relationships between reason and faith, the more interesting it is to know whether he believes that this *sight* of credibility, the notion of which he so forcefully identified, can be achieved by only natural powers, so that indeed it would be possible to move from this preliminary term to the assent of natural faith, which would be objectively certain. I think the texts force us to answer negatively. For Aquinas, there is no faith that is really certain outside of infused faith.

In the question of the *Summa* entitled *De Causa Fidei* [On the Cause of Faith] Aquinas teaches us that there are two things necessary for faith: the determination of the truths to be believed and the assent of the believer. The *determination* always comes ultimately from God, either because he speaks directly to a prophet or because he communicates himself to the crowd through the ministry of those He sent. The *assent* of the believer remains unexplained if we only consider the reason to believe that is presented to the believer. There needs to be added to it the action of a principle of grace that makes the believer inclined to say yes. Here is the text:

> Quantum vero ad secundum, scilicet ad assensum hominis in ea quae sunt fidei, potest considerari duplex causa: una quidem exterius inducens, sicut miraculum visum, vel persuasio hominis inducentis ad fidem; quorum neutrum est sufficiens causa: videntium enim unum et idem miraculum, et audientium eandem praedicationem, quidam credunt, et quidam non credunt. Et ideo oportet ponere aliam causam interiorem, quae movet hominem interius ad assentiendum

his quae sunt fidei. Hanc autem causam Pelagiani ponebant solum liberum arbitrium... Sed hoc est falsum: quia cum homo, assentiendo his quae sunt fidei, elevetur supra naturam suam, oportet quod hoc insit ei ex supernaturali principio interius movente, quod est Deus. Et ideo fides, quantum ad assensum, qui est principalis actus fidei, est a Deo interius movente per gratiam. [Now in regard to the second, namely to the assent of a human to those things which are of the faith, a twofold cause can be considered. One indeed of external inducement, such as a miracle that is seen, or the persuasion of a human inducing us to the faith: neither of which is a sufficient cause. For of those seeing one and the same miracle or hearing the same sermon, some believe and some do not believe. And so it is necessary to put forth another internal cause, which moves a human internally to assent to those things which are of the faith. Now the Pelagians held that this cause was free will alone... But this is false: because as humans by assenting to those things which are of the faith are raised above their nature, it is necessary that this would occur to them from a supernatural principle moving internally, which is God. And thus faith, in regard to the assent, which is the chief act of faith, is from God moving humans internally by grace.] (*Summa theologiae* 2a 2ae, q. 6, a. 1).

[17] Once again there are two elements of one unique act that have to be explained: determinate objects and the subject who adheres. Aquinas says: "one needs supernaturalized eyes in order to adhere to supernatural truths."

This article does not have a better commentary than another passage of Aquinas, which shows its conformity with his general doctrine of human knowledge, characterized by the distinction of two elements: the determination of the knowable object and the active synthesis of the knowing subject. The importance of this passage is unrivalled; I quote it entirely.

Quandocumque acceptis (homo) aliquo modo assentitur, oportet esse aliquid quod inclinet ad assensum; sicut lumen naturaliter inditum in hoc quod assentitur primis principiis per se notis, et ipsorum principiorum veritas in hoc quod assentitur conclusionibus scitis, et aliquas verisimilitudines in hoc quod assentimur his quae opinamur; quae si fuerint aliquantulum fortiores, inclinant ad credendum, prout fides dicitur opinio iuvata rationibus. Sed id quod inclinat ad assentiendum principiis intellectis aut conclusionibus scitis est sufficiens inductivum: unde cogit ad assensum et est sufficiens ad iudicandum de illis quibus assentitur. Quod vero inclinat ad opinandum qualitercumque, vel etiam fortiter, non est sufficiens inductivum rationis; unde non cogit nec per hoc potest haberi perfectum iudicium de his quibus assentitur. Unde et in fide qua in Deum credimus, non solum est acceptio rerum quibus assentimur, sed aliquid quod inclinat ad assensum; et hoc est lumen quoddam, quod est habitus fidei, divinitus menti humanae infusum; quod quidem sufficientius est ad inducendum quam aliqua demonstratio, qua etsi nunquam falsum concludatur, tamen frequenter in hoc homo fallitur quod putat esse demonstrationem quod non est; sufficientius etiam quam ipsum lumen naturale, quo assentimur principiis; cum lumen illud frequenter impediatur ex corporis infirmitate, ut patet in mente captis. Lumen autem fidei, quod est quasi sigillatio quaedam primae veritatis in mente, non potest fallere, sicut Deus non potest decipere vel mentiri. Unde hoc lumen sufficit ad iudicandum. Hic tamen habitus non movet per viam intellectus, sed magis per viam voluntatis: unde non facit videre illa quae creduntur, nec cogit assensum, sed facit voluntarie assentiri. Et sic patet quod fides ex duabus partibus est: a Deo scilicet ex parte interioris luminis, quod inducit ad assensum, et ex parte eorum quae exterius proponuntur, quae ex divina revelatione initium sumpserunt: et haec se habent ad cognitionem fidei, sicut accepta per [18] sensum ad cognitionem principiorum, quia utrisque fit aliqua cognitionis determinatio. Unde sicut cognitio principiorum accipitur a sensu, et tamen lumen quo principia cognoscuntur est innatum, ita fides est ex auditu, et tamen habitus fidei est infusus ....

[Whenever (a human) assents in any way to accepted views, it is necessary that there is something that would incline one to the assent; as the naturally given light results in one assenting to first principles known through themselves, and the truth of the principles themselves results in one assenting to the conclusions known through them, and some probabilities result in our assenting to these things about which we have opinions. If these probabilities were somewhat stronger they would incline us to believe, for faith is said to be an opinion aided by reasons. Yet that which inclines us to assent to understood principles or known conclusions is an adequate inducement; whence it compels us to the assent and is adequate for judging about those things to which one assents. Indeed what inclines in any manner, or even strongly, to the forming of an opinion, is not an adequate inducement of reason; whence it does not compel nor through it can a perfect judgment of those things to which one assents be had. Hence also there is in the faith by which we believe in God, not only the accepting of the thing to which we assent, but something that inclines us to the assent. And this is a kind of light, which is the habit of faith, divinely infused into the human mind. This indeed is more capable of inducing assent than any demonstration, which even though it never leads one to a false conclusion, however, the human in this matter is often mistaken in believing something is a demonstration that is not. It is also more capable than the natural light itself by which we assent to principles, since that light is often impeded by an infirmity of the body, as is clear in the insane mind. Yet the light of faith, which is as it were a certain faint stamp of the first truth in our mind, cannot fail, as God cannot deceive or lie. Hence this light is adequate for judging. This habit, however, does not move by way of the intellect, but rather by way of the will. Hence it does not cause us to see those things which are believed, nor compel an assent, but causes us to assent voluntarily. And so it is clear that faith occurs in two ways: namely from God by way of an internal light that induces us to the assent, and by way of those things that are proposed exteriorly, which obtained their source from divine revelation. And these are related to the knowledge of faith as the things received by the senses are related to the knowledge of principles, because both make any matter of knowledge certain. Hence just as the knowledge of principles is received by the sense, and yet the light by which principles are known is innate, so faith is from what is heard, and yet the habit of faith is infused] (*In Boetium de Trinitate*, Q. 3, a. 1, ad 4. Vivès, vol. XXVIII, p. 508).

The grace of faith is thus a light which is at the same time an inclination. Now, the role of this inclination is, according to Aquinas, so necessary that when infused faith is absent, he introduces another support of the *voluntary* kind in order to explain the assent to the doctrine of Christianity. The assent of the heretic not only to the point that makes up his heresy, but even to the Christian truths which he holds in common with the Church, is for Aquinas the effect of an arbitrary preference, and not of a demonstration. This point of view brings a remarkable confirmation of what I said about the essential role love plays in faith:

> Alios articulos fidei de quibus haereticus non errat, non tenet eo modo sicut tenet eos fidelis, scilicet simpliciter inhaerendo primae veritati; ad quod indiget homo adiuvari per habitum fidei; sed tenet ea quae sunt fidei, *propria voluntate* et iudicio. [A heretic does not hold the other articles of faith about which he does not err, in the same way as the faithful person holds them, namely by adhering simply to the first truth, for which a human needs to be helped by the habit of faith. But he holds those things which are of the faith *by his own will* and judgment] (*Summa theologiae* 2a 2ae, q. 5, a. 3, ad 1).

> Manifestum est, quod talis haereticus circa unum articulum, fidem non habet de aliis articulis, sed *opinionem* quandam secundum *propriam voluntatem*. [It is evident that such a heretic in regard to one article does not have faith in the other articles, but a kind of *opinion* according to *his own will*] (Ibid. corp.)

The reason for the necessity of a voluntary support is the imperfect connaturality of human reason with the truth that is proposed; because the object is of the supernatural order, the natural movement of intelligence is not sufficient for affirming it:

> Homo enim *ad ea quae sunt supra rationem humanam* non assentit per intellectum nisi quia vult. [For humans do not assent *to those things which are above human reason* through the intellect unless because they want to] (*De Virtutibus in communi*, q. 1, a. 7).

It is thus not exactly because I *believe* (as I *believe* in the existence of Peking or of Timbuktu), but because I believe in *a supernatural given* that a determinate influence of the will is necessary.

In addition let me point out that this influence of the appetite can [19] be unconscious, that it can be habitual, that it can be social as well as individual, and can have charmed intelligence so well that intelligence takes as a demonstration what is only plausible, that it can be solidified into blinding prejudices (individual, communal, national). Aquinas does not deny that one could show him a heretic who believes to have rigorously proved the truth of Christianity (in the same way that he does not deny that there are Catholics who believe they have a true certainty of the Catholic truth independently of any influence of the will). Subjective certainty is not in question.

The only thing that matters here is that for anybody who does not see the supernatural being through a supernaturalized[20] intelligence, the assent to Christian faith only has in principle the value of an *opinion*.[21] What the heretic believes, he believes, according to Aquinas, *ex aestimatione* [from estimation] ... *ex ratione humana* [from human reason]... *per aestimationem humanam* [through human estimation] (3 d. 23, q. 3, a. 3, sol. 2 and ad 1.). As we know the word *aestimatio* [estimation] designates in Aquinas an act of human reason that does not give the true certainty as science and as faith do.

Aquinas ventures to compare this human "estimation" that makes the heretic adhere [20] to his perverted Christianity to the estimation that makes pagans adhere to their fables. In heresy one believes in Christianity in the same way as outside Christianity one believes in mythology:

---

20   The French text says "surturalisée," which we take to be a typo for "surnaturalisée" (Translators' note).

21   The same holds for hope as for faith. There is no need for a heavenly help in order to make a silly presupposition. A child does not need grace to want the moon. Similarly grace is not needed for making mistakes. Without grace one can stubbornly adhere to Islam or be satisfied by an insufficient demonstration one gives of Christianity (founded for example on a false miracle or a flawed reasoning). Aquinas denies nothing like this when he establishes the necessity of theologal virtues and writes: "Habere fidem et spem de his quae subduntur humanae potestati, deficit a ratione virtutis. Sed habere fidem et spem de his quae sunt supra facultatem naturae humanae excedit omnem virtutem homini proportionatam" [Having faith and hope in those things which are subject to human power falls short in the nature of virtue. But having faith and hope in those things which are above the capacity of human nature exceeds all virtue proportionate to a human] (*Summa theologiae* 1a 2ae, q. 62, a. 3, ad 2). What he wants is that natural faculties be necessary for the acts of loving, hoping, believing to have their sincerity, truth, and legitimacy. Now the legitimacy of the act of believing is its objective certainty. That is why divine light is no less necessary to certain faith than the presentation of truths. In the above mentioned article he says in this regard: "Quantum ad intellectum adduntur homini quaedam principia supernaturalia, *quae divino lumine capiuntur*; et haec sunt credibilia, de quibus est fides ..." [In regard to the intellect, certain supernatural principles are added to the human *which are grasped by a divine light*. And these are the things to be believed about which faith is concerned] (*loc. cit.* in corp.).

Quod haereticus aliqua credat quae supra naturalem cognitionem sunt, non est ex aliquo habitu infuso... sed ex quadam aestimatione humana; sicut pagani aliqua supra naturam de Deo credunt. [The fact that the heretic believes some things which are beyond natural cognition is not from any infused habit ... but from a kind of human estimation; just as pagans believe some things beyond nature about God] (*De Veritate*, q. 14, a. 10, ad 10).

He writes further:

Formalis ratio objecti in fide est veritas prima, per doctrinam Ecclesiae manifestata; sicut formalis ratio scientiae est medium demonstrationis: et ideo, sicut aliquis memorialiter tenens conclusiones geometricas, non habet geometriae scientiam, si non propter media geometriae eis assentiatur, sed habebit conclusiones illas tanquam *opinatas*; ita, qui tenet ea quae sunt fidei, et non assentit eis propter auctoritatem catholicae doctrinae, non habet habitum fidei... Ex quo patet, quod qui deficit in uno articulo pertinaciter, non habet fidem de aliis articulis: illam dico fidem quae est habitus infusus; sed oportet quod teneat ea quae sunt fidei, quasi *opinata* .... [The formal reason of the object of faith is the first truth, manifested by the doctrine of the Church; just as the formal reason of knowledge is the means of demonstration. And thus just as someone holding geometrical conclusions in memory does not have a knowledge of geometry, since this person does not assent to them on account of the means of geometry, but instead will possess those conclusions as *supposed*; so too someone who holds those things which are of faith and does not assent to them on account of the authority of Catholic doctrine, does not possess the habit of faith ... From which it appears that someone who is persistently lacking in one article does not have faith in the other articles (I speak of that faith which is an infused habit); but it is proper that such a one would hold the things that are of faith as *supposed*.] (*De Caritate*, a. 13, ad 6).

As in one of the texts quoted above Aquinas affirms here the necessity of the infused faculty in order to grasp in the proposed object the formal reason of *dictum a veritate prima* [(what is) said by the first truth]. One who admits this cannot acknowledge any consistency in the "scientific faith" or the "natural faith" of modern theologians. Aquinas also calls acquired faith *opinio fortificata rationibus* [an opinion strengthened with reasons] (*Prol. Sent.* a. 3, sol. 3).

One can easily understand with this doctrine that Aquinas does not present the perception of credibility as the fruit of a rational demonstration that would precede the act of believing, but that he believes the perception of credibility to have been produced by the light of faith (*Summa theologiae* 2a 2ae q. 1, a. 5, ad 1, see a. 4, ad 3; q. 2, a. 9, ad 3; *Quodlibetum* 2, a. 6; see *Recherches*, 1910, no. 3, p. 254).

Here is another consideration. Aquinas does not grant that besides the case of divine revelation, a human being could know with certainty that he has charity. We always run the risk, [21] he believes, of mistaking a natural sentiment for a supernatural act of love coming from God. But he teaches us on the other hand that we can be certain of having faith. Thus, it seems that he does not admit the possibility of a natural faith that we could confuse with infused faith. Without this, his reasoning would be overturned. Here are the texts.

And first the difference affirmed between the two cases:

> De ratione scientiae est quod homo certitudinem habeat de his quorum habet scientiam; et similiter de ratione fidei est quod homo sit certus de his quorum habet fidem; et hoc ideo, quia certitudo pertinent ad perfectionem intellectus, in quo praedicta dona existunt. Et ideo quicumque habet scientiam, vel fidem, certus est se habere. Non est autem similis ratio de gratia et caritate, et aliis huius modi, quae perficiunt vim appetitivam. [It is of the nature of knowledge that humans would have certainty of those things of which they have knowledge; and similarly it is of the nature of faith that humans would be certain of those things of which they have faith. And this is the case then because certainty pertains to the perfection of the intellect wherein the aforementioned gifts exist. And hence whoever has knowledge or faith is certain of having them. But the nature of grace and charity is not also similar to other things of this kind which perfect the appetitive faculty] (*Summa theologiae* 1a 2ae, q. 112, a. 5, ad 2).[22]

Here is the reason given for charity:

> Non oportet quod certitudinaliter percipiatur (caritas); quia actus ille dilectionis quem in nobis percipimus secundum id de quo est

---

22 Rousselot incorrectly lists this as *Summa theologiae* 1a 2ae q. 12 a. 5, ad 2. Translators' note.

perceptibile, non est sufficiens signum caritatis, propter similitudinem naturalis dilectionis[23] ad gratuitam. [It is not necessary that it
(charity) be perceived with certainty; for this act of love which we
perceive in ourselves according to that whereby it is perceptible, is
not an adequate sign of charity, on account of similitude between
natural and gratuitous love.] (*De Veritate*, q. 10, a. 10, ad 1).

Against those testimonies and reasonings it would be vain to mention the passages where Aquinas proclaims the [22] perfect rationability [*rationabilité*] of Christian faith, the objective sufficiency of
history and miracles in order to establish the foundation of Christian
faith. There is not a shadow of an opposition between all this and the
absolute necessity of the light of grace: these signs of the supernatural
world are, on the contrary, like the colors susceptible of being illuminated by this light, according to the general theory of intellective
light and formal object.

Only one text may seem to represent a serious objection to the
interpretation I propose of the Thomist doctrine. It can be found in
the article on the faith of demons (*Summa theologiae* 2a 2ae, q. 5, a.
2:

Intellectus credentis assentit rei creditae, non quia ipsam videat vel
secundum se, vel per resolutionem ad prima principia per se visa,

---

23 The natural love [*dilection*] the text mentions here is not, following
Aquinas's principles, a natural love of God above all. Aquinas believes that
the will of the fallen man left to his own powers is incapable of such a
love. It can then only be an incomplete and imaginary love which conceals
a streak of subtle self-love [amour-propre] in a non-believing philosopher
or covers over with a fragile appearance the internal void opened up by
the loss of charity in a fallen Christian (See *De Veritate*, q. 17, a. 1, ad 4
in contr.: "Ex actibus infusae caritatis generatur aliquis habitus dilectionis,
vel praeexistens augmentatur" [A certain habit of love is produced from
acts of infused charity, or a preexisting habit is strengthened]. Once charity has vanished, this habituation [*accoutumance*] that Charity sustained by
incorporating it into itself ceases to be a "habitus,' loses its consistency and
solidity. It is no longer anything except an external trace and as it were a
prolongation of mechanical movement, a "disposition on the way to cor-
ruption," similar to those dispositions for evil left by the vicious habits in
the recently justified sinner (See Aquinas, *Summa theologiae* 1a 2ae, q. 95, a.
3, ad 2; *De Virtutibus Cardinalibus*, a. 2, ad 2, a. 3, ad 12; *De Virtutibus in
communi*, a. 10, ad 16).

sed propter imperium voluntatis. Quod autem voluntas moveat intellectum ad assentiendum, potest contingere ex duobus: uno modo ex ordine voluntatis ad bonum, et sic credere est actus laudabilis; alio modo quia intellectus convincitur ad hoc quod iudicet esse credentum his quae dicuntur, licet non convincatur per evidentiam rei; sicut aliquis propheta praenuntiaret in sermone Domini aliquid futurum, et adhiberet signum, mortuum suscitando, ex hoc signo convinceretur intellectus videntis, ut cognosceret manifeste hoc dici a Deo, qui non mentitur.... [The intellect of the believer assents to the thing believed, not because it sees it either according to itself or by its resolution to first principles seen through themselves, but on account of the command of the will. Now the fact that the will moves the intellect to assent could be due to two things. In one way through the order of the will to the good, and so to believe is a praiseworthy act. In the other way because the intellect is convinced for the reason that it judges of those things which are said ought to be believed, although it is not convinced by the evidence of the thing. Just as if some prophet would have foretold in a sermon on the Lord something about the future and made use of a sign by raising the dead, the intellect of a witness would be convinced by this sign such that the witness would clearly recognize this to be said by God who does not lie.]

Three remarks needs to be made:

1) The example Aquinas mentioned here of a faith that is absolutely certain, but not produced by the love of good in the will, is not an example of an intrinsically supernatural truth. *Aliquid futurum* [something about the future], Aquinas simply says. Now, as I claimed above, the supernatural essence of the object of Christian preaching is what makes this object inaccessible to naked reason. Here, Aquinas abstracts from the diverse states in which human condition can find itself and, given his object in this article, he did not have to deal with it. The example helps us understand the faith of demons. It leaves untouched the question of the faith of human beings.

2) It is possible moreover (and this has been already indicated in a previous article) through a close examination of the way Aquinas [23] conceives the faith of devils to draw interesting inferences about his general conception of the relation between intelligence and the will. The faith of demons is all at once a faith that is compelled and voluntary. It is compelled: this is what is said by the words *convincitur*

[is convinced] (corp.), *quodammodo coacta* [in a certain way forced] (ad. 1), *magis coguntur* [rather they are forced] (ad. 2), *ut compellantur* [that they are compelled] (ad. 3). It is *voluntary*: this is what is indicated by the general affirmation which dominates the whole article: "Quod voluntas moveat intellectum ad assentiendum potest contingere ex duobus...." [The fact that the will moves the intellect to assent could be due to two things]. Thus, the sufficiency, the *evidence* of the signs which the author here concedes does not suppress the necessity of a certain voluntary disposition, but this voluntary disposition does not seem to be in the power of the subject. The subject does not seem able to escape it. Now, according to Thomist theology, there is a voluntary disposition which has as it were passed into nature in demons. It is the *aversio a Deo* [aversion to God], the definite hatred of God. One is thus naturally led to say, according to the analogy of the Thomist doctrine, that the voluntary repulsion toward the supernatural produces the same effect of clearsightedness in demons as the loving acceptance of the same supernatural produces in believers (See *Recherches*, 1910, no. 5, p. 475). One may ask: "But could there not be in a human who is still a wayfarer an invincible conviction of faith of the same kind, an experiential certainty, hating and quasi-diabolic, that is to say through repulsion and not through attraction?[24] There would then be faith without good will." One can concede this hypothesis without detriment to what I defend: it would always remain that this certainty would be the effect of a grace, but under which the human being would struggle, instead of collaborating with it. God, infinite truth, would struggle with him through mercy in the same way that He oppresses demons through justice.

3) If one objects that nothing is lacking in assent, neither the intelligence of the terms nor the uncertainty of the connection, one would have to answer, as I already did (*Recherches*, 1910, no. 5, [24] p. 474), that there is no subject able to see, no faculty capable of operating the synthesis and that then everything is lacking. We here touch on the most fundamental postulate of the dualist theory, a

---

24   As a curiosity of this kind, see the case of Balaam discussed in the *Miscellaneae* by Scotus (Q. 6, no. 9: *An prophetia sit libera* [Whether prophecy is free], vol. V, p. 409).

postulate which is of a philosophical order. All the texts by Aquinas I quoted would, I think, leave no serious doubt in anybody's mind if a great number of people were not persuaded, by the habit of a theory of knowledge wholly immersed in the object, forgetful of the intellectual activity and of the *lumen* [light], that by renouncing a natural faith that is certain, they would sacrifice the rationability [*rationabilité*] of faith itself.[25]

After the 13th century the Scotist theory of faith did not take long to insinuate itself little by little, creeping even into Aquinas's school. Capreolus, "the prince of the Thomists" in the 15th century is rather close to Scotus, but not yet with him. He denies that acquired faith suffices to make one believe "perfecto et discreto assensu, et consimili assensui fidei infusae... discrete, prompte, firmiter, delectabiliter" [with a perfect and distinct assent, and similar to the assent of infused faith ... distinctly, promptly, firmly, delightfully] (3, d. 24, q. 1, Tours edition, 1904, vol. V, p. 316, 318). Cajetan goes further and admits the possibility and the objective certainty of both faiths ... I have given elsewhere (*Recherches* 1910, no. 3, p. 245, n. 1) some references to contemporary theologians; it would be easy as well as useless to multiply them.

It is not the case that no effort was made in the School to escape this naturalization of supernatural knowledge to which the Scotist opinion seems to lead, which is, besides, in such a bad harmony with experience and which seems to sacrifice the freedom of faith to its certainty.[26] Two ways of escape in particular were attempted. The [25] first attempt consists in negating the strict demonstrability of the fact of revelation in order to preserve a place for the will. This

---

25　In the *Dictionnaire de théologie*, art. *Crédibilité*, col. 2275-2276 one can see the reasons Fr. Gardeil gives to prove that Aquinas taught the demonstrability of the truth of faith through reason alone.

26　This drawback had little effect on a certain number of modern Scholastics, who are so preoccupied with exalting the rationality of faith that "compared to this primordial interest," "the difficulty of bringing the freedom of the act of faith into full light" seems to them "secondary," as one of them wrote to me. I confess that I cannot enter into this manner of approaching theological questions. The Church defined both the freedom of the act of faith and its rationability [*rationabilité*]: we have no right to give a preferential treatment to one of them at the expense of the other.

is what Lugo attempted. But it should not be believed that these theologians acknowledge thereby the necessity of grace, or, to put it otherwise, the physical powerlessness of natural reason to reach on this point a true certainty. For by negating the *evidence* of the demonstration of credibility, they usually add that the proofs one can elicit exclude *prudent doubt,* which they understand as even natural prudence. This leads them sometimes to declare expressly that such an assent, which is fully reasonable, does not surpass of itself natural powers. The second attempt is the very interesting, although insufficiently clarified, theory of Suarez. Suarez saw that in the case of the simple, grace can be an operator of certainty without a miracle.[27] He did not venture to generalize this explanation to the point of rejecting natural faith that is certain, but he made a step in this direction when he claimed that this natural faith does not have the authority of God for its formal motive.[28] The transformed Suarezian explanation has become nowadays the theory of the faith of homage.

One can only find in modern theologians fleeting reminders and traces of the doctrine of Aquinas, which rigorously requires grace either in order to believe or in order to see that one has to believe. Nevertheless, they do not impose any theological censure on it when they mention it. Still they do not seriously discuss the philosophical prejudice which put almost all of them beforehand in Scotus' camp by preventing them even from clearly conceiving the thought of their opponents. One can read for example in Gonet [26] (*Clipeus theologiae thomisticae,* tract. 8, de Gratia, disp. 1, art. 2, par. III, n. 97. Antwerp, 1744, vol. IV, p. 27):

---

27   *De Fide*, disp. 4, sect. 5, n. 9-10.

28   Ibid., disp. 6, sect. 7, no. 7 "Duobus modis possunt credi res fidei. Primo resolvendo assensum in externa vel signa credibilitatis, tanquam in rationem credendi, *et ad hoc genus fidei sufficere potest voluntas naturalis,* quia non transcendit fidem acquisitam, neque certitudinem humanam. Alius modus credendi est, pure sistendo in auctoritate divina, *et ad hunc modum dicimus esse necessarium voluntatem supernaturalem ...*" [The things of faith can be believed in two ways. First by fixing the assent on external things or signs of credibility, as it were on the reason for believing, *and the natural will can suffice for this kind of faith* because it does not go beyond acquired faith, nor human certainty. The other way of believing is by standing purely on divine authority, *and I hold that the supernatural will is necessary for this way*] (See disp. 3 sect. 12).

Addunt aliqui, praedicta concilia [Trident. et Arausic., ut notum est]... addere verba illa sicut oportet ut indicent, posse quidem hominem PER SOLAS NATURAE VIRES assentiri veritatibus fidei sibi exterius propositis ASSENSU QUODAM OPINATIVO, ita ut ratio propter quam illis assentitur, non sit divina revelatio, sed motivum aliquod PROBABILE, ut in haereticis contingere cernimus; NON TAMEN ASSENSU CERTO EST INFALLIBILI, auctoritati et veracitati Dei revelantis innixo, qualis requiritur ad justificationem. [Some add to the aforementioned councils (Trent and Arausica, as was noted) ... adding these words that they indicate, *as it is necessary.* Indeed a human BY THE POWERS OF NATURE ALONE could assent to the truths of faith themselves exteriorly to the propositions WITH A KIND OF CONJECTURAL ASSENT, so that the reason on account of which one assents to these things, is not divine revelation, but some PROBABLE motive, as we see happening in heretics. THIS IS NOT, HOWEVER, WITH A CERTAIN INFALLIBLE ASSENT, resting on the authority and veracity of the revealing God, as is required for justification].[29]

IV

Let us cross three centuries and leave the School. From Lugo and Suarez we move to Newman.[30] It may seem that we enter a new world.[31] Still, the opposition between dualist theory and organic

---

29　Saying this means to exclude "certain natural faith" or "scientific faith." In other words, it means to affirm that the only fully certain and fully reasonable faith is supernatural faith (whether it is formed faith or unformed faith). I am surprised that the author of remarks on "Les yeux de la foi," published in *Civiltà cattolica* of August 5, 1911 (*Rassegna Teologica*, pp. 330-333) constantly considered as new in the School this safe opinion. The same censor attributes to me as an expression of my own thought, and puts it even in quotation marks, as if reproducing my words, this assertion: "Sembra che si debba rinunziare al fondamento scientifico della fede" [It would seem that one would have to renounce the scientific foundation of faith]. This expression leads readers to believe that, in my view, faith should not be founded on reason. Now, this is precisely the mistake I fight in my essay and the words alleged as mine are not found there.

30　Rousselot uses the English edition of Newman and quotes him in English. Translators' note.

31　It would, however, be a grave mistake to believe that Newman did not study and appreciate the Scholastics's discussions on the act of faith, especially in the Scholastics of the last centuries. As is well known, Amort

theory makes up so much of the vital [27] and natural core of the treatise *De Fide* that we will find it again at the heart of the difficulties raised regarding the Newmanian conception of faith. Everybody feels that this theory is admirable and that it is incomplete. The idea I attempted to bring to the fore will maybe help us understand why it is admirable and why it is incomplete.

"We believe because we love. How plain a truth!"[32] Why then do several people who were not shocked by even more imperious formulations of Aquinas who says exactly the same thing (*Voluntas imperat intellectui, credendo* [In believing the will commands the intellect], and others), feel a sort of defiance or uneasiness when reading these things in Newman? Because they fear that this motor causality of love in the act of faith does not let subsist in his doctrine the objective causality of the reasons for belief; because they fear that if love has for its essential role *to color* the demonstration (as Newton says in his own terms), reason finds itself more seduced than convinced,

---

is quoted with honor in the *Grammar of Assent*. Several letters of Newman recently published by Ward in his great *Life* testify to a similar appreciation for other Scholastic authors, in particular for Perrone and Lugo. "They take," he writes about the Roman theological milieu in 1847, "a broad *sensible* shrewd view of reason and faith" (*Op. cit.,* vol. 1, p. 172). And eleven years later, when speaking of the problem of speculative certainty in vital questions: "When I came to read catholic theology, I found that it was solved in a way which I felt to be satisfactory." This is followed by the distinction between complete (and direct) proof and proof of credibility (p. 442, See vol. II, p. 276). See also the letter, dated from Rome in 1846, where he explains that in his thought *probable* is opposed to *demonstrative*, and not to *certain* (vol. I, p. 168-69. See p. 249). In order to be complete it should not be overlooked that he further wrote: "At least one Jesuit attacked me as a probabilist in doctrine, though I am not conscious of dreaming of being one; and certainly I should be afraid that I might say things which, though distinctly contained in de Lugo, are contrary to the tone of the day" (p. 248). These last words recall recent complaints by Fr. Gardeil. Nevertheless Newman never found himself enough at home in Scholastic theology so as to take the tone of a professional. "Ward and Faber, as well as myself," he wrote, "never had a course of theology" (He means a complete course. Ward, vol. II, p. 104, note). He acutely felt the difficulty of keeping a perfect balance when treating theological subjects: "To write theology is like dancing on the tight rope some hundred feet above the ground ..." (Ibid., p. 125).

32 *Oxford University Sermons,* sermon XII, no. 20.

and that in this way the reasonable character of faith would be compromised. They admire—and who would not admire it?—the subtle Newmanian psychology. They suspect his theory of faith to be fideism.[33] I believe [28] that even if he is sometimes unfair to the believer's reason or the reasons for belief, the reason for that is that Neumann did not push with enough rigor and consistency his fundamental principle of the necessity of love.

The Newmanian theory of faith essentially consists in saying that an antecedent spiritual sympathy is what allows human beings to interpret in the affirmative sense the proofs of religion. But this can be understood in two ways. If we understand this sympathy simply as a natural refinement of moral life, however exquisite, however delicate one may wish, one is exposed to the peril of taking a complacency for a certainty and the agreeable for the true. Moreover, the supernatural character of adherence disappears or becomes extrinsic again. If this sympathy is the effect of faith, one still has to show how this grace heals reason itself, and how then the sympathy in question, instead of simply changing the habits of the soul, causes the soul to move properly from the state of blindness to the state of clearsightedness, and so justifies the change in the eyes of reason.

Toward which one of these two interpretations would Newman be inclined? The notes that he added [29] to his most suggestive

---

33 "Because he was a dogmatist of blind faith and feared reason, Newman had to construct a theology where faith and reason would be two distinct faculties, without any compenetration, reason being always kept on leash. He had to construct an apologetics where the intellectual reasons for belief would be without essential import..." (E. Baudin, *La philosophie de la foi chez Newman*, p. 33). As is well known Leclère is even harsher: "Relativism, individualism are at the heart of Newman's doctrine like humanism and naturalism; whether we like it or regret it, they are there" (*Pragmatisme, modernisme, protestantisme*, p. 100). This judgment seems to me absolutely unfair. Traces of relativism and individualism can be found not *at the heart* of Newmanian doctrine, but at its outbuildings and surroundings; or, without metaphors, not at his fundamental intuition, but at the learned philosophy he used as a means of expression. With regard to the latter two "isms" [humanism and naturalism. Translators' note], either they are put there simply as logical consequence of the former two "isms" [relativism and individualism. Translators' note] or I have absolutely no idea what the author means when using them about Newman.

sermons[34] after his conversion show that he liked to compare his *antecedent sympathy* with the *pius affectus credendi* [pious affection of believing]. Besides, I do not recall that he ever affirms the possibility of a faith that would be absolutely non-voluntary. Even where he concedes that Christian faith is demonstrable, he is careful to observe that this demonstration is not irresistible.[35] On the other hand, the overly narrow conception he formed of "reason" prevented him from clearly seeing the real identity of *intellectual perception* which is required by theology, with *anticipation,* which is wholly penetrated with love and which he so well described. This appears with evidence from the opposition he establishes between "presumption" (the effect of antecedent sympathy) and "proof": *He goes so far as to contrast* "the impression legitimately made upon the mind by facts" *with the coloration that the spontaneous anticipation of the right heart places on it.*[36]

34　In the sermon already quoted, the notes of pages 224 and 236, published by Longmans, 1900.

35　*Grammar of Assent,* p. 410: "Truth, certainly, as such, rests upon grounds intrinsically and objectively and abstractly demonstrative, but it does not follow from this that the arguments producible in its favour are unanswerable and irresistible... The fact of revelation is in itself demonstrably true, but it is not therefore true irresistibly...," etc. This passage on the possibility of demonstration (See p. 411: "Let those demonstrate who have the gift") is suitable for reassuring those who would be frightened by the passages where the "cumulative" and "transcending" probability seems proposed as the only way (*Apologia,* p. 199). But neither in the case of strict demonstration, nor of certainty arising from probabilities, is the conviction of the truth of Christianity, according to Newman, independent of the will. Against scientific faith and the dualist theory, see also *Oxford University Sermons,* X, 12 (p. 182).

36　"To maintain that Faith is a judgment about facts in matters of conduct, such as to be formed, not so much from the impression legitimately made upon the mind by those facts, as from the reaching forward of the mind itself towards them—that it is a presumption, not a proving—may sound paradoxical, yet surely is borne out by the actual state of things as they come before us every day" (*Loc. cit.,* no. 5, p. 224). For me, on the contrary, to be legitimately impressed by moral and religious facts is nothing else than to interpret them as signs of the truth of Christianity. If Newman had only wanted to oppose the greatest subjective activity of the mind in faith to the relative passivity of reason toward "proofs" (for example, mathematical), which leave no room for freedom, then I would be fully in

Besides, in all of [30] the descriptions he gives of the state of the soul that is well disposed for faith, he hardly speaks of pious *moral* dispositions.[37] One does not see clearly, it seems, that there is a rectification of reason itself, which was blind before and now sees things in their *true* essence; one does not recognize at first glance this grace of faith, which, according to Catholic theology, "perfects intelligence." Here and there God seems to play, so to speak, with very diverse dispositions of good souls, directing their imagination in such a way that in the end they happen to meet with the truth. I know it would be a true injustice to take these passages and to leave aside their correctives. But the correction always seems a little bit *extrinsic*, as if it were through the will again that Newman would resolve to recognize a serious value to reason.[38]

To be sure, all of this is not said to downplay the charm and the seriousness of Newmanian psychology. On the contrary, I would like to bring to the fore the *theological* suggestive value of so many immortal passages, to which I am indebted to a large extent for the theory expounded in this work. But for the doctrine that makes a spiritual sympathy the operator of the assent of faith to appear and be in fact absolutely without danger, one has to push it to its limit. One [31] has to give to the psychological observation its rigorous and intransigent theological expression. It is not enough to describe with a marvelous sensibility this secret *connaturality* that in advance puts the subject in unison with Christian truth. One has to call by its true name the soul which animates it and which is the grace of Jesus Christ. One has to say this frankly: If the light of Grace were

---

agreement with him. But the contrast between "reaching forward" and the "impression legitimately made" can hardly be reduced to that.

37   "Faith is a test of man's heart ... it shows what he thinks likely to be and what he thinks likely depends surely on nothing else than the general state of his mind, the state of his convictions, feelings, tastes, and wishes" (Serm. XII, already quoted, no. 7, p. 226). See also (Ibid., no. 35, p. 248): "That whole body of opinion, affection and desire, which made up, in each man, his moral self..."

38   If he once affirms the existence of a "dead faith," which is *fides formata ratione, non caritate* [a faith formed by reason, not charity] (*Oxford University sermons*, X, 37), he strongly opposes elsewhere the duplication of living faith in an act of reason and a supernatural act (Ibid., XI, 1).

not there, all the most exquisite refinements of the moral life would not raise the assent to Christian truth beyond an uncertain opinion. As long as we have not stated this, we can be accused of violating the intangible candor of intelligence, and of wanting to substitute the interested biases of the heart for the views of reason. But when we have called by its true name the habit which truly sympathizes the soul with the truth, and which is the Grace of Christ, healing of intelligence, we can also easily see what natural and normal role the exterior proofs play in the genesis of faith; and we do not run the risk anymore of making of these proofs superadded parts that are tacked onto his system because they are required by the documents of the magisterium, but remain outside the real economy of thought.

One more word on the subject of Newman. Where is the cause of this important lacuna, or to put it better, of this incompleteness of his theory of faith? It seems to me to lie in his disdain[39] for technical speculations, especially those pertaining to the theory of knowledge. When reading the *Grammar of Assent* one can only be struck by the sporadic character of his references to great philosophers, who to a great extent in a way treated the same problem. One ceases to be a philosopher, to be sure, to the extent that one is interested in the opinions of people instead of dealing directly with things; but to show little interest in what specialists have said is to expose oneself either to [32] rediscovering America or to misunderstanding secret connections and the deep meaning of the most precious elements one discovers. Such an indifference has its price, and Newman paid the price. Regardless of what a superficial anti-intellectualism thinks about it, *to systematize is to deepen* when the system is not arbitrary, because it means seeing things as they are, not as isolated but as connected. The 19th century philosophy could have offered Newman great assistance for a technical, philosophical,[40] and theological sys-

---

39 On this lack of curiosity, see Bremond, *Newman, essai de biographie psychologique*, p. 102. The judgment of Bremond about Newman's youth is to be tempered by the testimony of T.-A. Froude in Ward, vol. 1, p. 62.

40 A remarkable letter to Henry Wilberforce (Ward, vol. II, p. 249) sheds an interesting light on what could have been the central idea of *Grammar of Assent*. Newman glimpses the fact that there is in the mechanism of all judgments something similar to what takes place in Aristotle's φρόνιμος: a certain concrete appreciation of the suitability of judgment to be pronounced

tematization of his theories of knowledge and faith. Perhaps he could have discovered at the end of his work the coincidence of his spiritual sympathy with the connaturality toward the truths of faith that grace brings about in the soul, according to the doctrine of Aquinas.

Let us end with a perfectly beautiful and accurate statement of the great cardinal: "Faith," he wrote, "is a venture before a man is a Catholic, it is a grace after it."[41]

V

I have had several occasions to quote in this work a theologian far removed from Newman and very harsh toward [33] him, Fr. Gardeil. I mentioned him in particular among the proponents of rational credibility in the strict sense, his assertions on this point being very clear (*Recherches* 1910, no. 3, p. 245, note). These assertions are, moreover, all the more remarkable that he emphasizes rather the "subjective substitutes" [*suppléances*] for credibility and especially the supernatural substitutes. Unfortunately, as I felt obliged to point out (*ibid.* p. 250 n.), he seems to consider too greatly this assistance as destined in general less *to make us see* than to *dispense us from seeing*. Gardeil has just published (1912) a new revised edition of his *Credibilité*.[42] While he mentions there some of my essays which only have a remote connection with the problem of the act of faith, he overlooks my articles of 1910. Nobody he says (p. xvii) reproached him for the too narrowly measured place of grace in his book of 1908. Now, the whole orientation of the work has changed felicitously and

---

by the subject. What assistance would have been furnished to him by the comparison with, on the one hand, the judgments *by connaturality* of Aquinas (the judgment by faith belongs to this category) and, on the other, the Kantian explanation of the perception of the beautiful, in order to draw a deepened and coherent theory from this intuition! *Das Vermögen durch eine Lust zu urteilen* [The power to judge through a desire]: this is the notion that would have allowed Kant to provide an expressed realist interpretation of his criticism and to spare himself the irrational moralism of the practical reason. This is the notion that reconciles the strict demands of objective truth with the partially appetitive character that knowledge always has in every potential subject.

41 *Loss and Gain*, p. 385.

42 *La crédibilité et l'apologétique.* Second edition. Gabalda, 1912. In-12, p XX-332.

the supernatural preparation takes first stage, and rightly so. However, despite some restrictions he still maintains the possibility of a "scientific faith" which would be purely natural and founded on an entirely rational judgment of credibility (See p. XIII-XVII, 37-38, 42, 51ff, 63, 65[43]). How is it that a theologian who is so independent of modern prejudices and so possessed, if I may say so, by the great theses of Aquinas, how is it that such a clearsighted opponent of the supernatural *quoad modum* [in regard to the mode], of the supernatural that is *tacked on*, still keeps this *morsel of Scotism* in his synthesis? Here again one can discern the *philosophical* prejudice. Fr. Gardeil seems to forget that in the intellective act, the causality of *light* (which belongs to the subject) cannot be counted alongside the causality of the notes which are perceived in the object and cannot thus be *opposed* to it. He seems to believe that to affirm the subjective necessity [34] of the light of grace would mean to deny the full objective sufficiency of the motives of credibility.[44] This philosophical inaccuracy, which weakens the whole doctrine of subjective substitutes, very sufficiently accounts for the repugnances it caused and for the fact that it seemed to render uncertain the rational foundation of faith among the uneducated, or more exactly among almost all human beings. If, on the contrary, we say that the light of grace, when falling on a sign which in the eyes of natural reason is only probable, makes of it an instrument of certain assent, then we realize that the

---

43　"Rational credibility is, as indicated by its name, and as I have already said, *naturally knowable*" (p. 65). And p. 51: "At the close of the council..., natural belief in the extrinsic truth of the proposed assertion: *this is scientific faith.*"

44　Regarding the"supernatural excitations which command the genesis of the act according to the Second Council of Orange and Augustine," we read in a note on p. 233: "To conclude that (the Catholic demonstration) owes its efficacy toward credibility only to these supernatural substitutes, and that rational arguments by themselves do not have the force of a demonstration, this is neither in the Fathers nor in the theologians nor, I may add, in Holy Scripture." Here we find a "by themselves" which marvelously betrays the latent postulate of the whole doctrine. Still the author knows fully well that rational arguments never have the force of a demonstration "by themselves," but only in conjunction with the intellectual light of a subject. What should this light be so that such a category of objects be illuminated? That is the question.

faith of the uneducated can be *intellectually as certain* while being *rationally less communicable* than the faith of the educated, and that there are not just five or six in the Church who possess reasons for belief that are objectively valid.[45] Before deriding as naïve and candid those who say that the legitimate motives for believing are always certain,[46] Gardeil could have examined whether those who speak in this manner did not have a more organic conception of the relationships between subject and object than he did. Every formal object is the correlate of a certain power of the subject. A sign that is merely probable for a [35] weak intelligence can be a sign that is certain for a strong intelligence. Similarly, an ambiguous sign for natural reason can be a very reliable sign of what is true for supernaturalized reason. The sign has not changed, but the subject has been raised. *Unus alio rem unam limpidius intellegere potest!* [One person can understand one thing more clearly than another]. When speaking of proofs of religion that are valid "in themselves," is it not arbitrary to understand *a priori* this "in themselves" in the sense of: "for the wounded reason"?[47]

---

45   But then these substitutes cannot be called any longer "the motives of subjective origin," which could ward off obstacles and facilitate adherence, but which were powerless to legitimate it adequately" (p. 319). And in order to reach full rationability one does not feel compelled to transform them into *objects*, into *seen reasons* (Ibid.).

46   *La certitude probable*, in *Revue des sciences philosophiques et théologiques*, April 1911, p. 237.

47   In the present state of humanity every reason that is not supernaturalized is a wounded reason, and there is no pure natural reason. But it may be that the opposition between the two theories of faith, the organic and the extrinsic, does not manifest itself to the eye more vividly than in the solution of the scholarly question: *Whether God could have revealed the Trinity to man left in the state of pure nature* (See in vol. V of Scotus' works Q. VI of the Miscellaneae no. 6, p. 407, and also the Q. *de Cognitione Dei*, p. 318). It is clear that the Scotist principles command the affirmative answer and the Thomist principles the negative answer. Let us note that those who concede the hypothesis confess that God indeed would not have done this without modifying in some way the last end of man, because God does not make anything useless. By an extrinsic principle they thus reach the same conclusion as those who deny it and who think, by starting from the very notion of truth and intellection, that if God reveals this mystery, the fact

I would be more inclined to insist on what brings me closer to Fr. Gardeil than on what separates me from him. One has to welcome happily the book of a theologian of such authority as a sign of the need that emerges in more than one way to see grace play the role it deserves in the theology of faith. After a long discussion about the play of natural causalities, it is not enough to *affirm* the reality of the role of grace, either to apply the glaze of the supernatural on the natural act or to abandon to the Holy Spirit the cases an ingenious psychology has found stubborn. One has to *explain* that grace can make us see and how it can make us see. But then is it enough to say: "I assumed as known the psychological theory of the influence of the dispositions of the subject on the character of the object"? In good faith I do not think so. [36] Fr. Gardeil[48] does not think so either, since he gives us so many scholarly explanations of the role played by the attractions [*attraits*]. For, if we are concerned with the vulgar *psychological* description, this leaves untouched the question of the *legitimacy* of such an influence, and this is a capital question in matters of faith. If we are concerned with the Scholastic theory, later theologians often conceived it in a way that is too mechanical.[49] In Aquinas himself, despite some numerous symmetrical and very remarkable points of attraction, the Scholastic theory is still too little developed.

Because of the parallelism between supernatural and natural psychology, a parallelism Fr. Gardeil clearly brought to light,[50] there can be no progress in the theory of the act of faith without corresponding progress in the theory of the human act. The immanence of volition in intellection is in this respect one of the notions that most needs to be elucidated. That is why I have tried to utilize some precious notions made available by modern philosophy and pertaining to po-

---

of this revelation presupposes or puts in the human a certain *connaturality* which makes us *interested* in it and makes *true intellection* possible.

48　From whom I borrow this phrase, but by extracting it from the context of a particular discussion, which determined its import (See *Revue pratique d'apologétique*, November 1, 1908, Vol. VII, p. 183, note 1).

49　As is the case with John of St. Thomas quoted in my first article, p. 249, n. 2.

50　*La crédibilité*, 2nd edition, p. 6 and passim.

tentiality, appetivity, and the voluntary nature [*volontariété*] of all conceptual knowledge. The imperfection of my endeavor does not escape me; if it is only a useful sketch, it would already be something. Besides, regardless of the value or failure of this attempt, it remains absolutely distinct from the principle of the necessity of grace for all certain perception of the truth of Christianity, a principle on which all the disciples of Aquinas should come to an agreement. This agreement would be near on the day one had understood by which mechanism of transposition the theory of scientific faith was born, to which philosophical attitude it corresponds, and how its arising, which divided the history of faith into two sides, marks one of the most important moments of this history.

[1066] "INTELLECTUALISM"[1]

The word *intellectualism* was repeatedly mentioned in the religious controversies that resulted in the condemnation of Modernism; in the mouth of the innovators it was a term of reproach addressed to traditional philosophy and theology. For this reason the word found a place in the encyclical *Pascendi*;[2] for this reason also it must appear in this *Dictionnaire apologétique*.

Littré defined intellectualism as: "A metaphysical doctrine according to which everything in the universe is subordinate to intelligence" (*Dictionnaire*, Supplement, 1886, p. 202). In the philosophical and theological discussions of the last twenty years, the word has usually been taken in a special sense, generally pejorative, and which does not have a necessary connection with this first meaning, as we will see: it designated the doctrine, implicit or expressed, of *the universal competency and sufficiency of conceptual and discursive thought*; one could also say: *the doctrine that envisages all reality on the model of a 'thing,'* meaning by 'thing,' the proper object of the concept, what is seen just as it is when it is conceived (*ens concretum quidditati materiali* [a concrete being of material nature], in the Scholastic language).

[1067] Those who attack intellectualism in moral and religious matters thus attack a doctrine which would grant conceptual and discursive thought in moral and religious matters either an absolute sufficiency, or a competency they deem exaggerated. I will show in what sense the Catholic doctrine rejects intellectualism (I), in what sense it sanctions it (II), and in what sense it leaves it a matter of free debate (III).

The fragmentary character of my study will not be surprising, if we recall that the main aspects of this subject have already been considered elsewhere (see the articles on Agnosticism, God, Dogma, and Faith in *Dictionnaire apologétique de la foi catholique*). For the same

---

1 *Dictionnaire apologétique de la foi catholique.* Paris: Gabriel Beauchesne, 1911, v. II, cols. 1066-1081.

2 See *On the Doctrine of the Modernists*, Boston: St. Paul Books, 1980. Translators' note.

reason, this study will be resolutely and brazenly technical: it would have replicated the articles cited, if it had not aimed above all at showing what the position of Catholic doctrine is towards the modern critique of the concept and discourse; this essay thus constantly presupposes a reader already familiar with this critique. I added a preparatory Note where I tried to distinguish clearly the main meanings of the word "intellectualism" whose reckless use created and still often creates the most deplorable confusions.

A – The historians of Scholastic take the term "intellectualism" to designate the metaphysical doctrine according to which intellectual operation is the final end of the universe, and allows us to grasp absolute being, by allowing us to possess God in Heaven. In this sense Krebs writes in his study on Meister Dietrich (Theodorus Teutonicus) that "he expressly proclaims intellectualism as his conception of the world when he states: "Maxime et potissime est homo propter operationem, quae est intellectus per essentiam; igitur per ipsam talis intellectus operationem maxime et immediate habet homo uniri Deo in illa beatifica visione" [In the highest degree and above all the human exists on account of the operation which by its essence is of the intellect; therefore the human being through the very operation of such an intellect possesses in the highest degree and immediately the state of being united with God in the beatific vision] (Krebs, *Meister Dietrich, sein Leben, seine Werke, seine Wissenschaft*, in Baeumker, *Beiträge*. Münster: Aschendorff, v. 5-6, p. 78). See also Rousselot, *L'intellectualisme de saint Thomas*, p. IX and what follows; English translation, *Intelligence*, pp. 5-6, etc.). In this sense, Augustine is a great intellectualist, because he places the end of the human being in the vision of the Truth. Now, it is very important to note the following correlation: a philosophy can be dominated by the idea of subsisting and divine Intellection, which it takes as the measure of being, or by the idea of beatific and deified intellection, which it takes as the ideal model and the end of every intellection; the more this is so, the more also the natural movement of such a philosophy brings it to develop a severe and contemptuous critique of the forms of inferior intelligence, and particularly of *rational* intellection, which is proper here below for the human animal (*rational*, that is to say by abstract concepts and by discourse). This is a pattern of thought that the Scholastics and especially Aquinas did not fail to follow.

B.—When the word *intellectualism* is applied to the philosophies stemming from Cartesianism (it is often used about Descartes himself, Malebranche, and Leibniz), the notion is already completely different. For, the Cartesians did not hold the same account as the Medievals, and especially as Aquinas, of the corporeal conditions of our present intellection. It follows that these philosophers, when taking intelligence as the measure of being, often tend to mean *human* intelligence. Although they are believers, they are led unconsciously to incline towards rationalism. "Anthropomorphic" Cartesian intellectualism is characterized by a tendency in metaphysics to isolate beings, and by the exaltation of evidence as the criterion of truth. Couturat writes of Leibniz that he takes as the fundamental principle of his philosophy the "*principle of reason*, whose exact and precise meaning is the following: '*All truth is analytic.*'" Consequently, he continues, "everything in the world must be intelligible and logically demonstrable by pure concepts, and the only method of the sciences is deduction. This can be called the postulate of universal intelligibility. The philosophy of Leibniz thus appears as the most complete and systematic expression of intellectualist rationalism: there is a perfect agreement between thought and [1068] things, nature and spirit; reality is entirely penetrable by reason, because it is penetrated with reason. To characterize this metaphysics by a single word: it is a *panlogism*" (*La logique de Leibniz*. Paris, 1901, p. xi).

C.—By making spirit the *adequate mirror* of being, Cartesian intellectualism presupposes an irreducible *dualism* between being and spirit. The philosophies stemming from Criticism proclaimed the *affinity* of the Spirit and things; by uniting them at their very roots with the soul, these philosophies also made them come out of their mutual isolation. The critique of intellectualism in the Cartesian manner is caught in the act in this assertion of Hegel: "The metaphysic of understanding is dogmatic, because it maintains half-truths in their isolation: whereas the idealism of speculative philosophy carries out the principle of totality and shows that it can reach beyond the inadequate formularies of abstract thought" (*Hegel's Logic*, trans. William Wallace. Oxford: Oxford University Press, 1975, p. 52, no. 32). However, Hegel himself fell into an idolatry of the understanding, of particular and conditioned intellection, that is much worse than the one for which he reproached Descartes; for, no longer understanding the necessity of the Personal and Creator God, Hegel came to turn human philosophical knowledge, which always remains conceptual and animal, into absolute knowledge. It thus comes as no surprise that minds imbued with Hegel—and, besides, dazzled by the wonderful progress of the natural sciences in the 18th and 19th centuries—attempted to explain the world following the methods of rationalist intellectualism, that is to say by accepting without examination the concept as the instrument of knowledge adequate to the world and by identifying *thing* with *reality*. This is the unconscious postulate of the intellectualism that flourishes around 1850–1860 and attacks religion head-on.

D.—In 1860, "intellectualism" is what is anti-religious. How is it, then, that at the time of the Encyclical *Pascendi* it is anti-intellectualism that is condemned by the religious authority? Religious defense was conducted in Protestant soil by separating more and more the domain of speculative truth, which pertains to reason, from the domain of religion, reserved for the heart (in a manner very much in conformity with the spirit of Luther, but especially since Kant, and after Schleiermacher and Ritschl). The Consequent Protestantism has, in this way, successively abandoned: 1) the age-old claim to demonstrate rationally the credibility of the Christian revelation, 2) the ancient dogmatic system itself. To cling not only to the ancient demonstrations, but even to the ancient dogmas, is thus now seen as sinning through "intellectualism", and this sin is that of nearly all Christian churches since the 3rd and 4th centuries at least. Harnack, for example, speaks about intellectualism in these terms: "Unter Intellectualismus ist hier aber vor Allem zu verstehen, dass hinter die Gebote der christlichen Moral und hinter die Hoffnungen und den Glauben der christlichen Religion die wissenschaftliche Erkenntniss der Welt gestellt wurde und man diese mit jenen so verknüpfte, dass sie als das Fundament der Gebote und der Hoffnungen erschien.

Damit ist die zukünftige Dogmatik geschaffen worden" [What we here chiefly understand by 'intellectualism' is the placing of the scientific conception of the world behind the commandments of Christian morality and behind the hopes and faith of the Christian religion, and the connecting of the two things in such a way that this conception appeared as the foundation of these commandments and hopes. Thus was created the future dogmatic (Harnack, *Lerbuch der Dogmengeschichte*. Freiburg: Mohr, 1894, I:2, 5, p. 50; English trans. *History of Dogma* by Neil Buchanan. London: Williams & Norgate, 1896, v. II, 4, p. 229). As we know, modernism was formed when these ideas crept into certain Latin minds and modernism for some years spewed waves of hatred and insults on the "intellectualism" of Catholic dogmatics and theology.

Besides theological intellectualism, the philosophical conceptions that it presupposed were also attacked. Faced with the idealist, sentimentalist, voluntarist and *mobilist*[3] theories of the innovators, the defenders of orthodoxy often accepted the word "intellectualism" to designate the realism and the dogmatism they professed, while adding to it this or that particular nuance these doctrines took in their systems. So, for example, Fr. Garrigou-Lagrange, in his effort to define the "intellectualism" that is common to Aquinas, Plato, and Aristotle, characterized it by *the priority of being over intelligence* (*Revue des Sciences philosophiques et théologiques*, January 1908, p. 30). Modern controversies even project their vocabulary upon the controversies of the past: for example, when speaking about the philosophical origins of Protestantism, Denifle-Weiss, calls *intellectualism* [1069] the doctrine according to which the intelligence can know what is (*Luther und Luthertum*, vol. II, pp. 298 and 299, note 3).

E.—Yet if it is a fatal error to sacrifice the objective value of conceptual knowledge, is it not also a fatal error to ignore the activity of the subject and to deny all immanence of the appetition in the concept? For twenty or so years some Christian philosophers branded as "anti-intellectualist" have vigorously risen up against this mutilation. Blondel condemns "a generic conception of which idealism and real-

---

3 Rousselot, following standard French usage, uses the adjective mobilist (*mobiliste*) to refer to theories that posited becoming or change as the ultimate reality, such as those of Heraclitus. Rousselot also uses the noun mobilism (*mobilisme*) to refer to such a theory of becoming.

ism in all their varied forms are only hybrid species and which can be labeled "intellectualism": This is summed up," he says, "in this fundamental error: the *fact* of thought is taken in itself, separated from the very *act* of thinking" (*L'illusion idéaliste*, excerpt from the *Revue de Métaphysique et de Morale*, November 1898, p. 19. English translation, Fiachra Long, *The Idealist Illusion and Other Essays*. Dordrecht: Kluwer, 2000, p. 87. See also by the same author, "Le Point de départ de la recherche philosophique," *Annales de Philosophie chrétienne*, vol. CLII, p. 232).

I. Intellectualism as contrary to faith

The doctrine that affirms the absolute sufficiency of human, conceptual, and discursive thought in moral and religious matters is nothing else than *rationalism* in its crudest form. To say that everything can be explained by reason is to deny divine *mysteries* and divine *revelation*; it is thus clearly to place oneself in contradiction with faith. For, the Church teaches not only that the known truth does not suffice for living well, that thought is not *sufficient* for salvation (but that in addition the will needs divine *grace*); this is how the Church is opposed to *absolute intellectualism* (to which one could relate with some qualifications the systems of Spinoza and Hegel). The Church also teaches that natural reason is powerless for the knowledge of the truth *necessary* (but insufficient) for salvation, and that this truth hidden in God has been *revealed* to human beings by His incarnate Son for their salvation.

Among the diverse forms of rationalism all incompatible with the belief in Revelation, one is sometimes more particularly called "intellectualism": the one that reached its apogee around the middle of the 19th century; it consists in this: in order to resolve the enigma of the world, in order to give the last word on being, this form of rationalism no longer trusted *Reason* in general (as in the 18th century), but more particularly *Science*, that is to say, a system of rational knowledge built upon the methodical study of material nature and history. The young Renan was one of the most influential leaders of this movement, although Renan's natural skepticism prevented him from sharing its illusions about everything. The dogmatic culmination of this trend of ideas is properly Taine's metaphysics: true reality is constituted by "facts" and "laws," and all being is governed by an "Axiom." According to the particular purpose described by the title of my essay, I do not need to refute this metaphysics here, but only to point out its fundamental illusion.

The disrepute into which this metaphysics of "intellectualism" has fallen nowadays (closely related to atomism in cosmology and to associationism in psychology) seems to dispense the Catholic doctrine from any "apology" on this point. Even outside the special world of philosophers and theologians, people realized quite well how arbitrary and narrow it was to claim to apply the principles proper to the sciences dealing with material things to the knowledge of the soul. "The error of Intellectualism," Bourget writes, "lies precisely in applying to [1070] phenomena of a certain order methods that were suitable for other phenomena" (*Pages de Critique et de Doctrine*, v. II, p. 313). The more technical and closely-argued critique by anti-intellectualist philosophers was also, to a large extent, instrumental in achieving the truth. By showing that conceptual knowledge is never exhaustive, it has proved anew, against Hegelianism, that the concept cannot be the organ of absolute knowledge. By showing that the concept is essentially relative to our limited nature as reasonable animals, it showed, against Taine, that absolute reality cannot consist in "facts" and "laws" essentially correlative to the concept; it has likewise dissipated the chimera of the eternal Axiom. One can even hope, it seems, that this idea of the relativity of the concept, gaining still more ground, will manage to make classical Pantheism intolerable to the contemporary philosophical intelligence; this Pantheism *consists in picturing the Supreme Being as a great "Thing,"* which amounts to imposing upon Him the conditions of the concept. (This reaction is sketched here and there in some essays of *polydemonism*, which are, besides, rather irrational in their constructive character, but interesting because they are the antipode of the "scientific" metaphysics of former times). It may be that this critical movement, if it continues, brings spirits back to the true notion of God, a living and personal Spirit. Be that as it may, it is certain that among agnosticism, modern "*mobilism*" and Catholic dogmatism, intellectualism in the fashion of 1860 has seen its place very much dwindle in our day.[4]

This modern critique of intellectualism, which, on more than one point, has gone too far, furthers the views of Catholic thinkers, and particularly the principles of Aquinas, in what remains legitimate in the relations among science, human reason, and religious truth. With respect to the present question, we can summarize these principles in two fundamental assertions. First assertion: *metaphysics does not depend per se on the sciences*. (The reason for this is that metaphysics has for its object *being* as such, while each science has for its object a qualified being, determined in a certain manner, taken under these or those conditions to the exclusion of all others. There follows this consequence, that the progress of the sciences does not necessarily and directly advance the question of the Supreme Reality, i.e., the question of God, since the sciences give an account of the different qualifications of beings, but the Supreme Reality is that which explains being as such). Second assertion: *the Supreme Reality is not seen such as it is through the concept* (see Aquinas on the vision of God, for example, *Summa theologiae* Ia q. 12 a. 11, or *Summa Contra Gentiles*, III, 45-57). These two assertions are extremely important, and one could not be too intimately convinced of these two assertions for the very sake of the conservation of the faith.

We should no doubt be pleased that the scientific pseudo-metaphysics is in decline; but we should not forget that a change of wind can put it in vogue again, the propensity to interpret the world in terms of *properly conceivable "things"* being profoundly rooted in the human mind. Of late, harsh and fair criticisms against universal mobilism have arisen; a sound rationalism appears to have regained favor in several fields, in literary criticism, for [1071] example, and in political science. Up to this point this reversal contains nothing that would not please the Church. Even if, by an accident that nothing foreshadows, it resulted in a revival of the naturalist intellectualism of the year 1860, Catholic thought should vigorously remain in its rightful middle path of truth: affirming the competence of the con-

---

4 The program of the old intellectualism and its opposition to contemporary mobilism are clearly defined by Jacob against Le Roy in the *Revue de Métaphysique et de Morale*, 1898, pp. 170-201.

cept within its proper limits, but stressing also with rigor these same limits, and pressing on with the critique of the concept in the sense of the two Thomist principles formulated above. Besides, it is clear that these two principles are sufficient neither to make a human being a Catholic, nor even to make a human being admit the necessity of a revelation. These principles only dispose the intelligence to do that by ridding it of grave errors.

II. INTELLECTUALISM AS GUARANTEED BY FAITH

"Modernists," the Pope said in the Encyclical *Pascendi*, "place the foundations of religious philosophy in that doctrine which is commonly called *Agnosticism*. According to this teaching human reason is confined entirely within the field of *phenomena*, that is to say, to things that appear, and in the manner in which they appear: it has neither the right nor the power to overstep these limits. Hence it is incapable of lifting itself up to God, and of recognizing His existence, even by means of visible things. Such is this doctrine. From this it is inferred that God can never be the direct object of science, and that, as regards history, He must not be considered as a historical subject. Given these premises, everyone will at once perceive what becomes of *Natural Theology*, of the *motives of credibility*, of *external revelation*. The Modernists simply sweep them entirely aside; they include them in *Intellectualism*, which they denounce as a system which is ridiculous and long since defunct" (Encyclical *Pascendi dominici gregis*, September 8, 1907, Latin Text in *Questions actuelles*, v. XCIII, p. 198, or in Denzinger-Hünermann, *Enchiridion*, 37th ed., no. 3475[5]; English translation, *On the Doctrine of the Modernists*. Boston, St. Paul Books, 1980, p. 10). Intellectualism appears here as the term that the modernists use to designate the contrary of agnosticism; more precisely, as the system that admits *natural theology* (which is more ordinarily called *theodicy* today), the *rationability* [*rationabilité*] of the faith proved by exterior signs of a divine manifestation, and finally the possibility of an *external revelation*, hence not enclosed in the heart of those whom God addresses, but expressible in concepts and communicable through words.

---

5 Rousselot uses the numbers of the old Denzinger edition; these have been updated.—Translators' note.

I cannot treat here these three questions to their full extent, already set forth in the articles Agnosticism (*Dictionnaire apologétique de la foi catholique* (vol. I, col. 66 f.), God (ibid., col. 943 ff.), Dogma (ibid., col. 1135 ff.), and Faith (vol. II, col. 65, etc.). On each of the three points touched on by the Encyclical I confine myself to adding certain details from my particular point of view here of the critique of the concept; that is to say, I will try to delineate exactly what sort of sufficiency of conceptual knowledge the Church affirms in each of the cases.

A. Natural Theology

The Pope first spoke of natural theology. By affirming the power reason has to know with certainty the existence of God through creatures, the Encyclical *Pascendi* has absolutely made no innovations; it explicitly refers (a few lines after the passage cited) to Vatican definitions that, in agreement with a constant tradition, had already established this significant point (First Vatican Council, session III, chapter 1, and canon 1 of *De Revelatione*, Denzinger, op. cit., no. 3004 and 3026). [1072] Let us observe only that a later document, which the first articles of the *Dictionary* could not take into account, again clarified Catholic doctrine, through an authorized interpretation. This is the oath formula prescribed by Pius X, September 1st, 1910, to certain categories of ecclesiastics (*Motu proprio: sacrorum Antistitum*). "I profess," we read there, "that God, principle and end of all things, can be certainly known and even demonstrated by the light of natural reason through what has been made, that is to say, through the visible works of creation, as a cause can be known and demonstrated through its effects." Two features deserve our attention: the insistence on the *visible* effects of the creative potency [*puissance*], and the term "demonstration" in order to explain the *knowledge* that is *certain*, of which the First Vatican Council speaks. This last teaching, besides, only ratifies a consequence already drawn in Catholic schools, where the equivalence of these two propositions was judged "theologically certain": "God is knowable with certainty by natural reason" and "the existence of God can be demonstrated." The affirmation of the demonstrability of God excludes every *uncertainty* in the proof drawn from the visible effects of the Divine

Potency; it does not exclude all *influence of freedom* on the conditions of its perception, and we are not compelled to believe that this demonstration is as evident and compelling as a geometrical demonstration for every intelligence no matter what its state. Extreme intellectualism would consist in believing that discourse acts here, so to speak, *ex opere operato* [from the work performed], i.e., that the moral state of the subject does not matter. Besides, whatever may be the importance we grant to good and free dispositions in this matter, we have to be careful, for if we conceived of these dispositions as *compensating for the insufficiency of the proof*, there would no longer be a *demonstration*; for the demonstration the Pope declares possible to exist, the free effort only needs to dispose the subject to perceive an objectively valid proof. This role of freedom thus consists in the removal of obstacles rather than in a positive efficacy.

The terms "light of natural reason" used by the First Vatican Council and repeated by Pius X, do not merit less attention, and have a fundamental importance for the question of intellectualism. These terms exclude the different *fideist* systems, which makes the certainty of the existence of God depend upon faith or even upon supernatural charity. In any approach wherein one necessarily requires a light that is intrinsically, *substantially* supernatural (in order to use the technical term) for the purpose of providing the certainty of the existence of God, one certainly falls into heresy. In the present case we would not escape heresy either if we started from the very legitimate distinction between the rational objective value of the proofs and the capacity to perceive them, and granted that assuredly the demonstration of the existence of God is valid, but that it can only be grasped with certainty by a supernaturalized intelligence. For, the Council did not make its definition directly bear upon the naturality of the known truth, but upon that of the organ of knowledge, of the means that makes something known. No doubt, for those who admit the Thomist doctrine of the formal object, these two notions are correlative. But someone who would deny this doctrine and claim that the natural truth of the existence of God can only be known through the supernatural light, would not escape from the anathemas of the Council. It follows from this that we cannot make the aforementioned certainty depend on the conversion of the heart to God, on justification (which immediately introduces infused faith into the soul).

[1073] The question then arises: is it the case that the human being whose intelligence is supernaturalized, whose reason is mended by faith, is in the same situation with regard to natural truths as someone whose intelligence still suffers from the effects of original sin, whose reason is still wounded? The answer is no. First, everyone admits that the revealed truths proposed by the teaching of the Church very effectively protect [*protectrices*] the natural truths concerning morality and the existence of God. And what is more, it is also conceivable that the infusion of the supernatural light straightens out a certain internal imbalance of the knowing subject with regard to the knowledge of any truth whatsoever. On this very sensitive issue, some defenders of dogma may have been mistaken for lack of familiarity with the anti-intellectualist philosophers, and it also happened that some Catholic philosophers used unacceptable formulas, even though their true thought contained nothing contrary to faith.

"To think," writes the author of *L'Action*, "that we can arrive at being and legitimately affirm any reality whatsoever without having reached the very end of the series which extends from the first sensible intuition to the necessity of God and of religious practice, is to remain in illusion" (Blondel, *L'Action*, Fifth Part, Chap. III, p. 428 of the complete edition; English translation, *Action* by Oliva Blanchette. Notre Dame: University of Notre Dame Press, 1984, p. 392).

At first sight this proposition, it seems, cannot avoid the qualifications of "erroneous" and "close to heresy." By "religious practice" does the author not mean the Catholic religious practice? By the knowledge that reaches the end, does he not mean the firm and supernatural knowledge faith gives about it? Now the Church teaches that the demonstration of God that is certain (which necessarily presupposes a knowledge of being that is certain) can be perceived outside this supernatural light. It is certain that before being resolved in Christian observances, and even before having adhered to Christian dogmas through faith, one can have a knowledge of God that is certain, demonstrated, that will not have to be corrected and that is therefore "legitimate."

Taken as it stands and out of context, the formula would thus rightly fall under censure as I have said; let me add that, even replaced in its context, this formula still offends by its unfortunate wording. However, the context, I believe, suggests an acceptable meaning.

However legitimate it may be as a rational proposition and authentic conclusion of a discourse, does the affirmation of God that is certain have its full share of truth in a reason wounded by original sin and not yet mended by grace? Even outside Blondel's school, several authors refuse to believe so. If philosophical research, they say, does not limit itself to the representative elements of the idea alone and at the value of the representation of the intellective act alone, it leads to the discovery of a new kind of knowledge, more intimate and more penetrating, and based upon a more perfect accord of subject and object. This knowledge is of the type of those that Aquinas calls *per connaturalitatem* [*by connaturality*], and more excellently imitates perfect intellection, which, according to this holy doctor, is not only a representation of an object, a gaze upon an essence, but a conquest [*conquête*], an embrace [*étreinte*], a grasp [*prise*] of a being. Now, in this particular case, this sympathetic knowledge requires a free and supernatural consent. In what sense then can it be called the only "legitimate" knowledge of anything whatsoever? In the following: this sympathetic knowledge alone establishes a balance between the real and the subject; it puts the real in "adequacy" [*adéquation*] not only with the subject determinately aiming at a given object, [1074] restricting the field of its vision to a partial problem; the adequacy is with the whole subject, completely present (since it is spiritual) in each of its intellections, with the subject that, beneath all the partial problems it deals with, pursues the solution of the primary problem which is identical with life itself: to gain its soul and to gain God. As we can see, this point of view goes beyond that of the current "criteriology," from which the value of particular and partial certainties is examined and which has often been adopted to criticize the formula cited above.

Nearly the same result can be reached through a different way, as follows. In the most primitive and spontaneous exercise of reason, analysis easily discovers a certain triumphant confidence in itself, a certain assurance that it can clarify being, a conviction that we, human beings, can manage *to be clear* about ourselves, the world, and life. This presumption (I use the word with no pejorative nuance) is natural, essential to intelligence; it is the *a priori* condition of its exercise, and forms as it were the moving spirit [*l'âme*] of each of its particular intellections. Now, here again, in the actual state of fallen nature, and owing to the ruin of the entire race through Adam, this presumption is unjustified outside of a grace illuminating the intelligence. Without a revelation from on high, without a healing which is not owed to it, intelligence cannot arrive at the truth concerning its *real* destiny. An imbalance ensues in the knowing subject as such; this imbalance *throws into confusion* all that the subject knows, and although it does not render each act of knowledge false or "illegitimate," it cuts these acts off from what should give them their full meaning and truth. Ignorance itself is healed by the teaching of the Church, which catechizes us from the outside and allows us to know our destiny; likewise, this life force [*élan vital*] of reason, this natural presumption that lies at the origin of all of its movement, is healed at its source by the power of infused faith, which rectifies reason by elevating it. If we envisage the situation in this way, we can appraise the benefit of supernatural faith alone, when considered as the perfection of the subject; this perfection restores its underpinning to natural reason and benefits the knowledge of any object whatsoever.

B. Motives of Credibility

With regard to the motives of credibility, the Encyclical *Pascendi* refers again to the First Vatican Council (*De Fide*, canons 3 and 4). The *Motu proprio* I quoted contains once again an important clarification on this point; it affirms the strict sufficiency, even for ordinary people, of external motives (such as miracles, prophecies, and actions of the Church). A communicable conceptual representation can therefore be the means chosen by God to bring the human mind to the rational assent to Christianity. If this is intellectualism, the Catholic Church is intellectualist on this point; it absolutely refuses to restrict the legitimate motives of credibility to internal phenomena alone, and it has proclaimed this doctrine in an infallible definition.

But in the interpretation of the documents, and because of a lack of a necessary philosophical distinction, there could be an excess of intellectualism here in the sense that a certain sufficiency of the concept might be affirmed, which is more extensive than the one the Magisterium defined. This is what we have to explain.

We assume that revelation has been made to human beings and admit that God did not bestow it upon our intelligence as though it were an innate gift; but instead God makes it reach each of us through tradition, through authority, and as [1075] St. Paul says, through hearing, supported by valid reasons. Still, this being granted, the question remains regarding the *manner of appropriating it*. Will reason suffice for this task or will the good will be absolutely required? Will nature suffice or will grace be necessary?

All are in agreement in admitting the following: the truth of Supernatural Revelation cannot be known *in the way required for reaching salvation* (Second Council of Orange, canons 5, 6, and 7; Council of Trent, canon 3, *De justificatione*. Denzinger, *op. cit.*, no. 375-377 and 1553) without a supernatural grace from God and without a good effort of the free will. To think otherwise would be to attribute salutary faith to the forces of nature and to fall consequently into the Pelagian heresy. All are also in agreement today in condemning the error of Georges Hermes, a less radical error yet one condemned nonetheless. Hermes did not say that a natural assent could be a salutary act; he even expressly denied it, and this was precisely the meaning of the distinction he drew between *faith of knowledge* [*foi de connaissance*] and *faith of the heart* [*foi du coeur*]. But this faith of the heart was only an abandonment, a resignation of the self to God: faith was natural as knowledge and faith without charity, "dead faith," was not a grace. This is what the Church condemned (Denz., *Enchiridion*, no. 2738 and 3035. *Acta Concilii Vaticani*, notes 14 and 17 in the schema of the theologians, col. 527 and 529 of volume VII of the *Collectio lacensis*). It must therefore be a constant among Catholics that good will collaborates with supernatural faith, *even insofar as it is a knowledge*. This will suffice to exclude the so-called "self-sufficiency" of the concept and thus to dismiss the most serious reproaches of excessive intellectualism directed against the Catholic theory of faith.

C. Revealed Dogmas

If the Catholic doctrine has been criticized for an excessive intellectualism in its manner of conceiving the motives of credibility, the attack has been still even more heated with regard to the content of the truth in which to believe. People have contemptuously denied that concepts, expressible in words and communicable, could be legitimate vehicles of the divine and salutary truth. This question was treated in the article Dogma; I will confine myself here to an observation that bears directly on the conceptual character of the dogmas that the Church proposes for our faith.

The Modernists asked in a tone of mockery if the truths that we claim to be "spoken by God" were received from His own mouth one day when He chatted with us with a sensible voice and articulated words. *According to the Catholic doctrine the answer must be yes.* For, whatever the possible means may be that the divine wisdom did not choose, as a matter of fact the conversation of the incarnated God with human beings is the basis of the whole doctrine of salvation. It is the doctrine of the whole of the New Testament. "No one has ever seen God," St. John says. "The only Son, God, [*the true reading seems to be: the only God-Son*] who is at the Father's side, has revealed Him" (Jn 1:18; see 6:46). "Who has known the mind of the Lord?" St. Paul says. "But we have the mind of Christ" (1 Cor 2:16). And the Epistle to the Hebrews states: "In times past, God spoke in partial and various ways to our ancestors through the prophets; in these last days, he spoke to us through a son" (Heb 1:1). And we also read in the Synoptic Gospels: "No one knows the Father except the Son, and *anyone to whom the Son wishes to reveal Him*" (Mt 11:27; see Lk 10:22).[6] Thus, all of the economy of Revelation consists [1076] in the fact that we, human beings, have heard the One who saw. The human who lies at the origin of our faith was not *believing*, but *seeing*, and without any veil, as the true Son of God. (See Aquinas, *Summa Contra Gentiles*, III, 40:4: "sive ipse homo proponens fidem immediate videat veritatem, sicut Christo credimus" [or human beings themselves proposing the faith see the truth immediately, as when we believe in Christ]).

---

6 Translation from *New American Bible*. New York: Oxford University Press, 1990. Italics added by Rousselot.—Translators' note.

The true Incarnation of the Word, and as we say now, the "metaphysical" divinity of Jesus is thus essential to the notion of Catholic revelation, and anyone who would deny these things would have to profess and to defend a faith different from ours. The consolidation and the consecration by Christ of the conceptual order, if I may use this expression, pertains to the most general plan of the restoring in Him of our terrestrial world and of all that belongs to it, which He has as it were stamped with His seal: *omnia in Ipso constant* [in Him all things stand firm], St. Paul says (Col 1:17). Hence, the *sacramental* [*sacramentaire*] principle of our religion, that is to say, the use of the corporeal nature itself for the conferral of grace. Hence, its *ecclesiastical* principle, that is to say, salvation made accessible to human beings through the agency of those humans who teach, govern, and dispense holy things. Hence also its *dogmatic* principle: that is to say, our poor forms of thought, infirm and animal,[7] raised to the dignity of expressing in full certainty the mysterious truths that concern the intimate nature of God.

Let me put it more precisely focusing on the subject matter at hand: if what lied at the origin of revelation was a confused experience of the Divinity, as Tyrrell imagines, if it was even a mystical illumination or an intellectual vision, similar to those about which the saints spoke to us, then the following suspicion would be legitimate: the conceptual explanation of revelation that would be given afterwards would be inaccurate, because the most spiritual human beings can mix something of their own human thoughts with the shafts of celestial light.[8] It would be asking much then, if the "prophets" could have with assurance excluded the false interpretations of their revelations after hearing those "secret words that human beings could not repeat" (2 Cor 12:4). The internal revelation would be from God: but its external expression and its communication to human beings would be from human beings who are fallible in themselves. Whether divinely established *words* were communicated, either then one

---

7 "Rationality," Aquinas says (that is to say, the specific attribute of spirits who know through concepts and discourse) "is a property of the genus animal" [*Rationale est differentia animalis*] (*I Sent.* d. 24 q. 1 a. 1 ad 4).

8 See Ignatius of Loyola, *The Spiritual Exercises, Rules for the Same Purpose, With a Greater Discernment of Spirits*, Rule 8, trans. George Ganss. St. Louis: The Institute of Jesuit Sources, 1992, no. 336, p. 128.

would have little choice other than to revere dead syllables, which is suitable for servants rather than for friends, or their interpretation would raise the same difficulty. Hence, no doubt, the small number of dogmas in the Old Testament, and the smaller communicability of the revelations made to the Patriarchs and Prophets (see Newman, *Essay on the Development of Dogma*. Notre Dame: University of Notre Dame Press, 1989, p. 347). The situation is very different in the case of Christian truth: its principle does not lie in a more or less confused experience, but in the vision itself in which the Son sees His Father, in which God sees God; the human being who communicates this to other humans is the same God, made flesh. Thus, the knowledge of the master as well as the "particularization he makes of his knowledge for the use of his disciples" (to use an expression of Aquinas[9]) [1077] are necessarily and absolutely joined with the truth. In other words, Christ was not born, nor did he come into the world, only in order to render testimony to the truth (John 18:37). He could truly and properly say: *I am the Truth* (Ibid., 14:6). Yet the concepts, the judgments, and the discourses of the One who is the subsisting truth define the created truth, so that they cannot deviate from it in any way. "I tell you what I have seen in the Father's presence" (John 8:38):[10] He could only speak sincerely, "naively", truly, of divine things. Put another way still. If, as stated in the proposition condemned under number twenty by the decree *Lamentabili*,[11] revelation could not be anything other than the consciousness acquired by human beings of their relation to God, it is perhaps right to undertake a rational critique of the expression manifesting such phenomena of consciousness. But if God is made human, the very manifestation of this consciousness, its transition into human categories is thereby sanctioned by the authority of God. As a consequence, the modernist objections which start with the difference between the original phenomena of religious experience and its "secondary forms," or said differently,

---

9 Aquinas, *De Veritate*, q. 9 a. 5, and passim.

10 Translation from *New American Bible*. New York: Oxford University Press, 1990.

11 See *On the Doctrine of the Modernists*. Boston: St. Paul Books, 1980.—Translators' note.

from the powerlessness of the human concept to translate divine realities, vanish before the reality of the Incarnation.

Let it be clear that I do not claim to prove the truth of the Catholic dogmas in all I just said. We do not prove all of the dogmas by affirming one dogma. Yet we do show how they hold together, or better how one particular dogma accounts for the other dogmas, and also explains this dogmatic boldness of the Church, when it prescribes for us so many and so specific assertions on the most hidden and sublime objects. The Church heard the Son. Conversely, our opponents, by making the general critique of dogma, take a stand upon one dogma. They begin by stating that Jesus was a field laborer who believed that the end of the world was near, and who combined a sublime dream with this crude imagination. They thereby take a stand upon the whole or rather against the whole of Catholicism. The Word is no longer made flesh, the material world has no longer been sanctified by Him, and there is no longer continuity between our human words when we say the *Creed* [*Credo*] and the human words of Emmanuel, of God Himself, when he conversed with His disciples.

It is also clear that what I said leaves intact the question of the identity of the dogmas taught today by the Church with what Christ said to his followers. This question lies outside of my present subject matter: all I had to do was show that the expression of our faith was conceptual at the origin of Revelation and in the very mouth of God. The distinction between vulgar concepts and learned concepts is, after all, accidental. Dogmatic intellectualism has successfully made its case, if it has shown that there can be homogeneity between its *Creed* [*Credo*] and the revelation made by God Himself. This homogeneity is guaranteed for us by the Incarnation of the Word. "Christus," Aquinas says, "secundum humanam naturam habet perfectionem aliis homogeneam, et est principium quasi univocum, et est regula conformis, et unius generis: ... haec complet in ipso rationem capitis" [Christ ... according to His human nature possesses a perfection homogeneous with others, and He is as it were the univocal principle, and He is the like standard, and of one kind: ... This in itself furnishes the nature of a head] (III Sent. d. 13 q. 2 a. 1 sol.).

As we know, the Holy Fathers often developed the notion of Revelation that requires the Incarnation of the Word, so that not only would we be redeemed, but also that we would be instructed in the divine truths. See Irenaeus, V, 1; [1078] and Athanasius, *On the Incarnation of the Word*, Ch. XIV, XVI, XLV, XLVI. The foundation of the doctrine I expounded in this section is summarized by Gregory the Great in these words: "Dum divinitas defectum nostrae carnis suscepit, humanam genus lumen, quod amiserat, recepit. Unde enim Deus humana patitur, inde homo ad divina sublevatur" [When the divinity took on the weakness of our flesh, the human race recovered the light that it lost. For whence God suffers as a human, thence the human is raised up to the divine] (*Hom.* II (13) *in Evang.*). Irenaeus also says that the Word becomes a child in order to converse with us: συνενηπίαζεν (IV, 38).

III. INTELLECTUALISM AS FREELY DISCUSSED

Now that I have expounded the kind of intellectualism the Church rejects and the kind it sanctions, it remains for me to say what kind the Church leaves as a matter of free debate.

It is enough for the Church that its dogmas remain intact, and that the consequences following from them pertain to the limited but real value of conceptual knowledge; besides, the Church imposes no determinate systematization on the nature and activity of the intelligence, or on the relations between intelligence and the will. As a matter of fact, the two most celebrated philosophical systems in its bosom, and which formed the basis for the two most distinct schools of theology, Thomism and Scotism, find themselves on these points in irreducible opposition. Will has the primacy in Scotus, and in the Franciscans in general; their system is commonly and rightly characterized as anti-intellectualist and voluntarist. Intelligence has the primacy in Aquinas; we can say that his philosophy is founded on an uncompromising and radical intellectualism.

Yet, when we speak in this way, it is important to observe that we take *intellectualism* in the metaphysical sense, in the sense Littré takes it in the definition cited at the beginning of this article. The heart of Thomist intellectualism is its thesis on the beatitude: it asserts that the Infinite Being, that God, the happiness and the Final End of human beings, is *possessed*, properly speaking, by intelligence, and not by the will.[12] The intuitive vision of God is where Thomist intellectualism sees the ideal of intellectual operation, and the final reason of every movement of the supernaturalized intelligence. The intuition of "Subsisting Intelligibles," of pure living spirits, is where Thomist intellectualism sees the most noble natural exercise of intelligence. Now, the idea that this intellectualism forms of ideal intellection leads it to criticize with an extreme rigor (and sometimes to belittle in very contemptuous terms) the intellectual knowledge proper to the rational animal, that is to say discursive, conceptual, and abstract knowledge, [1079] which is submitted to the conditions of time and space. The recent interpreters of Thomism insisted on this aspect of the doctrine with predilection. (See Rousselot, *L'intellectualisme de saint Thomas*. Paris, 1908; English translation, *Intelligence*; Sertillanges, *Saint Thomas*, in the collection of the *Grands Philosophes*. Paris, 1910; English translation, *Saint Thomas Aquinas and His Work* by Godfrey Anstruther. London: Blackfriars, 1957). This latter author very felicitously sums up the Thomist critique of the concept according to ideal intellection, in this formula: "The more something is intelligible, the less it is conceivable" (*Op. cit.*, v. I, p. 49). In this way the most substantial and the most enthusiastic metaphysical intellectualism is precisely what provides the most drastic and deci-

---

12 "Happiness is the laying hold of our ultimate end, and this is not done by the activity of the will. For the will is charged with its object whether it be absent, and then desired, or present, and then rested in and enjoyed. Obviously the desiring an end is not the possessing it, but a moving towards it. And while the delighting in an end comes from its presence, the converse does not hold, namely that the presence of an end comes from the will's delights in it. The act, then, which brings about this presence to the lover must be other than an act of the will. To take an illustration from the world of sense. If money could be got by the willing, a needy man would straightway have all he wanted. But he starts by lacking it, and then has to set himself to secure it by the work of his hands or other powers, and then he may come to enjoy its possession. So it is also in the world of intelligence. The will's desire starts for an end, but it is reached by its becoming present to us by an act of mind, and then, when it is already gained, the delight of will rests content with it. In conclusion, then, an act of mind forms the essence of happiness" (*Summa theologiae* Ia-IIae q. 3 a. 4; contra Scotus, *Opus Oxoniense*, IV d. 49 q. 4). English translation. Thomas Gilby, *Summa Theologiae*. New York: McGraw-Hill, 1969, vol. 16, p. 71.

sive antidote against the narrow and "anthropocentric" intellectual-ism which idolizes animal intellection and the concept.

One would seek in vain for the principles of a similar critique, me-thodical and merciless, in Scotus. "Scotus thinks, against Aquinas, that the possession of God is realized formally through the will. He is thus consistent with himself in denying the perfect coincidence of the intelligible order and the real order: this is the meaning of his famous formal distinction *ex natura rei* [from the nature of the thing]. Because he lacks the Thomist notion of possessing intellec-tion and intellectual immanence, he tends to envisage all knowledge on the model of our *abstract and representative conception*: this is what explains his theories on the univocity of being, and on the human knowledge of the divine attributes. If we define intellectualism by the tendency to equate all knowledge with human knowledge, then we would have to say that Scotus is more intellectualist than Aqui-nas" (Rousselot, *op. cit.*, p. xxiii, note 1; see English translation, *Intel-ligence*, p. 11, note 10). We see how dangerous it is, judging on first appearances, to invoke the Scotist tradition in regard to the modern critique of the concept. A similar confusion is possible in the ques-tion of the act of faith, where Scotus attributes to the will a role less decisive than Aquinas. Here some essential distinctions have to be made that those who only have a limited knowledge of Scholastics can easily overlook (see Le Roy, *Dogme et Critique*, pp. 123-124, and see note 8). Besides, once again, and whatever may be the very special favor shown by Rome to the system of Aquinas especially nowadays (see the article Thomism in *Dictionnaire apologétique de la foi catholique*), the system of Scotus enjoys complete freedom in the Church.

Moreover, whatever their ideas were on the metaphysical preemi-nence of intelligence or of the will, the Scholastics were in agreement in using the method of rational dialectic in theology. On this point Aquinas is no more intellectualist than Scotus. It may not be useless to note, at the end of this section, that the Church has disapproved, in Bonnetty, of the idea that the method of the Scholastics led to ra-tionalism. And although it has still been repeated from time to time, this assessment remains condemned by Rome (Denzinger, op. cit., no. 2814).

CONCLUSION

What does the Church think about intellectualism? In all that has been said so far, the reader sees that this question cannot be settled through an abrupt and brief response, but that multiple distinctions are necessary in order to resolve it. The task is relatively easy when we deal with either an intellectualism drawn in rigid and clear-cut lines, as with the intellectualism of Taine, or a definite anti-intellectualism which is still rational in its method and therefore limited, as the intellectualism professed in the school of Scotus. The anti-dogmatic principle can be easily recognized, identical to itself in its [1080] weakness, either as it scoffs with Voltaire at the dogmas for the alleged benefit of morality, or as it proclaims with Ménégoz that "faith saves independently of beliefs": in these two writers, who differ in everything else, there is the same powerlessness to believe in the power of the truth. Yet there was a vague and diffuse anti-intellectualism, rather of the literary order, which was very fashionable in the heyday of modernism and earlier. "Formulas are a great evil," they said, "the soul, the unspoken soul that one places there ... is all that matters ... it would be immoral if faith could be formulated ... knowing before doing is our evil temptation; let us only undertake to be people of good will ..." "Do not ask him for a system," said one Protestant theologian about another Protestant; "he is too rich to be coherent. Life cannot formulate itself; it has neither the leisure nor the need for this." I could easily multiply citations of this kind; but I have had my fill of them *ad nauseam*. Now, with these detestable counter-truths, they mixed some lesser truths, "The primordial concern is not to speculate on the universe, but to conduct one's life," etc., and some truisms expressed poetically, as with the saying of Goethe, "My dear friend, every theory is gray, but the golden tree of life is of a lush green," without forgetting the inevitable distich where Hamlet warns Horatio that there are, on earth as in heaven, more things than his philosophy can account for. This medley constituted anti-intellectualism in the state of a diffuse mentality. What sought expression in this manner was ordinarily less a thought than a vague state of sentimental annoyance, now with the excessive presumption of reasoning reason [*la raison raisonnante*], now with the legitimate intransigence of the truth, now with one and the other confused in one and the same repulsion. Of this indistinct and confused state of the soul, nothing can be said for certain. It can indicate the end of a narrow and lofty rationalism; more often it indicates, perhaps, a disease of the intelligence, incapable of gaining and preserving its own good, the truth, in peace. The duty of the physician of souls [i.e. the confessor,—Translators' note] is to treat each of them according to their diverse disabilities. The duty of the Catholic philosopher and theologian is to distinguish carefully the diverse intellectual forms of anti-intellectualism, *ut sciat reprobare malum et eligere bonum* [so that one would know how to refuse evil but choose good][13]; the Catholic philosopher and theologian, first, must keep free from all harm the absolute rights of the divine truth; next, they must integrate into Catholic speculation everything that seems well-founded in the modern critique of the concept. Those who apply themselves seriously to this twofold task, find themselves wholly delighted with the admirable balance of Catholic thought, so sensitive to all errors, so fair toward all truths; this scene marvelously finds confirmation in faith. *Omnia consonant vero* [Everything harmonizes with what is true].[14]

"That there is a truth then; that there is one truth; that religious error is in itself of an immoral nature; ... that it is to be dreaded; ... that the mind is below truth, not above it, and is bound not to descant upon it, but to venerate it; that truth and falsehood are set before us for the trial of our hearts; ... that 'before all things it is necessary to hold the Catholic faith;' that 'he that would be saved must thus think,' and not otherwise; ... this is the dogmatical principle, which has strength" (and is in force). "That truth and falsehood in religion are but matter of opinion; that one doctrine is as good as another; that the Governor of the world does not intend that we should gain the truth; that there is no truth; that we are not more acceptable to God by believing this than by believing that; that no one is answerable for his or her [1081] opinions; ... that it is enough if we sincerely hold what we profess; that our merit lies in seeking, not in possessing; ... this is the principle of philosophies and heresies, which is essential weakness."

---

13   *Isaiah* 7:15.—Translators' note.

14   Aquinas, *Sententia libri Ethicorum*, I, l. 12, 139.—Translators' note.

These words of Newman (*Essay on the Development of Dogma*, ch. VIII, sect. 1:1, Notre Dame: University of Notre Dame Press, 1989, p. 357) admirably express the first principle of what we are entitled to call Catholic intellectualism, the principle of strength, harmony, and peace, and, despite what a superficial critique may say about it, the principle of *life*. The blessed Angela of Foligno says the same thing more briefly: "*One who knows in truth, loves in fire*" (*Complete Works*, trans. Paul Lachance. New York: Paulist, 1993, XXXIV, pp. 300-301, cf. XXIX, p. 290).

Appendix

On the facing page is a photocopy of a
full page of Rousselot's manuscripts.

[…] il n'a une dans […] autres […]. Mais […] l'esprit, qui croit […] apercevoir dans la psychologie rationnelle la fallacia […] substantiale. De quel droit, dit-il, attribuer la permanence substantielle, la durée, à cette "âme" […] existante? N'est-ce pas la traiter, à […], comme un objet?

Voici la réponse. Si cette objection porte, il faut remonter plus haut, et dénier à l'âme […] l'existence ([…]) Or, on ne peut pas dénier à l'âme l'existence, s'il est vrai que […] est dite existante […] rapport (actuel ou possible, […] ou représenté) avec elle. — […] Donc cette objection ne porte pas.

(Cheap l'art de 2 pp.)

Preuve de la majeure. Identité de l'affirmation de "dénué substantielle" avec l'affirmation d'"existence." — En un sens véritablement […], nous devons dire de l'âme (comme de Dieu) que nous ne connaissons d'elle non son essence mais son existence, non quid est, mais seulement quia est. — J'avoue qu'il y a là […] et […] et […] de […] aide beaucoup, elle a […], à fait compenser la […]. […] que je conteste la légitimité d'une autre manière de dire, d'après laquelle on attribuerait la connaissance quia est à la conscience directe, et l'on désigne sous le nom de connaissance quid est la construction conceptuelle subséquente. — Une même objet gît, en fait, sous ces langages différents. — Nous ne disons pas contre Kant (ça serait assurément la façon expéditive et […] de ce lieu d'affaire), nous ne disons pas qu'il suffit de considérer, de fixer la […] de l'opération indifférenciée de la synthèse perçue, pour envisager l'essence de l'âme, (ni même pour percevoir, tels quels, les attributs qu'il s'agit, contre lui, de justifier.) Mais nous disons qu'une fois […] perçu la nature de l'idée d'être (de […] relation transcendantale à l'âme intelligible) et une fois que […] idée d'être est appliquée à l'âme comme en […] corrélatif principal, à l'analogum princeps de ce couple qu'on […] extrait de l'unité indifférenciée de la "vie", — une fois cela fait, dis-je, toutes les déterminations qu'on appliquera à l'idée d'âme ne seront que des déterminations ([…] positions en […]) (explications) de l'idée primitive d'être, — l'explication si l'on veut, de cet (à meilleur droit), de cet "ipsum magis" immanent à la première application qu'on fait à l'âme de cette idée, — la fixation seule […] utilisation légitime de cette […] dans laquelle flottait la "vie" au moment […] de la […] primitive transparence, et qui demeure sans emploi dès qu'on a fixé le concept à la "chose". Les prédicats discutés se réduisent à trois, en somme: immatérialité, substantialité, immortalité. De chacun d'eux nous dirons quelque chose. Mais ce n'est pas eux qu'il faut envisager tout d'abord. La première transition que nous devons examiner pour voir s'il est légitime, c'est celle par laquelle on passe de la connaissance vitale et inexprimable à l'affirmation: l'âme existe. […] sous un double forme […] le qui paraît en lui discutable c'est qu'on y trouve déjà introduite, à ce qu'il semble, un quid est, un quiddité, (car on ne peut répondre à la question an est sans avoir déjà […] conception, quelque représentation qui réponde à la question quid est; ou, pour s'exprimer scolastiquement, l'âme y est déjà soumise à la catégorie d'essence et d'[…] — c.-à-d. à cette fonction dualité de l'esprit qui fait sortir de l'affirmation primitive et concevoir la différence du possible et du réel.[+] Quelle est la nature de ce premier quid est, extérieur au quia est, et néanmoins […] qu'il présente un sens? (s. Thomas le décrit ainsi: "en non dicitur quid […] sit […] sens où quid nomine vi signification") Ce premier quid est, expliqué organiquement dans l'affirmation: l'âme existe signifie tout simplement que l'âme est être, c.-à-d. que l'âme est objet de l'âme, que l'âme est intelligible, ou tout au moins représentable: nous avions donc raison de dire que c'est à ce premier pas, si jamais, que l'âme est transformée en objet. — Mais si

[Left margin footnote:]
[+] Je ne prétends pas qu'une chose n'est existante que par son rapport actuel avec l'âme, mais que c'est ce rapport, […] au passé (actuel[?] si ce possible) qui a tous au fond de l'affirmation de l'être ou de la possibilité d'une "chose". […] je […] je veux, […] de ma vie, etc. si ne […], etc. d'autres et le système. à son aperception). Assurément, on peut dire en […]: "j'imagine bien […] être qui ne fait […] un être absolu. Il y a d'ailleurs à […] un être impossible l'[…] absolue […] actuel. — Mais tout être […] représenté, faut-il être envisagé, tout objet de […], faut-il être objet d'intuition ou d'[…]?

[Bottom footnote:]
[+] Bien en fait nous […] la solidité de la […] métaphysique thomiste, que de voir quelles limitations et distinctions d'essence et d'[…], de nature et d'hypostase, […] sur la problème de la connaissance, et à […] de la problème de l'être. Une […] comparaison de […] avec la […] légitimiste serait ici nécessaire, pour faire toucher du doigt les richesses latentes dans les […] les plus […] de la […] thomiste, et qui […] se […] par de la complexité de la vie ou […] à montrer […] d'être […] Kierkegaard. […] cette […] rocher […] — Voir le […] de nature et de sujet, […] de toute la […] des choses […], v. Delfgaauw […]

U